D0302952

EQUITY AND EXCELLENCE IN THE
PUBLIC LIBRARY

For Hazel

Equity and Excellence in the Public Library

Why Ignorance is Not our Heritage

BOB USHERWOOD
The University of Sheffield, UK

ASHGATE

Published by
Ashgate Publishing LimitedAshgate Publishing Company
Gower HouseSuite 420
Croft Road101 Cherry Street
AldershotBurlington, VT 05401-4405
Hampshire GU11 3HRUSA
England

Ashgate website: http://www.ashgate.com

British Library Cataloguing in Publication Data
Usherwood, Bob
    Equity and excellence in the public library: why ignorance
    is not our heritage
    1. Public services (Libraries) 2. Public libraries
    I. Title
    025.5

Library of Congress Cataloging-in-Publication Data
Usherwood, Bob.
    Equity and excellence in the public library : why ignorance is not our heritage / by Bob
    Usherwood.
        p. cm.
    Includes bibliographical references and index.
    ISBN 978-0-7546-4806-2
    1. Public libraries--Great Britain. 2. Public services (Libraries)--Great Britain. I. Title.

Z791.U84 2007
027.441--dc22

2007020568

ISBN: 978 0 7546 4806 2

Printed and bound in Great Britain by MPG Books Ltd, Bodmin, Cornwall.

Contents

Preface

...this is of consequence because it contributes to a feeling that nothing matters, that nothing should be taken seriously. This leads to an infantilization of public discourse, exemplified by the sneering combination of irony, populism and kitsch...

McCrum (2000)

The starting point for this book was a nagging feeling that the public library profession no longer has confidence in its core values and is confused about how to defend them. I began to explore this situation by examining the challenges and opportunities facing public library services that seek to prioritize equity and promote excellence in their services and collections. In order to obtain the views of current practitioners I sent an electronic questionnaire (Appendix 1) to all the English public library authorities on the CEPLIS[1] database. The same research instrument was also completed by Sheffield postgraduate students taking a dedicated public libraries module. The quantitative and qualitative data generated by this exercise, together with research undertaken by the CEPLIS team and a number of Masters and Doctoral students at the University of Sheffield have contributed to what are preliminary conclusions. In addition, I surveyed the library literature and a wide range of relevant material written by academics, writers, and commentators from outside our professional world.

The result is a text that is rather more polemical than I had planned. The tone is the result of a sense of frustration. As I reviewed and reflected on the material obtained from the sources outlined above, the evidence of wasted opportunities and limited horizons increasingly disappointed me. This is far from being the whole story but in a strange way my knowledge of some of the visionary public librarians working today made matters worse as I wondered who is going to fill their shoes. At the start of my career, I was inspired by a City Librarian who told me that I had joined the greatest profession in the world and by an educator who opened my eyes to the value of the library in society. I know that such inspirational people can still be found today but at the same time, there is much to suggest that many current policy makers and professionals are failing to recognize the full promise of the public library. This in turn limits the expectations of users and potential users. In other fields, public service professionals and policy makers argue that everybody should have access to the best. Thus, doctors argue that people should have local access to the best hospital treatment and educationalists proclaim that every child deserves the best school. Public librarians are different. Many appear to reject the concept of 'the best' and denigrate professional standards and qualifications. As you will see from

---

1   Centre for the Public Library and Information in Society.

the text that follows, some even regard it as elitist to advocate that public libraries should provide the best.

I found it, by turn, amazing and depressing that it is regarded as elitist for public libraries to redistribute the wealth of information and ideas. Do those who hold this view really advocate a service that reflects the unequal distribution of the private sector? Do they believe that public librarianship is little more than an adjunct to the retail trade? Some do appear to regard it as a routine, administrative activity, which simply responds to the demands of the market. They apparently see it as their role to merely give the public, or more likely in modern management speak 'the customers', what they want. I feel particularly uncomfortable when people who have clearly benefited from access to quality material and educational opportunities advocate policies that would exclude others from similar opportunities. I am sure that it is not intentional but it is an attitude that reflects a mean spirited attitude to other people's life chances reminiscent of Reaganomics or life in Thatcher's Britain.

Although for the first time in many years, I have had the opportunity to write, read, and think without being encumbered by academic or professional responsibilities I still feel that I need more time to reflect on what I have found, but to do so would test the patience of my publisher. I regard the text that I hope you are about to read as no more than an early step in what I hope will be a productive discussion on the future of the public library. A future that will demonstrate that 'ignorance is not our heritage'. That sub-title was inspired by Howard Jacobson who, in a newspaper article on the antics of the so-called celebrities on *Big Brother*, told readers that, 'knowing nothing is not your heritage'. It was a phrase that spoke to me as I examined my data and attempted to set down my thoughts on the role of the public library. It is certainly not fitting for professional librarians to go along with the current culture of ignorance. Ignorance is the enemy of equity and the friend of prejudice. It excludes people from full participation in a democratic society.

The former Chancellor of Sheffield University and Library Association President, the late Lord Dainton, argued that 'the plain fact is that modern societies will need, even more in the future than in the present, professionals with their insistence of high standards, knowledge, skill, personal commitment and sense of responsibility to the individuals they serve' (1977). He made those comments three decades ago in a memorable Presidential address. They are even more relevant today as public library professionals deal with the challenges and opportunities of the twenty-first century. If they are to be successful in that task, they will need to be guided by a firm set of core values. They will need to be flexible enough to deal with a changing world, but be strong enough to resist the fads of fashion and the seductive voices of populist commentators and others who neither know nor care for the library service. I hope that this book will promote debate and do a little to help the future leaders of our profession, understand the dangers of present circumstances, formulate a professional response and develop an appropriate vision for the future.

Acknowledgements

Thanks are due to all those who completed the questionnaire used as part of the research for this book. I am grateful for their time and comments. I must also acknowledge a huge debt to my former colleagues and students in the Department of Information Studies at the University of Sheffield. For 30 years, the Department provided fertile ground for discussion, debate, and it was a privilege to work alongside such generous and talented people. It was great to be part of the Sheffield family.

Some of the ideas expressed in this book appeared in an early form in the professional press and on conference platforms, and the comments from readers and audiences have proved to be a valuable source of inspiration. I have attempted to identify and acknowledge all my sources but fear that in over 40 years of professional practice, teaching and research the occasional phrase or idea may have slipped into my notes or memory and gone unacknowledged. If that has occurred I trust that the people concerned will accept my apologies and thanks. Particular thanks are due to Mike Cheadle for keeping my computer going and to Briony Birdi (née Train) for helping test the questionnaire and talking to me about public libraries. I have also received help from a number of libraries and would like to thank members of staff at, the British Library Colindale, the RSA Library, Sheffield City Library and the University of Sheffield Library. I am also grateful to the archivist at the Dartington Hall Trust, Angela St. John Palmer, who opened a display case so I could see the document quoted in the Postscript, and to Yvonne Widger, the archive administrator for clarifying some details. Thanks too to Helen Grindley for providing an index and to Dymphna Evans and Nikki Dines at Ashgate Publishing Ltd.

As ever, I owe more than I can say to the support and patience of my daughters, Julie and Tania and to my wife Hazel for, finding material, proof reading, discussing 'light fiction' and just about everything.

Author's Notes

In the questionnaire sent to library authorities respondents were asked if they wished to be identified or not. In the event there was a very mixed response to this request and in order to protect the identity of those who did not want to be named it has been decided not to identify individual respondents but to give a broad indication of the background and experience of the person quoted. Respondents have been divided into the following categories:

HoS   [Head of Service or equivalent]
Dep   [Deputy Head of Service, Chief Assistant or equivalent]
SP   [Senior professional]
PG   [Postgraduate student on a dedicated public library module]

A number indicating the respondent's professional experience in years follows each code. These have been divided as follows.

10+ [10 − 20 years]
21+ [21 − 30 years]
31+ [31 − 40 years]
41+ [41 years or more]

The experience of the postgraduate students is between one and four years

Thus, a quote followed by [HoS 31+] indicates that the statement was made by a current Head of Service with between 31 and 40 years professional experience.

It has also been decided to include the identification codes in respondent quotations taken from other research projects. In most cases, these are self-explanatory where this is not the case they have been expanded as appropriate.

Comments from respondents are included as supplied and not edited for grammar, etcetera except to aid clarity of meaning.

Chapter 1

Equity and Excellence –
The Librarian's Dilemma?

Modern civilization is a mess and we all know it. Much of the deterioration of our culture and society impacts significantly on librarianship and makes the achievement of our ideals all the more difficult.

Finks (1989)

Recent years have seen a proliferation of intellectual arguments, political policies and management structures that emphasize the need for public library services that, in the language of the times, meet the needs of the many and not just the few. As part of a modernization agenda, public libraries are required to satisfy a range of ambitious objectives. Officially perceived as a service that is inclusive and based on the ideas of social equality, they are expected to contribute to reading and education, to enable digital citizenship, and promote social inclusion. Such worthy ideas, along with many others were rehearsed in *Framework for the Future* (DCMS, 2003) and subsequently reflected in a variety of upbeat reports and publications from the Museums, Libraries and Archives Council (M.L.A), the Department for Culture Media and Sport (DCMS) and a variety of other public and professional bodies.

According to many of those involved such policies are urgently needed if public libraries are to find a place at the heart of modern life. It is argued that if these ideas are to be successfully implemented then public libraries must identify and remove barriers to access and develop inclusive services and activities. It is a direction that receives substantial support in parts of the literature, where writers argue the case for public libraries respecting, 'the various pop culture tastes and interests of adolescents' (Rothbauer, 2006); and, to quote Fox (2006), 'one of the most important government strategy papers [states that] "libraries must now include cafes, lounge areas with sofas and chill out zones where young people can watch *MTV*, read magazines, and listen to CDs on their listening posts"'.

However, despite the plethora of official pronouncements, and the activities of energetic Ministers, serious doubts are being expressed by some professionals, policy makers, and the public at large. These are not about improving access and inclusion but about the direction the service is being asked to take in order to achieve this. A wide array of publications and public statements demonstrate a state of unease and uncertainty. The nature of the problem was nicely illustrated by an exercise undertaken by participants on a recent course designed to develop public library leaders for the future. Those taking part were asked to, 'consider the senior manager who is working to implement the vision outlined in *Framework for the Future*, while long-standing library users are lobbying local politicians for more of a traditional service, and staff feel their professional skills are being undervalued' (*Leading Modern Public Libraries*, 2005). The different elements of that task reflect some of the tensions that exist in the public library world, notably the perceived neglect of established users and services, and the fashionable dislike of professional values and standards. Moreover, its inclusion on a leadership training programme is perhaps indicative of a profession that feels the need for a greater sense of direction.

From outside the immediate professional community critical friends and cultural commentators complain that, 'The library service has lost its soul and desperately seeking some justification veers between pop marketing in imitation of the big chains – and trying to be a sub brand of information processing' (Hoggart quoted in West, 1991). The recent rebranding of some service points as 'Idea Stores' or 'Discovery Centres' is seen by others as part of a fashion 'to turn our great national museums and libraries into entertainment centres, ostensibly to justify their public expense' (Kerevan, 2004). In so doing, public libraries, in the words of former ALA President Sarah Long (2001), have been 'fitting in with a tide of stylish opinion that was sweeping the country, opinion that was both anti intellectual and anti authority'.

In other fora professionals and users have expressed various anxieties and concerns. Although the past decade has seen the emergence of some splendid new buildings, there are still serious worries about the deterioration of the public library infrastructure. A survey by the Museums Libraries and Archives Council (MLA, 2006a) found just under a third of public library premises to be inadequate. It identified crumbling buildings, maintenance backlogs, and a need for major investment to bring them in line with health and safety legislation. At the time of writing, and despite much evidence to the contrary, broadsheet and populist newspapers in the UK regularly carry headlines predicting the end of the public library. In 2004 Tim Coates, formerly a managing director of the Waterstones chain of bookshops famously suggested that public libraries in the UK would all be shut down by 2020 because of a lack of demand. He argued that they had 'failed to meet the need for a broad range of books; [and] to be open at times when users are able to visit'.

The physical and psychological state of the public library service can be seen as symbolic of the condition of cultural institutions in general. In a post-modern age where little is taken seriously and professionals, be they broadcasters or bibliographers, are urged to implement increasingly philistine agendas many will share the concerns of the fictional Professor Stewart who, when he listens 'to the talk about cultural institutions and how they need to be renewed, and the importance of visitor figures... wonder [s] if we are forgetting their ultimate purpose' (Waterfield, 2003).

In the United Kingdom the discussion about the library service reflects, in many respects the current debate about the future of another cultural institution, the BBC. In the words of one Head of service, 'The Library Service has great synergy with BBC programme aspirations. These include reaching into different and more diverse communities, being accessible and opening and widening the base of media literacy skills' (Cordwell quoted in Slane, 2006). At the same time, Aspden (2004) has written about how the BBC is, in 'a tricky position hovering between several expectations: as a guardian of the cultural cannon [and] as a mass broadcaster that has to win the approval of several different elite groups...'. Like the BBC, public libraries also face competition from new technologies, commercial imperatives and, some would suggest, changing public attitudes.

A letter to the *Daily Telegraph* arguing that, 'the vast majority of British adults no longer need the traditional library service', and advising that local authorities, 'sell them off and give the council taxpayers a break' (Keene, 2005), almost certainly expresses an extreme view, but it does reflect a contemporary argument that questions the public provision of cultural and educational institutions be they libraries, museums, galleries or public service broadcasters. It is argued by some that such organizations are out of touch with the values, aspirations, and beliefs of a population that no longer seeks enlightenment or self-improvement.

Indeed, in some sections of the British population education is now held in such low regard that bright children deliberately under perform so as not to be bullied by fellow pupils. This rejection of education has been examined by the sociologist, Michael Collins, who has defended the materialism of white working class 'chavs' who, in his opinion, 'have been branded because they have made it into the lower–middle class via money instead of education' (2004). Others seem to imply that ordinary people, especially those from the working class, have a low attention span and little interest in the world around them. Richard Littlejohn provides the archetypal view of the tabloid journalist when he claims: 'does anyone give a monkeys about what happens in Rwanda... If the Mbongo tribe wants to wipe out the Mbingo tribe then as far as I am concerned that is a matter for them' (quoted in Sweeney, 1994).

This is part of a broader, and what many might regard as patronizing, argument that suggests that only the upper or middle class are interested in the world around them and can appreciate high art or aesthetic values, and that the poor and disadvantaged crave escapism of the easiest kind, or material that provides an instrumental outcome. Howard Jacobson (2004) examined this populist scenario in a lecture at The University of Sheffield. He gave the example of a barmaid in a television soap opera who says of a visit to see Hamlet, 'it bored the life out of me... it was about this king who had the ghost of his father hanging over him. It really did 'is 'ead in.' Jacobson asks, 'why does she speak about it so cretinously? Would it be a sin against class solidarity to have a barmaid know a play by Shakespeare and admit to liking it?' Some professionals, who currently work in public libraries, appear to view the average library user in a similar way to the writers of soap operas. A librarian interviewed by Goulding (2006) observed that, 'People get upset that the library is not a quiet, studious temple of culture. But in this day and age, if you provided that then nobody would come through the door.'

At the very least this indicates that there are some worrying attitudes around in contemporary library services. Indeed, the existence of these kinds of opinions amongst colleagues appears to suggest that some public librarians are content with a professional world that has little regard for intellectual content, prefers style over substance, and promotes choice over quality. They appear to be happy to be part of what John Tusa has called 'the flight from intelligence' (in Gibson, 2005). Because of such views we have, librarians 'gutting the book collections (both adult and juvenile) of classical literature... with the rationale that such things were "too sophisticated for today's readers". In other words, we're directly contributing to the dumbing down of society' (Burnell, 2005). It is a situation that justifies the prediction of a leading British librarian Thomas Callendar who over three decades ago stated, 'We have corrupted the taste of one generation and are well on the way to corrupting that of a second' (quoted in White, 1971).

Ironically, it is currently library users who complain that their 'local library... is now like an amusement arcade' (Hockin, 2004) or, that 'our library is full of old books – mostly, soppy romances and the like', and ask the professionals and policy makers to, 'Please take care of this great asset' (McDonald, 2006). Where a public library might once have been regarded as a place for study and reflection it is now primarily seen by some as a place for entertainment. Those in the profession who dare to argue against this current orthodoxy are attacked as traditionalists, and accused of ignoring social exclusion.

The holders of such opinions are routinely identified by the weasel word 'elitist'. A *Radio Times* trailer for a BBC radio discussion described the situation as one where: 'Anti-elitism is the new Spanish Inquisition.' In its holy name, public libraries are turned into 'ideas shops' (Lebrecht live 2005). Indeed, it is now routinely argued that 'public libraries... are run by elites and attended by a disproportionately large number of upper and middle class patrons' (Harris, 1973). As Holden (2004) writes: 'The use of the word "culture" itself now begs the immediate response "whose culture"?' In the same way Pachter and Landry (2001) observe, 'Judging quality in terms of culture is out of fashion, yet strangely when we buy a commercial product or service from the mundane to the special we focus on characteristics of quality as a matter of course.' Cultural judgements have become relative, suspect and tainted. Almost everything is to be regarded as relative and, in such a world, the professional judgement of the librarian is suspect. Moreover, it is apparently only members of the middle and upper class who are able to appreciate excellence. This is the true elitism of the age, 'when you hold people's capacities in contempt' (Bob 1982).

More recently, Lynne Truss made a similar point when she observed, 'a lot of people are being held back from learning in the name of egalitarianism' (quoted in Byrnes, 2005). Egalitarianism is of course different from equity. 'A strictly egalitarian society would be unjust... if it meant unfair equalities prevailed.' The focus of our concern are what A.C. Grayling (2006a) has called the 'crucial equalities – such as equality of opportunity, equal rights and equality of citizenship status irrespective of age, ethnicity and sex [these are] the foundation of the just society and therefore non-negotiable'.

Political Dimensions

Such matters have a political dimension, but these are often over – simplified in debates about literature and the arts. The Left is portrayed as saying that providing material of high intellectual quality is culturally exclusive, and the Right as complaining about the closing of the American, or for that matter, the British mind (Bloom, 1987). In reality the situation is far more complex. Writers from quite different political persuasions often make the same arguments and make them in startlingly similar ways. Ideas and practices that used to be criticized by the political right are now also attacked by some on the left. Thus, a contributor to a predominately right wing

Adam Smith blog complains that, 'a book that has not been taken out in six months has to be put in storage' (Oli, 2005) while, from a completely different political perspective, the long time leftist librarian Sanford Berman is unhappy about, 'an ongoing epidemic of wanton mindless weeding [...] for the past 4 or 5 months' (Berman, 2001). Also from the left of the political spectrum, a *New Statesman* writer complains that, 'Some libraries appear to have settled for becoming community information points with coffee shops attached', and suggests that 'a statement that literacy is at the heart of what libraries are for would be welcome' (Clee, 2005).

Similar political confusion can be seen in the way that the market driven commercialism of the right, which seeks to justify everything in economic terms, can be seen to equate with the views of those on the left who reject as 'elitist' attacks on popular often populist culture. Thus, some left leaning librarians defend a populist culture, which more often than not is produced by an organized, and often manipulative, media industry. What some, but by no means all, on the left regard as the empowerment of the user can also be seen as an acceptance of the market forces beloved by the right. An Ideas Store Manager, quoted in a broadsheet newspaper, illustrates this perfectly by arguing that, 'our residents want us to talk the language of retail' (quoted in Dyckhoff, 2004). The worry for many is that such retail-led, access-driven policies may degrade the library experience and have a debilitating effect on the educational aspects of the public library.

At some time in the recent past the Right's obsession with choice, and the Left's suspicions of authority, became merged in an unhelpful co-alliance. This is seen in the poverty of much of what we now recognize as post modernist thought, with its dated sense of irony and shallow criticisms of experts and professionals. On parts of the left there has been a form of counter-cultural thinking. This is sometimes based on the ideas of French philosophers like Foucault, who believed that there is no such thing as empirical truth but only a series of equally valid opinions. The political picture is further confused by Habermas' (1991) critique of postmodernism as neo-conservative, irrational and potentially fascist.

Parkin (1972) argued that, 'the musical, literary and artistic tastes of the dominant class are accorded positive evaluation, while the typical cultural tastes and pursuits of the subordinated class are negatively evaluated'. However, matters were never quite as simple as that. The present author recalls quoting the passage to a class of library school students in the early nineteen seventies, but a marginal comment in the lecture notes suggests that students were invited to debate Parkin's point of view. There are alternative perspectives, Rose (2001) for example observes, 'If the dominant class defines high culture, then how do we explain the passionate pursuit of knowledge by proletarian autodidacts, not to mention the pervasive philistinism of the British aristocracy?' More recently, Eagleton (2000) suggested that, 'The traditional class structure and the traditional cultural pecking order, has never been simply correlated.'

A related debate is also taking place amongst some of those responsible for public library policy. In the UK the government's policy, at one level, still invokes the ideas of Ruskin. In its strategy for cultural policy, arts, and the creative economy The Labour Party (1997) expounds his belief that a 'person who everyday looks upon a beautiful picture, reads a page from some great book, and hears a beautiful

piece of music will soon become a transformed person'. Ministers from the DCMS
maintain that, 'it is the content delivered that matters to people' (Jowell, 2004), while
at the same time insisting that libraries promote social inclusion (Department for
Culture Media and Sport, 1998). Members of library user groups also argue that,
'libraries are a major force in combating social inclusion' but are equally concerned,
'at the preponderance of cheap and "popular" fiction and non-fiction on the shelves
[and] the dumbing down of the service' (LLL, accessed 2006). In similar fashion,
the Deputy Editor of *The Big Issue*, a magazine for the homeless, fears that libraries
will be subject to 'an explosion of populism, with 10 copies of the latest blockbuster
novel made available at the expense of one useful but expensive reference book'
(MacKenzie, 2002).

Professionals and policy makers, facing this confusing situation confront
complicated questions that are not always adequately reflected in the populist
debate. They face a subtle and complex set of issues which often cross the political
and or professional divides. There are numerous areas of concern. Will members of
the library profession be able to meet the demands of policy makers to open up the
service without destroying it? Should libraries, at least in part, be evaluated by their
contribution to the population's understanding of the arts and enjoyment of literature
and music? Have egalitarian aspirations hindered attempts to create public libraries
as centres of excellence? Indeed, should public libraries be centres of excellence? Is
it the role of the public library to select, stock, communicate and promote material
that is not entirely dependent on the whims of the market place? Should it be a
place where every one can access minority tastes, a place for the unpopular and the
experimental? Should it contain works that are untried and untested, and promote
ideas that will disturb, question, and on occasions offend?

The literature and agendas for professional meetings indicate that librarians are
keen to attract more users to their service and want to make it more accessible. Fewer
people appear willing to question if this can be accomplished without changing the
service beyond recognition. There are of course people who feel that such radical
change is required. However, the experiences of professionals in other closely
related areas demonstrate the dangers of simply sleepwalking into the future. Even
those who want change need to ask if our public libraries are in danger of being
downgraded and their values eroded by a combination of commercialism, cultural
relativism, and mistaken egalitarianism? The way the profession decides to deal
with these issues will have significant implications for the future identity of public
libraries. In essence such questions are about, what the fictional professor quoted
above called, the ultimate purpose of the service.

In the current climate, simply raising such matters can put an author at risk of
being mistaken for some kind of right wing apologist. Some feel that these questions
should not even be asked. One person responding to the survey undertaken as part of
the author's research wrote: 'I really disagree with the tone of some of these questions
– it has never been the role of libraries to dictate a highly cultural/educational model
on its customers' (HoS 31+). That is a conclusion that library historians may wish to
debate, but it is true that the present writer is concerned at his possible association
with what are apparently now regarded as reactionary ideas. However, he takes some
comfort from Bob's (1982) observation that, 'as librarians we show our contempt

for people's capacities by over-emphasizing the lowest common denominator'. Moreover, as Eagleton (2000) comments: 'Those radicals for whom high culture is *ipsofacto* reactionary forget that much of it is well to the left of the World Bank.' A.C. Grayling (2002) too has argued that people of left-liberal political sympathies can 'believe that high culture has special and superior value which justifies state support...'. It is also worth recalling that it was at a low point of Thatcherism that Norman Tebbit declared it was impossible to tell the difference between a page three girl and a Titian nude.

The present author's own point of view has been shaped by the experience of growing up as part of a working class community in London's East End. That experience included weekly visits to the local public library and regular access to the BBC, which, at that time, radiated public service values. It is now fashionable to regard such values as paternalistic but those two organizations and later the Open University, provided gateways to a richer and more rewarding world. It would be a tragedy if the kinds of opportunities that they provided were not available to, and used by, present and future generations. Of course those future generations will inhabit a different landscape and the public library will need to respond to that, but it should do so in a way that reflects what Gorman (2000) called its 'enduring values'.

This book sets out to explore and analyse some of the issues set out above by examining the views of library professionals, and the observations of writers and commentators from outside, but related to, the library world. Many of these matters have been the subject of Masters Dissertations undertaken by the author's Sheffield students, and some of their work is also drawn on in the text that follows. In the somewhat limited debate that the British profession has had so far there has been a degree of over generalization. The argument is often simply portrayed in terms of, left and right, relativism, elitism, equality and that easiest of targets, political correctness. For the purposes of this present text, librarians' views were obtained via the professional literature and through a questionnaire which was sent to senior practitioners and postgraduate students with a particular interest in public libraries. Their disparate views have been considered in the context of a wider discourse provided by reference to the work of a variety of academics, practitioners and policy makers who have dealt with similar issues, sometimes in other arenas. It is an appropriate time for such a discussion because as Etzioni (1995) remarks, 'The best time to reinforce the moral and social foundations of institutions is not after they have collapsed but when they are cracking.' The public library service is not in a state of collapse, but there are definite cracks in its edifice, and it is perhaps not unfair to suggest that a number of these have been caused by some contemporary professionals who have neglected to look after its foundations.

The book is not intended as a practical manual and the aim is certainly not to produce yet another management tool kit, but rather to encourage professional colleagues and policy makers to engage in debate. That having been said, for those who do seek a managerial perspective, the arguments contained in the pages that follow are relevant to the way public libraries are presented to the public in terms of accessibility, service marketing, funding, and publicity. However, the primary intention is to stimulate and encourage discussion so as to inform and perhaps influence political, professional, and practical judgements. It is hoped that readers will find the basis for that exercise reflected in the text that follows.

Chapter 2

Equity and Excellence Around the World

The changing nature of the world means that this discussion is timely, because not just us but many countries are debating the future of libraries

Lammy (2007)

In the preface to his book, *Where Have All The Intellectuals Gone?* Furedi (2004) observes that, 'Discussions with friends in the United States suggested that institutional dumbing down was not merely a British problem.' Indeed, a brief review of the relevant literature confirms that the issue is not just confined to Britain or even the United States. There are reports from many parts of the world that reflect a growing concern at the onward march of philistinism. A few years ago, Emeritus Professor Geoffrey Bolton (2002) warned Australian librarians of, 'the tyranny of ignorance'. He suggested that his audience look at 'the opinion columns of our tabloids, counting the number of times the words "academic" or "intellectual" are used as terms of contempt, usually linked with some epithet such as "airy-fairy", "ivory-tower" or "do-gooder"', and went on to cite, 'the crude over-simplifications of talkback radio' as part of his argument. In Spain 'telebasura' or 'tele-rubbish' has been described by one spokesperson for the left as 'demented' and, there it is argued that, 'this degradation on the television screen shows how low our society has got' (Seco in Keeley, 2006).

In similar terms the Watergate journalist Carl Bernstein warned a Kansas Press Association's annual convention that, 'the consequences to a society that is misinformed and disinformed by the grotesque values of this idiot culture are truly perilous'. He argued that, 'the weird, the stupid, the coarse, the sensational and the untrue are becoming our cultural norm – even our cultural ideal' (quoted in Ranney, 2005). From a different geographical perspective, Paul Danahar (2006), the editor of the BBC South Asia bureau reports that in India: 'TV news channels are now setting the standards for the whole industry. There is more demand for coverage of the rich, famous, and beautiful [and] the editors of good old fashioned Indian newspapers and magazines, where the standards of journalism are among the best in the world, are looking-on in horror.' In April 2002, *Helsingin Sanomat*, the Finnish daily paper, announced that trash television had arrived in Finland. This, said its reporter, is television that features programmes that 'wallow in scandal involving the less tasteful aspects of human relationships. Others involve certain types of reality TV in the genre – including various matchmaking programmes for singles' (Isohella, 2002).

As Burton (2005) says the 'conduct and effects of media policies across Europe are a cause for concern to... citizens who fear the erosion of a genuine choice of material and ideas'. In fact, that concern is felt across the world and it would be all too easy to provide many more examples. However, for public library professionals and policy makers, the central issue is how the public library service should react to the situation. As Nailer (2002) observes libraries exist in a world of threat and: 'The habit of creativity and the spirit of inquiry, the interest in and concerns for others which define civilized society, are in retreat around the world.' In the US it is argued that, 'Library policy must not be controlled by outside agendas or cascading fads of popular thought; for above this ebb and flow of life styles, there are basic principles that are inherent in the very nature of the public library' (Taber, 2000). Others are fearful that 'Librarianship which has prided itself on its vital role in democracy – is turning that crede into empty lip service through its avid adoption of the customer driven model' (Buschman, 2003).

Many would agree that this type of model is inappropriate for the public library sector. A Swedish cultural commentator argues this case maintaining that public libraries are precisely the type of 'institutions that are expected to bear in mind the good of individuals and the community as a whole without being concerned with short-term economic goals' (Kleveland, 2005). Such worthy ideas are still to be found in the library literature in most parts of the world and, in Scandinavia at least, there is a feeling that in 'recent years the old moralistic ideology has been creeping back through the back door' Mäkinen (2001). However, this may well be the exception that proves the rule because all too often the evidence suggests that in practice: 'At the turn of the twenty first century in many parts of the United States', and the present author would argue elsewhere, '...the prevailing political climate appears to favor individual consumer expenditure over the collective provision of public good' (Pawley, 2003). By coincidence, quite literally as this is being written, research just published by the Henley Centre shows that the latest generation of United Kingdom graduates put their individual needs before those of the community at large. The attitudes of what is termed 'Generation Y' are demonstrated in the City of London where 'soaring bonuses have become synonymous in the public mind with new levels of greed as bankers share an estimated bonus pot of £8.8 billion' (Booth, 2007).

The Scandinavian countries have attempted to fight these trends for longer than most. Less than two decades ago Vakkari was able to write that: 'The library still plays a central part in the Finnish literary culture. It is the main channel of books to readers. The library in Finland has a central role in guaranteeing the availability and accessibility of high quality, varied literature' (Vakarri, 1989). It is then not too surprising to find that in contemporary Finland: 'The effort of the state to promote art and culture is a conscious social development strategy' (Schwanck, 2003). Likewise, an official from the Norwegian Archive, Library and Museum Authority, was able to tell a recent IFLA conference that: 'In a society with obvious social and economic divides, and an expanding cultural and media market, the aim was to offer children conditions of equality and leisure centres free of commercial influences' (Indergaard, 2005).

State Support

As *The Complete Review* observes: 'Without state support of this sort it is unlikely that the majority of large cultural repositories and institutions – museums, opera houses, libraries, and many theatres – could survive in this "market economy" – surely a devastating indictment of the idea of capitalism being what's best for culture.' A similar indictment of the market economy has been observed by Augst (2003a). When considering libraries as agencies of culture he notes that: 'Community in post modern America has itself become a function of niche marketing, in which "culture" has become synonymous with leisure and consumption.'

Across the North American border, in Canada, it is argued that: 'The health of the literary community is inextricably linked to the health of public library systems' (Canadian Publishers Council quoted in Fitch and Warner, 1997). In addition, public libraries in the North-west Territories help preserve Inukitut as a living language (McMahon and Fiscus quoted in Fitch and Warner, 1997). Local issues are also important in Portugal where 'the Public Library is situated at the core of the local cultural policy. And equally so, stimulating the establishment of libraries is considered to be, right from its starting point, the most successful programme of the Governmental cultural policy' (Moura, 2004). Libraries and culture are also closely linked in Germany where most librarians tend to think of themselves as cultural workers. The same is true in Italy where libraries are often thought of as cultural institutions, although some are now keen to adopt an information role. In France, the goals of municipal libraries were recently set out as: culture, information, heritage, training, self-improvement, leisure and pleasure. Here, as in much of Europe, it is seen as the role of the state to provide financial support. The IFLA Country report shows that 'Every new building or renovation is supported by the Ministry of culture for around 30 per cent of the total investment cost in France', and emphasizes the state's role in developing libraries 'in poor urban areas or in rural areas, where the population has less resources and a rather bad quality of access to services ...' (Poncé, 2004.)

In the United States, some academics and policy makers are critical of this kind of government support for cultural institutions. For example, Cowen (2000) in his book *In Praise of Commercial Culture* maintains that it is not only wasteful of public money but also stifles creativity. He writes:

> Germany and France... deliberately sacrifice contemporary popular culture to both older, high culture and to the contemporary avant-garde. These governments restore old cathedrals and subsidize classic opera and theater, while simultaneously supporting the extreme avant-garde, such as Boulez, Stockhausen, and Beuys. Yet European popular culture, especially in cinema and music, is largely moribund and lacking in creativity.

Conflicting Expectations

The existence of such differing professional and political perspectives tends to support Vestheim's (1994) view that 'public libraries in the industrialized world of today are institutions on the crossroads between conflicting expectations...'. There are conflicting opinions too in Africa. There librarianship is described as having 'the option of slowly falling into oblivion or of adopting a new paradigm based on a rigorous re-assessment of priorities and a concentration on the most important aspects of service' (Mostert, 2001). Issak (2000) in her comprehensive report on public libraries on that continent concludes that:

> The consensus of opinion seems to be that African librarians need to rethink what a public library is all about, in terms of what is needed, what will be used, and what is sustainable in Africa. Perhaps some new and more viable visions will result. In particular, public libraries in Africa need to start to be more aggressive and introduce services that are attractive to the users. Librarians must begin to know their potential users, and not only assume that they are school children. More dynamism and more involvement of the user community, extended to all users – school children, adults, literates, non-literates and neo-literates – are required for the improvement of public library services.

She notes that, 'because of the existence of basic problems related to high levels of poverty', that, the condition of the public library service is among the 'lowest priorities' in the African countries that she studied.

The evidence suggests that most African governments have not recognized the role that libraries in general, and public libraries in particular, can play in reducing this poverty. Mchombu and Cadbury (2006) however, present a powerful case that links libraries, literacy and poverty reduction to African development. They argue that:

> Libraries play an important role in the acquisition, maintenance and development of literacy skills. They achieve this through offering access to reading materials that are relevant, stimulating, enjoyable or useful. Pleasure in reading, which in turn helps to foster a lifelong reading habit, is often experienced in the library in which readers gain their first opportunity to pick a book of their own choice. Libraries are also important for providing practical information that can be used to facilitate development, whether for seeking employment, understanding rights, learning a skill, checking a fact or gaining health information.

These functions are also important in the more Developed World.

Trivialization of Public Libraries

In all parts of the world social commentators, library practitioners, and the users of libraries worry about the trivialization of public libraries, and there is a simmering debate about the future direction of the service. In the words of Dowlin and Shapiro (1996): 'The public expects a major urban public library to continue its traditional role as a repository of knowledge and wisdom, providing access to information, knowledge, learning and the joys of reading.' This is exemplified by an Australian contributor to an on-line debate who tells of his disappointment of visiting a library and:

> finding that the work of literature I'm looking for has been thrown away because it's no longer regarded as "relevant" – which was the sad explanation given to me in Sydney

recently while looking for a copy of Lawrence Durrell's *The Black Book*. It and several hundred other great volumes had been removed in order to accommodate newer books which were deemed more modern and "inclusive" (Donovan, 2006).

Some American librarians, according to an article in the *Washington Post* appear to have automated this process using, 'A software program developed by SirsiDynix, an Alabama-based library-technology company [which] informs librarians of which books are circulating and which ones aren't. If titles remain untouched for two years, they may be discarded − permanently' (Miller, 2007).

This policy provoked an angry response from users (*Washington Post*, 2007). One commented that, 'Librarians have always been the last bastion of hope for education, as far as I am concerned. Now they are getting dumbed down with everybody else.' Another respondent in a comment that contradicts Cowen's view quoted earlier, argued that, 'the market model is antithetical to the basic premise that underlines their [public libraries] existence... . We wonder why we as a society are so ignorant not only of our past but our present day, and this article provides one answer.' A further contribution highlights the difficulties of, 'finding a copy of one of the more obscure classics that were mentioned in the article at your local big-box bookstore. The library may be the only source − but not if they keep throwing books in the dumpster.' Similarly at Providence public library in the United States, where there are plans to create a 'popular' library, users 'fear dumbing down of the library because of a lack of attention to its intellectual core' (Jones, 2004).

Such comments reflect many of the issues to be discussed in the chapters that follow. They also demonstrate how far the public library profession has moved, some might argue declined, since the time, when in 'Phoenix Public Library under Dr Ralph Edwards, collection development was the number one priority' (Alabaster, 2002). Similarly, there was a time in Finland when 'there were hardly any library meetings, where a discussion about [the selection of books] did not take place' (Wigell, 1994, in Mäkinen, 2001). Choy (2007) maintains that, in Singapore, 'librarians consciously apply criteria base(d) on our social, cultural and collective values to enhance the usefulness of the collection and help users...'. On the other hand it is argued that in Norway, 'public libraries have now abandoned the concept of public education and are left with the ill-defined mission of providing information and experience to those who may seek them out, as well as taking special responsibility for providing information to the so-called less well served groups in society' (Egeland, undated). Likewise, although public libraries were once 'the crowning success of Scandinavian cultural policy... the egalitarian aspiration effectively blocked all attempts to create cultural centres at a level of international excellence in some parts of Sweden' (Nilsson, undated). This perceived, although it is argued by the present author, unnecessary, conflict between equity and excellence is a central theme of the present text.

Serving Civic Society

On a more positive note, another Scandinavian expert notes that, 'in the service of civic society':

The public library is undoubtedly the cultural institution with which most representatives of ethnic minorities are in touch. The libraries have catered for immigrants and refugees through special services, and the public libraries play an important role in the integration process in the Northern countries as a whole (Skot-Hansen, 2002, 2002a).

Other countries also emphasize the importance of the public library to multi cultural communities. For example, the National Library Board of Singapore when outlining its plans for the future states that 'Singapore is also a multi-racial society. To maintain our social cohesion we need to ensure that no segments of our society become marginalised by lack of access to knowledge or opportunity.' It also pays particular attention to providing support for 'those who need us most – those with reading or learning difficulties' (Singapore National Library Board, 2005). In their plan for the future, New Zealand librarians similarly argue that: 'It is important for the social cohesion and cultural identity of New Zealand that all citizens, whatever their ethnicity or culture, have access to information and reading materials in their own language. Public libraries provide a significant resource with which local authorities can strengthen their diverse communities' (*Public Libraries of New Zealand. A Strategic Framework 2006–2016*). New Zealand colleagues like those in Singapore also focus on the requirements of 'those with physical or intellectual impairments' arguing that, 'libraries need to provide information systems and processes sensitive to their needs'. In India too it is claimed that the 'positive use of library material will lead to a widening of perspective and the development of a community which is intellectually alert and socially aware' (Madiman and Parekh, 1978).

Although it is often thought to be a British pre-occupation the question of class and public library use is, if not universally, regularly raised in library literature throughout the world. For example, Berelson's (1949) study on the use of American public libraries, of over half a century ago concluded, 'the library is pretty much a middle class institution'. Nearly two decades later Ward (1977) in his study of public library users argued that middle-class users were 'over represented' in Australian, French and German libraries. From present-day France it is reported that:

> Municipal libraries are making efforts to conquer new audiences by increasing their cultural actions (book fairs, writing workshops, meetings with authors) and partnerships (social services, early child care, retirement homes, prisons, and so on). Despite the progress achieved, there are still disparities in access to books: between different communes, departments and regions, and social and economic disparities (Desjardins, 2006).

New audiences are also sought in India, from where it is argued that their importance 'would be felt more strongly, if the public libraries attract common citizens and younger generations and such librarians meet the information needs of all walks of users' (Das and Lal, 2006).

Mostert's (2001) literature review of African public libraries suggests that it was believed that the library needs 'of the African people would match those of library users in Europe and America [and that] Services based on these presumptions led to libraries isolating themselves from the general public, content to serve only a small, mainly urban-based, relatively well-off, educated elite'. According to Alemna (1995), Davis (2005) is of the opinion that libraries are 'useful to an educated elite

– [but] of much less utility to the mass of people. He suggests that most people choose to solve their problems through oral means.'

In other parts of the world library professionals are concerned about much newer forms of communication. Information technology is often cited as an issue. An Indian commentator suspects that, 'The Internet, made several Indian school and college kids not miss the public library… But [he argues] the experience of being in a public library is irreplaceable' (Sebastian, 2004). In the United States there is also concern that 'although libraries today receive more visitors than ever, it often seems that their most crowded spaces are where people sign up and patiently wait their turn at the computer terminals made available for public use' (Augst, 2003a).

Professionals, Roles and Values

It should be clear from the evidence presented in these first two chapters that, 'libraries, museums, and public broadcasters face an extraordinary challenge in the coming century. A surge of new populations, languages, and cultures has placed added demands on the content and quality of the services these institutions provide' (Walker and Manjarrez, 2003). Faced with this situation, people in different parts of the world are beginning to ask if the people who work in those institutions are equal to the task. Although it can be argued that 'librarians remain idealists and missionaries, keen to demonstrate their knowledge and skills and how these can be employed' (Egeland, undated), other problems have to be acknowledged. For example, the 'library and information profession in Australia, and indeed throughout the world, is rapidly aging […] [and] The issues associated with an aging workforce include the need for effective succession planning and the development of new leaders' (Hallam and Partridge, 2005). Scandinavian colleagues argue that, 'the librarian needs – not necessarily detailed knowledge of the textual canon of her cultural sphere – but a general orientation of literature and epochs, beyond the often fragmented information given in public education. This orientation should include the possibility to become familiar with different modes of expression, media and genres.' The need to reach out beyond the established boundaries of the profession is demonstrated by the fact that in some countries, including the United Kingdom, there has been a growth in policies that 'merge libraries with other cultural organizations to create new cultural centres, such as combining libraries with theatres, archives, museums or centres for art education. This has been initiated by a reorganization in which a cultural entrepreneur, often without a library background, is put in charge of the new centre' (Nijboer, 2006). This last finding re-introduces the questions surrounding professional leadership noted in Chapter 1.

A recent report from the United States maintains that 'there is a rich tradition of public service that infuses citizens with great respect for the mission of libraries' (Public Agenda 2006), but there, as elsewhere, the service faces political, financial and technological challenges as it attempts to combat a culture of ignorance, and social exclusion. Throughout the world, people who are responsible for public libraries, together with those who use them are, to varying degrees, concerned about the quality of library collections and services. They perceive that established library values are in danger. Ragnar Audunson speaks for many when he argues that, 'while it is important to be undogmatic and open, it is of decisive importance that we hold on to the core principles of the library's role and value platform' (quoted in Kleveland, 2005). As Fink (1989) reminded us, the deterioration of our culture makes the achievement of this much more difficult. It also makes it more important, and in meeting the demands of policy makers to open up the service, public librarians must not sacrifice their core principles or values. Rather they must seek to manage and organize their institutions in a way that ensures both equity and excellence.

Chapter 3

Value versus Demand

In my experience... serious readers prefer seriously good books. They will choose
Toni Morrison before Plum Sykes... with a bit of luck, an appetite for good books will
balance the temptations of trash.

McCrum (2004)

Writing some years ago Hoggart (1988) observed that at 'librarians' conferences
nowadays you are likely to hear an argument between those who still put first the
traditional idea of the library's role, and the 'democrats' who challenge the librarians'
right to choose between books by their own scales of judgements'. Hoggart regarded
this exercise of professional judgement as part of 'the great tradition' and contrasted
what were then contemporary attitudes to those of, 'Four or five decades ago [when]
most librarians saw themselves as offering, no matter what else they made available,
a good selection of the best that has been thought and said especially for young
people who were unlikely to have that access. They made sure that they had well
stocked shelves of the classics, good fiction, poetry and drama' (Hoggart, 1988).

Sadly, the debate over this issue has never been as thorough in the United
Kingdom as Hoggart's observation suggests. It is true that in other eras Ernest
Savage (quoted in Black, 1999) wrote about the tensions between 'the technicians
and the "cultured"' and Eric Clough once demanded that it was, 'time we stopped
issuing rubbish' (quoted in White, 1971). More recently, adverse public comment
on the quality of titles being borrowed from public libraries led the official CILIP
journal to ask, 'Are public libraries dumbing down?' (*Library + Information Update*
2007). Only one contributor thought that they were. In general, members of the
British profession, with the exception of those working with children, have never
been as concerned about the quality of public library collections as their colleagues
elsewhere. In the UK, there has never been the depth or quality of debate such as
that engendered by the American Public Library Inquiry. A product of the post-
Second World War years the Public Library Inquiry set out to study and document
the successes, strength and weaknesses of American librarianship. In so doing, it
'struggled with the same questions of identity purpose and strategy that confronts
today's public librarians' (Raber, 1997). The final result was seven books and
five supplementary reports which were published between 1949 and 1952. These
suggested that libraries should focus on material of 'quality and reliability' and on
services to 'serious groups in the community, however small'. The authors argued that
such an approach would bring benefits to all by contributing to sound public policy
decisions affecting individuals and communities. Although these recommendations
were later described as 'unforgivably elitist' (Raber, 1997), in the United States, they
remained a subject of professional discussion to the end of the twentieth century and

beyond. Indeed, in 2006 some American library school students were apparently taking part in a seminar which asked: 'Why were the results of the Public Library Inquiry relegated to the history shelves? Were they invalid? Or did they reveal things about the situation that people just didn't want to have to confront?' (University of North Carolina, 2006).

In the United Kingdom, few of the respondents quoted in Ann Goulding's (2006) survey of public librarians' opinions seemed to be terribly worried if public library book lending should be driven by quality or quantity, value or demand. In the same way many of those taking part in the survey associated with the present text were equally reluctant to claim any special expertise in this area. When asked if public libraries should aim to make the best material available one respondent asked, 'Who is to say what the best is – let the people decide, even if it's the *Sun* or BNP manifestos. Then we can start having the debate about what is "best"' (HoS 21+). Another agued that 'It is disingenuous to assume that the professional librarian knows what quality is on a diverse range of items' (PG).

This unwillingness, on the part of so many, to acknowledge any kind of professional expertise in terms of the selection of material suggests a serious gap in our professional development. In the words of James Jatkevicius (2003), 'What on earth are we doing in this profession if we are unwilling to pass value judgements on books and other information media?' Such reluctance is perhaps indicative of a kind of anti intellectual pragmatism that is sometimes evident in the British profession. Over the years, this has been a recurring theme in some student dissertations supervised by the present author and it is somewhat dispiriting to see that the attitude persists. It shows itself in a number of ways. It can be found for example in a routine dismissal of theory and research and can also be seen to have an impact on day-to-day practice. For example, Abigail Phillips (2005) in a dissertation, recently supervised by a Sheffield colleague, found 'that there was reverse discrimination by stock selectors regarding quality, or highly regarded literature'. One of her respondents commented: 'There is a certain amount of anti-intellectualism. Stock selectors can be turned off by anything they think is too highbrow or demanding for their readership.'

The Demand Debate

Even at a time when it appears that many librarians and policy makers are more concerned with the cost rather than the value of selection it is worth asking if a public library's stock and services should be designed simply to satisfy user demands. Those who argue in favour of just meeting demand tend to question the right of librarians to impose their standards on the public at large. They maintain that members of the general public pay for the service and should be able to obtain what they want and argue, that even if a major role of the library is to educate, material reflecting a wide range of quality should be made available. Moreover, the proponents of this position suggest that it is a waste of public money to buy items that are not regularly used. It was a view that was strongly reflected in the opinion of one respondent to the present study who stated that: 'Only the most popular and frequently used materials that meet the needs of local communities should be purchased – the rest can be borrowed via ILL' (HoS 21+). It was also recently stated that in economic terms libraries have to be tough minded about storing stock that is no longer issuing (LASER, 2004). Others suggest that providing unchallenging material may lead people on to 'better things'. However, as Levy (2000) points out what he calls 'the taste–elevation theory' had, in some parts of the world, been largely abandoned well before the end of the nineteenth century.

Certainly, it would appear that in the contemporary public library world the emphasis is now very much on satisfying public demand. Many of those responding to the survey undertaken as part of the research for the present book pointed out that: 'Public libraries are used voluntarily. If libraries cease to satisfy public demand then they have failed' (HoS 21+). It was stated that, 'It would seem nonsensical... to defend a service that was clearly unable to satisfy public demand' (SP 31+). This reflects a significant change in professional attitudes. As Raber (1997) comments: 'That the public library might someday base its legitimacy precisely on the ability to satisfy public demand is a condition that could scarcely be imagined by the authors and supporters of the [U.S.] Public Library Inquiry.' It is however the predominate, and apparently preferred, model for the present day. In a recent electronic article, Parry (2003) argued that librarians should:

> Find out what your customers want, and give it to them. Be extremely suspicious of words like 'need' and 'should' and 'ought' with respect to patron borrowing. It's none of your business what they should, or ought, or need to read. Your business is giving them what they want. You have no more business deciding for your customers what they will read than the most militant censor has. Your job is to sense what they want, not censor what they get.

Degrading the Mission of the Public Library

This reflects a change of direction that still concerns what now appears to be a minority in the profession. They argue, as did one respondent, that the library 'can do so much more [than satisfy demand]' – leading the way to new services and facilities before a demand is ever recognized. It would be a shame to stifle innovation and creativity (HoS 31+). Another asked, 'How do they [users] know what they want? From the media for example? Libraries need to acknowledge demand but also go beyond what people think they want to offer more than what is known' (PG). McCabe (2001) argues the case most forcefully when in *Civic librarianship* he argues that to 'surrender to the demand approach to selection will clearly degrade the mission of the public library'.

In practical terms meeting short term user demand for populist titles will result in too many copies of these titles in the future. Moreover, simply responding to demand can often work against the needs of individuals and communities. Such 'democratic' selection can result in public libraries supplying the lowest common denominator. In addition as D'Angelo (2006) reminds us:

> it is wrong to identify consumer demand with the democratic will of the people because democracy operates on the principle of one vote per person whereas the market operates

on the principle of one 'vote' per dollar, favoring the rich over the poor. Nor do consumer markets permit the kind of rational, public deliberation that most democratic theorists have believed is necessary for democracy.

In the United States the critic Clive Harris cited television as an example of 'the first truly democratic culture – the first culture available to everybody and entirely governed by what the people want'. He concluded that 'the most terrifying thing is what people do want' quoted (in Sweeney, 1994). As this is being written that comment is exemplified by the fact that books by Dan Brown, and Jeremy Clarkson, a yobbish television personality with a penchant for fast cars who finds mobile libraries 'quaint' (2006), are high in the UK fiction and non-fiction best seller lists respectively. A fact that brings to mind a comment by a character in Jonathan Coe's excellent novel *The Closed Circle*. Describing Britain in 2002 he observes, 'the obscene weightlessness of its cultural life, the grotesque triumph of sheen over substance'. It is a world in which celebrities have replaced thinkers and academics as public commentators.

A review of correspondence in the British press shows that many library users, unlike some professionals, are aware of the dangers of an over concentration on populist material. It is rare to find letters from members of the public complaining that a library collection does not contain enough populist material, rather they express concern that, 'public libraries now actively discourage users seeking titles which are outside a narrow populist mainstream' (Binns, 2004). This is a view that mirrors the opinion of one of Black and Crann's (2000) mass observation correspondents who observed, that, 'though the building is large, the main library is pretty much last year's mainstream fiction. It's not that I'm a snob, it's just that I've read most of the decent genre fiction they have, and I have never chanced on anything else of interest'. Similarly, in *Checking the Books*, a study examining the value and impact of public library book reading undertaken by the University of Sheffield (Toyne and Usherwood, 2001), a library service that stocked a large amount of popular material was criticized by respondents for not providing material for those who sought a more challenging read or 'aesthetic escape'. In the same way when Phoenix public library created a system-wide adult circulating core collection of material 'universally accepted by librarians' it was found that 'most of the much maligned core titles did circulate and in some cases even ended up increasing branch circulation' (Alabaster, 2002).

Serving the Serious User

Clearly, there are many who do not want libraries that pander to populism, and it is quite wrong, not to say patronizing, for library professionals to assume that their users are unable or unwilling to read material that is more challenging. As Jacobson (2004) has written, 'those who lose the most [are] those in whose name populism is practised'. To quote Tessa Jowell, 'in seeking access, we want to make sure we are supplying access to the best. Access to the substandard is access to disappointment' (Jowell, 2004a).

The argument for concentrating on value rather than simply responding to demand appears to place emphasis on the needs of the serious user. This is a concept which appeared to antagonize and even anger some respondents to the present study. When invited to comment on the statement, 'The proper business of the library is with the serious user', a large number asked: 'Whose place is it to judge what "serious use" is?' (Dep 31+) and, 'How would you define "serious"?' A Mills and Boon reader may be as 'serious' a user as a PhD researcher (HoS 21+). A few months earlier Philip Pullman (2006) had provided a definition of 'seriousness' in a piece written in support of the Love Libraries campaign. He said, 'There's a seriousness about library buildings and the atmosphere they contain – not a solemn hush-hush disapproval, but a feeling that people come here to go about the business of thinking about important things, of finding out truths, of extending their knowledge'. This seems to be a reasonable rationale for a public service.

The strength of feeling expressed by respondents to this aspect of the present study was somewhat reminiscent of the reaction to a brief comment in the foreword to *Reading the Future*. This document was based on the final report of the Aslib Public Library Review and published by what was then the Department of National Heritage (1997). It argued that: 'The original concept of the British Public Library system was one of high seriousness and importance. In more recent years, there has been a shift away from that high seriousness towards entertainment. Information technology should help to restore the profound importance of public libraries in our society.' The topic was also touched on by Iain Sproat at the official launch of the document. This may have increased the professional antagonism to the idea because, at the time, Sproat was a very unpopular Junior Heritage Minister in a very unpopular right-wing government.

However it would be a fundamental mistake to see the issues he raised as only of concern to those on the Right. It was very much, an issue on which commentators from quite different political perspectives expressed strong views. Richard Hoggart and Dame Barbara Cartland, for example went 'head to head' in *The Guardian*. In an editorial the paper itself, although surprised that a government so in favour of market forces should call for 'seriousness' at the expense of materials for which there is popular demand, approvingly quoted Iain Sproat as saying, 'The Government will want to look at a general return to high seriousness' (in Stainer, 1997).

Those who place emphasis on serious use argue that such use improves individuals and communities by increasing their stock of knowledge and providing opportunities for growth, development, and greater understanding of the issues of the day. It suggests that the public library has a responsibility to educate, and this provides part of the justification for public funding because the people who use the service 'are therefore made better or wiser people and contribute to the whole of society. The whole is taxed and the whole is enriched' (Library Board of Western Australia, 1966). In addition the public library can and should provide people with the opportunity to benefit from material they might not wish to search out for themselves. For one respondent: 'This is our USP – chain booksellers/the economics of the publishing world are reducing the availability of many titles/the range of titles on a subject. We must maintain the depth and breadth of our collections, including appropriate retrospective collections' (Dep 31+). Such provision gives people the opportunity to take risks. As Michael Grade (1999) has argued, 'Public service involves taking risks to make it relevant for people's lives. It should not be wall to wall instant gratification… there is the capacity to do much more than that!' He was talking about public service broadcasting but the same applies, or should, to the public provision of library services.

The provision of a wide range of material was thought by many respondents to the *Checking the Books* study to encourage people to experiment and take risks with their reading. It enabled readers to develop and grow because in the words of one, 'it is economical to try out books in the library. [People] are not wasting their money. They are safe to try out new books or authors.' One user told the researchers: 'It broadens what you read, I've read new writers, I wouldn't have done if I had to pay every time' (Female 45–54, North Midlands). An Arts and Cultural worker participating in the study also maintained that:

> Libraries are vital in ensuring that people experiment in their reading. I've run readers groups and people are adamant that they won't like something. You persuade them to read it and they love it. Choice and availability is vital, as otherwise people would get very bored. Readers change, so they need the range to assist them in their changes.

Other respondents felt that through taking such risks they had progressed as readers. Often this progression was from popular fiction to what they regarded as a more challenging read. This view was also confirmed by some respondents to the current study who argued that, 'Libraries offer a place where people can expand their horizons and take risks in their reading material – in disadvantaged communities, free access to such material may make the difference between trying it out and sticking with something "safer"' (HoS 31+). The use of, 'This material will broaden people's horizons and promote social cohesion and understanding in all possible levels (local, national, international)' (PG). It suggests that a good public library is one that provides people with an increased awareness and provides opportunities for personal fulfilment.

Those who argue differently, 'fail to appreciate the extraordinary delight felt by the self taught when first stumbling across Ruskin or Marx, Beethoven or Rembrandt' (Hoggart, 1998). This kind of approach is open to fashionable accusations of paternalism but, as the above examples demonstrate, it has provided many people with the chance to grow and develop. Moreover, if one has to make a choice between the accusations of so called paternalism levied at (say) the BBC, libraries, or other cultural institutions and the free market products of Murdoch, media moguls and others on the cultural relativist wing then paternalism does not seem such a bad option.

A minority of respondents warned against going 'overboard on this [providing challenging material]' arguing that 'we do tend to traditionally'. They felt that it was, 'better to provide a good range and lots of popular material too because that is how people will get hooked on self development/love of literature, and so on' (Dep 10+). Of course, library users will want to make use of both ephemeral and quality material. However, in today's economic climate, it is not possible for any one service to acquire everything and judgements have to be made. In making such judgements those responsible for library services should be concerned about the ultimate needs of society. They need to be concerned about the overall importance of service and collection development. John Ruskin once argued that there were two kinds of books: the books of the hour and the books of all time. It is a major role of the public library to concentrate on volumes of lasting value. It is important to remember that, 'what the public values *today* may compete with the idea of intergenerational equity' (Holden, 2004). The public librarians of the present day need to reflect on their responsibility to maintain and sustain the quality of material available for future generations.

It is, from this perspective, wrong to spend a large amount of what is always going to be limited public money on material of limited quality. The value of a public library and the material it includes is not just about the present day but extends into the future. Demand is often short term and the vast majority of ephemeral populist publications are readily available from many other sources. In practice most libraries will acquire a reasonable amount of popular titles for those unable or unwilling to use alternative outlets but such items are rarely time sensitive and requests can be adequately satisfied via a reservation system. In some circumstances libraries may wish to adopt the American practice of 'speed reading' whereby high demand material is lent for shorter periods, say one or two weeks, and attracts higher fines to encourage a swift return. Some libraries in the United Kingdom have developed Bestseller collections. These are short loan collections containing multiple copies of the latest bestselling books. There can however be problems with such an approach, especially if this type of material is bought at the expense of work of more lasting quality. Similarly, suggestions for pay collections or fee based premier membership are contrary to the principle of equal access.

Cartwright's research (2001) suggests that public library stock is often valued for its archival nature and in the broader perspective, it is the overall quality of the collection, its breadth and scope that matters. As one respondent observed 'This may not be new material. The joy of public libraries is the depth and breadth of their collections and the opportunity they provide for people to discover unknown and unfamiliar material' (HoS 21+). Another argued that:

> We must maintain the depth and breadth of our collections, including appropriate retrospective collections. Similarly, we need to ensure the provision of minority interest/community language/BME interest materials LGBT interest material, frequently unavailable elsewhere, as well as large print materials which have a very limited commercial distribution and the lack of which severely reduces the quality of life (Dep 31+).

As a public service, the public library has a responsibility to keep predominantly to the higher ground. It is not enough to argue for the purchase of multiple copies of an item simply on the grounds that it is popular. That kind of measurement of popularity could apply to tabloid newspapers such as *The Sun* and *The Daily Mail*, and television programmes such as *Footballers' Wives* or books such as *The Da Vinci Code*. High numbers and high quality do not always go together, and a public library collection should not be put together primarily on that basis. As Stauffer (1999) reminds us, 'the literary quality of a fictional book is based not upon its popularity or the ease with which it can be read, but upon the quality of the literary elements found in the book'. David Spiller (2000) in his review of the principles of stock selection quotes T.S. Eliot who said that, 'Those who claim to give the public what the public want begin by underestimating public taste; they end by debauching it.' In twenty-first century Britain that is demonstrably true and rather than join television companies and newspaper proprietors on that slippery slope public librarians should concentrate on the acquisition of material that enriches the user. As Akey (1990) reminded an American audience, when public libraries become, what he termed 'McLibraries, the serious reader gets shelved.'

However, many in the profession today, perhaps many who read this text, would argue that promoting and prioritizing high aesthetic standards would make libraries culturally exclusive. The argument comes in many forms. From one, often a left of centre perspective, it is regarded as undemocratic to promote high, often described as elitist, culture at the public expense. It was argued by one respondent that. '… the current standards are set by the white middle class and are both exclusive and elitist' (HoS 21+). Those who argue this case often appear to confuse excellence with elitism, an all too common fault in contemporary Britain. Their view seems to be based on an arrogant and patronizing assumption that ordinary people lack the capacity to discriminate. As such, it is a confusion that is in danger of disadvantaging many of the most vulnerable in our society.

Professional Responsibility

Public librarians who are responsible for the public provision of information, ideas and works of imagination will always be faced to varying degrees with difficult decisions reflecting the dichotomy of value *versus* demand. Essentially, do they give the public what it wants, or do they concentrate on material of quality? Such arguments are brought into sharper focus at a time of declining resources and rapid developments in ICT. Of course, some popular material can be of high quality and high quality material can be entertaining and popular. It is too simplistic to assume that popularity and high quality are always in opposition. There is a balance to be struck and public libraries should select the best of the popular in addition to providing a comprehensive range of high quality material. They must also contain a wide variety of material that is not readily available elsewhere.

At the time of writing this issue is being discussed in terms of the provision of audio visual material. Subscribers to an email discussion group have argued in favour of libraries, 'supplying the less "popular" genres – world music/cinema, key directors, classical'. They maintain that 'AV collections should be regarded as part of the core "stock" of a library' – and that buying such material will, 'encourage the production of a greater variety of product range in the DVD market place where libraries have got a clear imperative, for example documentaries, DIY, travelogues, biography, world knowledge, etc., etc.' (Metcalfe, 2006). Given the ready availability of populist material, another subscriber suggests that, 'the library service will need to offer something distinctive or give up media as a lost cause. This could be… a high quality, distinctive media service that majors on world music, art house films, and specialist publications and out of print classics' (Heywood, 2006). Interestingly contributors to the discussion list demonstrate a sound knowledge of the range of material available and, unlike some respondents to the present study, a willingness to make value judgements about the quality of material that is available. In Scandinavia, after two decades of debate about the nature of the music libraries: 'They have adopted the common user-centred attitude but not a totally demand-based acquisition. They advocate a wide-ranging collection... there exists an astonishing unity in the views of the librarians and the users. Both librarians and users accept a pluralistic view: it is not only demand that counts' Mäkinen (2001).

Public librarians should also be expected to know what constitutes quality in books and other library material. One respondent felt that there was a lack of 'mechanisms/training available to ensure librarians were taught book selection' (SP 21+). David Spiller made a similar point suggesting, in 1991 that book provision as a subject had moved down the agenda as the study of management and information technology moved up. Stock management, he argued, had been neglected in practice, education, literature and research (Spiller, 1991). A respondent to the present study also argued 'that some of these issues are not considered at library school anymore, or adequately debated' (SP 21+). This may have been true in some places but this author would point to the example of the practical public library stock selection exercise which, with the help of local public librarians, was an integral part of the public library course at the University of Sheffield. It is also true that in the last few years, reading and reader development have reappeared on professional and political agendas. In addition, the Public Libraries Stock Quality Health Check, pioneered by *Opening the Book* was developed as a practical tool to help libraries assess the relevance, depth and range of stock they hold in relation to the profile of the communities they serve. Unfortunately, it now appears unlikely that this potentially valuable initiative will receive any further support from the MLA.

In other times and other places public librarians were, 'encouraged to take as much part as possible in the selection of books for their libraries' (Library Board of Western Australia, 1966). However, it appears that over the past few years a combination of market forces and a misplaced fear of elitism has meant that rather too many in the library world have been unwilling, or at worst unable, to differentiate between the good and the bad. Indeed, it is true that for a brief period, especially in the 1980s and early nineties the range of stock available in many UK public libraries was narrowly populist. This was, in part, the result of a reduction in public sector budgets that often led to reduced book funds, and the market orientation of the times that frequently caused performance to be judged simply and simplistically in terms of book issues. It was a time when some public librarians, 'in a welter of management speak, ICT and strategic plans, possibly may just have forgotten the importance of reading and its development' (Conway, 2001). For a while it was almost as if the public library profession had a kind of collective guilt at any mention of ideas such as standards or literary quality. It was and sometimes is, as one contributor to a *Guardian* discussion list suggested, easy to 'get the impression that a large number of people think watching *Big Brother* or *EastEnders*, not to mention drinking, is more important to our existence than reading. And it also seems that anyone who dares suggest otherwise is an elitist snob who supported the Iraq invasion and wants to privatise the air we breathe' (In Front, 2006).

The selection process requires continuous adjustment and librarians need to undertake a detailed analysis of their current provision. Good professionals prescribe for a particular set of conditions, they do not always simply give people what they want. As Bob (1982) writes 'the notion of consumer sovereignty overlooks the question of consumer competence'. Focusing on the user does not necessarily mean that librarians always have to purchase what the users say they want. 'Wants' may have to be mediated in order to provide what is appropriate for a particular community or an individual. A professionally qualified public librarian should be expected to know what constitutes good quality in writing, and the staff of a large public library system should also include expertise in other areas such as music. Stock selection and management may not be an exact science but it is an integral part of the library profession, and an art that deserves serious consideration.

As Spink (1989) reminds us, 'Book selection involves decision making. No one can opt out. Books on the shelves of any library reveal something of the ideas or lack of ideas behind the selection.' As part of the *Checking the Books* project, stock managers were asked to describe the philosophy which determined stock selection, and the means they employed to decide selection. Some earlier work had suggested that a philosophy behind stock management policies has been lacking (Cole and Usherwood, 1996) but the findings from *Checking the Books* demonstrated that more recent stock policy documents had adopted a more philosophical approach, outlining the principles which govern the aims and objectives of a particular authority. Stock managers confirmed that the policies were used as a practical tool to govern their selection practice. Damiani's (1999) work suggests that librarians often talk about having a 'feel' or 'instinct' for what to select. It remains to be seen just how far this trend will continue if and when libraries adopt the stock procurement ideas recently advocated by the MLA.

It is reasonable to suggest that the library user, like the Doctor's patient or the lawyer's client, will gain benefit from the advice and guidance provided by a properly educated professional librarian. In many other spheres of life members of the public recognize the value of recommendations and suggestions from professionals. For example, much attention is given to the advice from the medical profession about how people should reduce their intake of junk food, take more exercise, and generally improve their health. In many parts of the world there is as great a need to counter the ill effects of the junk food of the mind. If junk food results in wide waistlines, a poor cultural diet leads to narrow minds. Both are likely to lead to an unhealthy, even an undemocratic society. As the Fabian thinker Beatrice Webb once remarked: 'Democracy is not the multiplicity of ignorant opinions.' Before dismissing this as 'elitist', it is worth recalling that the Stephen Lawrence murder suspects were largely illiterate and had few educational qualifications, and that tabloid-inspired vigilantes have been known to attack the homes of paediatricians because they didn't know the difference between a paediatrician and a paedophile. Lynne Truss (2005) is also making a serious point when she states that: 'People are turning out like Wayne Rooney, and we are in deep trouble.' Popular culture she suggests, 'is fully implicated in the all-out plummeting of social standards'.

In this situation, society requires properly funded agencies to provide materials and experiences that encourage reflection, explain and celebrate excellence. Agencies such as public libraries that have the ability to challenge attitudes and transform lives. In ancient Thebes the inscription over the library's entrance read, 'Medicine for the soul'; at Alexandria the medical imagery was maintained as the library proclaimed itself a 'hospital for the mind'. Today it is important that public libraries, and the professionals and policy makers responsible for the service support and promote a lifestyle that helps develop a taste for healthy and sustaining cultural diets. To do so will not only help people as individuals but do much to improve communities and the overall health of the nation. It is important to maintain and strengthen those few organizations that provide people with the opportunity to experience things they may not have imagined, and develop a fuller understanding of the world in which they live. Libraries at their best are, as Meredith (1961) reminded us, 'remarkable transformer(s) of energy, for the "fuel" which goes into [them], in the form of books and journals... gives out a steady flow of power through... readers'.

That is not to suggest that public librarians need appear superior and 'academic' when confronted with demands for a new racy title from Black Lace, or the ghosted memoirs of a celebrity footballer. There is however a need to recognize the worth of experience, professional knowledge and values. What is required is a generation of public librarians who will combine their enthusiasm for equity, community and public service with the rigour and mission of the informed professional. Such librarians will be aware of the balance between different types of material in their collection and be prepared to explain it to their users. They will aim at a collection that serves the needs, rather than underestimates the capabilities of their community.

In so doing they may well take advantage of tools such as a Stock Quality Health Check. They will need to ensure that the 'classics' are available and consider the consequences of changes in reading habits and preferences. There will be other considerations such as the needs of people from different age groups, cultures and backgrounds. Although, that having been said, they need to be aware of the dangers of taking decisions based on stereotyping different user groups. Although the precise nature of the boundaries between high and lowbrow, literary and popular material will and should always be the subject for debate, those with a professional responsibility for public collections must have, and be prepared to justify and use, some criteria of quality.

Who Should Select?

The professionals who were contacted for this study were invited to consider who should be mainly responsible for selecting material for the library. They were asked to indicate their strength of agreement or disagreement with three approaches. The first suggested that professional librarians should be mainly responsible, the second suggested that librarians should let the 'customer' select and the third said that all but a very small amount of materials should be selected by library suppliers. The results indicate that the majority of today's librarians no longer wish to exercise the kind of judgement that Hoggart regarded as part of their great tradition (Chart 15).

Only 14.3 per cent of those responding agreed that the professional librarian should be mainly responsible for stock selection while over 67 per cent appeared to have little time for what was once considered a fundamental professional responsibility. One said bluntly, the 'we know best culture is not relevant in a customer led society' (HoS 21+). Another was of the opinion that, 'selection should not be carried out by professional staff because they do not reflect local communities – selection should be carried out by the community, with advice and guidance from library workers' (HoS 21+). Many wanted to involve para professional staff arguing that, 'the person on the counter who deals with the public and their needs on a day to day basis also has a vital role to play' (HoS 31+).

A quarter of those responding to the survey linked to this book were in favour of letting the 'customer' select (Chart 16). 'Local involvement' it was argued 'strengthens links, gives a sense of ownership, extends our understanding of local needs and improves perceptions of relevance' (Dep 31+). One respondent asked, 'who better to recommend stock for purchase than the service user themselves – particularly those people we sometimes have difficulty identifying with, like teenagers?' (HoS 31+). There was particularly support for involving children and teenagers, one respondent had had, 'lots of good examples of getting help from these groups' (SP 21+). However, it should be noted that just over half of those responding were neutral on the matter of customer selection, and that in their written comments many expressed concern that, 'all needs are addressed, not merely the mainstream or [those of] the most vociferous' (SP 31+). A respondent who had experiences with adult customer selection found that 'it is usually people with narrow interests' who take part. Another was worried that, 'Customer selection could lead to a bias of stock rather than a wide ranging stock' (SP 21+). From outside the profession Webster (1999) advises that: 'Librarians should take courage in their convictions, arguing that, as gatekeepers with finite budgets that they must discriminate in what is stocked. They will have procedures to effect this, and these ought to be transparent, but librarians should insist that consumer demand is only one dimension of this process.'

One respondent thought that selection mainly by library suppliers was, 'inevitable in the current financial, organizational, political and commercial climate' (SP 31+), and the survey showed that 46 per cent of respondents were in favour of this approach (Chart 17). It was felt that, 'Suppliers have enough knowledge and skills for 90 per cent of the things libraries need' (Dep 10+). That having been said respondents emphasized, 'the need for good specifications' and strongly argued that selection by library suppliers can only be as good as the specification provided by the library authority. It is also true that the literature suggests that supplier selection can and does lead to unadventurous stock selection. As the figures suggest, the survey of staff indicated that there were some differences of opinion regarding the practice. One of those replying had had a long and happy experience of supplier selection and had found that, 'they are unbiased, have no preconceptions about customers' tastes, and are closer to the publishing industry than we are'. Another respondent was, 'Not sure I agree with that!' adding that 'our experience is that where teams select books the needs fill rate is lower than where the librarians select for their own community. I'm willing to be convinced but to date the jury is still out' (SP 21+).

Wherever the responsibility for selection resides the visitor to a public library has the right to expect a collection of high quality material. The aim should be for a library service that is able to guarantee diversity both in terms of its collections and the people it serves. There is a balance to be struck. The library should include the best of the popular, and a comprehensive range of material that has stood the test of time. It is a function of the public library to show people other worlds and to help users in their choice of material. It should provide the opportunity for them to stumble across a challenging but rewarding read. Even John Carey (2005) who has something of a reputation as an anti-intellectual admits that great literature 'enlarges your mind, and gives you thoughts, words and rhythms that will last you for life'. Words that coincide with the sentiments of Radice (2006), the Director of the American Institute of Museum and Library Services, who recently told a Carnegie Hall gathering that, 'literary reading has special power. It moves us; it explores the human condition; it helps us see ourselves and others in new ways.'

Decisions about the quality of library collections and materials are at the heart of the debate about the role and function of the public library service. The profession must decide if it wants to maintain public libraries as social institutions serving the public good or as *quasi* retail outlets that simply seek to maximize their popularity by responding to populist demands. To argue the case for the former is not to suggest that users should be faced with shelves of material that is unremittingly highbrow but that they should be given equality of access to collections of high quality material. Collections that are the result of well founded policies and procedures that strike the right balance between value and demand.

Chapter 4

Self-Improvement, Complex Culture, and the Public Good

The idea of a free library presupposes value, to the individual and to society.

Jacobson (2005)

Ed Murrow, the journalist portrayed in the recent award-winning film *Good Night and Good Luck*, once said of television that it 'can teach, it can illuminate... it can even inspire. But it can only do so to the extent that humans are determined to use it in that way' (quoted in Evans, 2005). The same sentiment can be applied to public libraries. Historically, they have been seen as places where people have educated and improved themselves. Many examples of this kind of behaviour are to be found in Jonathan Rose's (2001) comprehensive study of the intellectual life of the British working classes. In this it is reported that: 'Once public libraries and cheap classics were widely available, motivated working class people were able to narrow the cultural gap separating them from the educated classes, at least in the realms of literature.' A Chief Librarian quoted in the same work observed that: 'People's curiosity had been awakened, they want to read and find out a few facts for themselves – they want to understand the world better, and so they have started to read.'

Later, Lionel White (1971) expressed the opinion that, 'the public library should take its place in the van of the fight for a better understanding of life'. The service has also been described as having 'a special role in preserving the spirit of inquiry' (Nailer, 2002), while a Finnish commentator has observed that, the 'golden age of the Finnish public libraries began when the dominant library ideology still was rather moralistic and intended to edify' (Mäkinen, 2001). Another writer from Finland argues that 'the idea of popular enlightenment has throughout the years been one of the cornerstones of the library world' (Lehtinenin in Vakkari, 1989). The service, he said had, provided 'light for the common folk'.

Although the language, and sometimes the means of delivery, are now a little different, such ideas still receive the support of many professionals and policy makers. A former UK Secretary of State, Chris Smith (1997) viewed the public library as, 'a platform for self development', while Tony Blair (1996) in his vision for a new Britain argued that, 'Just as in the past books were a chance for ordinary people to better themselves, in the future online education will be a route to better prospects. But just as books are available from public libraries, the benefits of the superhighway must be there for everyone.' Another British politician, Phil Woolas (2006), told the All-Party Parliamentary Group on Libraries that, 'to those who have missed out at earlier stages in their lives. The library has been the place to go to improve your prospects and realize your ambitions.'

From across the Atlantic, Terry Buford, the Director of the Irondequoit Public Library in Rochester, New York, made a similar argument when he told students at the School of Information Studies at Syracuse University:

> You will NEVER get a better opportunity to improve the lives of your fellow citizens than working as a public librarian. When people want to cast an informed vote, get a job, start a business, advance their career, get ahead, get healthier, learn how to do or get better at anything, they can start at the public library. If they want to enrich their lives with literature, the arts or the humanities they can start with the public library. No other local government department does so much, for so many, with so little (Buford, 2004).

Self-improvement – A Thing of the Past?

Given such testimony it would appear reasonable to conclude, as did a respondent quoted in an Insight Research (1998) project, that 'People are probably tending more to use libraries for what they were originally intended for, which is sort of self-improvement, education...'. There are however a number of contemporary commentators and professionals who take rather a different view. They have decided that the culture of self-improvement is outdated. They suggest that we have lost, 'the Arnoldian, indeed Fabian idea that culture improves people' (Holden, 2004). Andy Duncan (2006) the Chief Executive of Channel 4, the broadcaster that gave British television *Big Brother*, declares for example that, 'the old Reithian idea of giving people what is good for them is impossible when there are so many other alternatives'. From the library community, Black and Crann (2002) go further and suggest that the idea of the public library as an agency for self-improvement is something of a myth. They argue that: '*Generally*, the working class has rarely looked to the public library as a potential source of improvement' (emphasis in the original). Such views are endorsed by some of the participants in the current study. A number are skeptical about the library's role. One for example argues that: 'Self improvement is alive and well among the working class but has become detached from public libraries which are perceived as being elitist and middle class' (HoS 21+).

That having been said none of the respondents to the survey undertaken for the present publication entirely agreed with the proposition that self-improvement was a thing of the past (Chart 9). Although their comments suggest that several found the term somewhat old fashioned, it was argued that, 'even if the phrase "self improvement" isn't used the principle still exists'. Indeed, it was considered to be, 'even more important now in this age of competitiveness and challenge'. In addition it was stated that, 'people are increasingly learning and developing independently and the library has a unique role in enabling this to happen' (HoS 31+).

Similar sentiments are to be found in a recent report from New Zealand which argues that, 'Supporting self-improvement, independent learning, and the attainment of new or higher skills for those not able to access formal learning, has always been a significant role of libraries.' There too, it is felt that, 'This role needs to be updated to take advantage of the opportunities afforded by the digital revolution and the appropriate technology' (*Public Libraries of New Zealand A Strategic Framework 2006 to 2016*, 2006). Support for this view is provided by Pachter and Landry (2001) who observe that: 'the self-improving social purpose remains but is framed in terms of bridging the gap between the information rich and information poor or tackling the digital divide with a focus on technique. An example is the Lasipalatsi cyber-library in Helsinki.'

A fashionable e-zine contributor has no problem with the age of the concept or the language used to describe it. In fact, Block (2004) describes the library as, 'The self-improvement place', arguing that, 'helping people acquire new skills and learn how to market themselves to employers should be an important goal for us. Libraries [she says] are also where immigrants have traditionally learned the language and history and culture of their new country.' In many countries, refugees and minority ethnic immigrants have used the public library. The former Whitechapel Library in East London is a fine example of what the service can achieve. During the post-war period it 'was open to… all, and opened doors that would take them away from deprivation and poverty' (Gorb, 2004). It has provided a haven for generations of immigrants including the writer Bernard Kops, who when he heard it was going to close and become an Ideas Store, wrote a play and a poem to mark its passing. Reflecting his experience the poem proclaimed:

> … I emerged out of childhood with nowhere to hide
> When a door called my name
> And pulled me inside
> And being so hungry I fell on a feast
> Whitechapel Library, Aldgate East
> (quoted in Gorb, 2004)

Now, as then, the needs of the immigrant community are immense and, in many parts of the world, newcomers to a country look upon the public library as a refuge and a conduit to understanding their new home.

Those who took part in the survey linked to this book identified three main areas where they felt that the library service contributed to 'self improvement'. The first was information and communications technology (ICT), with respondents citing examples such as, 'the take up of Peoples' Network ICT by 'silver surfers'. The second was adult education. A student librarian argued that, 'the old fashioned term of "self improvement" has been replaced by the contemporary phrase of "lifelong learning" so [it is] very much alive' (PG). The third area dealt with more general ambitions. As such it could be seen as lending support to Tessa Jowell's (2004) view, as expressed in, *Government and the Value of Culture*. In this she argued that, 'complex cultural activity' is the means by which the 'poverty of aspiration' can be overcome. As an example of this a respondent reported that, 'evidence from [name of authority] learning partnership surveys shows that people see the library as a non threatening place where they can learn by themselves. Libraries and other providers are key players in the raising aspirations agenda' (HoS 21+). Another reflected that, 'while LSC policy seems to focus on employability skills, there is still a demand for "self-help" titles, hobby books, and so on [and] still a strong demand for certain areas of non-fiction books (biography, history, genealogy, and so on) reflecting a general, non-academic interest, which I would define as "self-improvement"' (Dep 31+).

Questioning the Public's Desire for Self-Improvement

Some commentators, however, question the public's desire for more general self – improvement. For instance, in his book on the purpose of the American public library, Patrick Williams (1988) states that the American Public Library Inquiry 'suggested, that the masses are content to be ignorant'. This, says Williams, raised the troubling question that 'American democratic theory may be seriously defective'. It is of course a question that applies elsewhere and the literature suggests that there are many reasons why people might not want to seek political knowledge and or intellectual development. Case (2002) for instance, discusses the idea of information overload as a possible cause. He argues that: 'We often think of information reducing anxiety, but such is not always the case... .' Other writers suggest that some people are willing to relinquish control of the discussion of important issues to specialists or experts. Brookes *et al.* (2004) on the other hand, argue that the media and politicians in partnership generate public disengagement and apathy by only offering the public a limited and passive role in political discussion and media presentation.

Kingrey (2002) believes that when seeking further information about, and greater understanding of an issue, people are forced to admit to what they don't know. In so doing, they are opening themselves to new knowledge, and this involves a negotiation between the self and the larger world in which their identity and social status can both be vulnerable. However, Owens and Palmer (2003) think that the Internet has provided people with the opportunity for greater political engagement and activism by altering the power relationship between the mainstream and alternative media. The World Wide Web, they argue, has altered the media landscape of protest by giving activists access to a mass medium that they control themselves. They suggest that this has, in turn, widened public discourse and laid the foundations for a more 'democratic public sphere'.

The repositories of public knowledge (RPK) project undertaken by researchers at the University of Sheffield, indicated that the degree to which the public library service is used and valued or, to reprise Ed Murrow's phrase, 'the extent that humans are determined to use it', is affected by a number of factors. None of these appeared to fit in to neat demographic variables such as age, social class or region. The research indicated that people often use a benchmark of personal relevance and importance when assessing their scale of concerns, and the lengths to which they will go to acquire further information. As a result, the researchers concluded that a person's choice of sources might say more about their sense of engagement with a particular matter than it does about the places from which they choose to receive their information.

The project went on to examine the kind of efforts people would make in order to develop a fuller understanding of issues of the day. Some respondents sought information through special interest groups, using organizations that reflect particular social, political, and ethical beliefs and concerns. Professional and educational status was also seen, in some circumstances, to encourage increased awareness of specialized sources, and importantly, access to them. In this respect, the Internet has increased access to professional journals and publications reducing the need to visit libraries for some, but not all, sources of information.

A person's lifestyle, in terms of their occupation and career was also shown to affect their general levels of interest in matters of the day. It can help or hinder a person's opportunity to discuss such topics with colleagues and peers. In some cases there may be an unconscious, culturally embedded behaviour which motivates people to be 'in the know'. Work by Fyfe and Ross (1996) on the use of museums appears to support this view. The extent of library usage was also affected by factors including parental responsibility, professional identity and societal influences such as educational achievement and upbringing. One respondent reported using the library, 'as a resource to fulfil my role as a parent and as a young professional working in the city' (Parent, Midlands). Parents in particular felt an obligation to encourage their children to become library users. They also suggested schools and education services as an obvious channel for promoting this activity. Some argued, 'it's up to the schools to teach children how to use a library properly and to the libraries to make them see how [much] fun and rewarding it can be' (Parents, South East).

Members of focus groups contributing to the Sheffield study were reluctant to concede that they were apathetic about the matters of the day. Many asserted that time, or rather the lack of it, was a huge barrier to becoming fully engaged with current issues. This restricted their use of the 'less immediate' information sources available to them. Other research on information seeking behaviours reveals a number of reasons that lead people to seek, or not seek, a fuller understanding about matters of contemporary concern. It shows a continuum of behaviours ranging from avoidance to active engagement. Gladwell (2002) has identified 'tipping points' that cause people to seek out richer information. One of these tipping points may simply be the proximity and ubiquity of resources. Evidence from the RPK study also indicates a more personalized 'tipping point'. It suggests that the scale and importance of an issue and the extent of personal relevance, are important when attempting to ascertain the real motivation for seeking a 'deeper understanding' of social and political concerns. The research also demonstrated that emotional and intellectual responses to political and personal events can influence people's use of material.

The RPK study and other projects have shown that libraries are regarded as one of the most trusted sources of information. They are thought of as one of the best places for people to seek out the truth, and to acquire knowledge about matters that are important to themselves and their communities. As one respondent to the present study said, 'Widening peoples' horizons, making them aware of opportunities, promoting community engagement all contribute to quality of life and to a local authorities general duty of promoting well being. It's what libraries do' (HoS 31+). Another added that, 'Providing we promote all cultures and not force-feed an isolating monoculture. We are a unique institution for increasing understanding of and between the diverse cultures in the UK. This is an aspect of the work we do which is often missed' (Dep 31+).

It is also an increasingly important function in a society in which ignorance is so often the basis of prejudice. As Block (2004) suggests: 'When we help individuals improve their skills and their lives, we make the entire community richer and healthier.' When public libraries promote 'complex culture', they contribute to the public good. Their stock and activities should be designed to enrich individuals and communities. A good public library is one that provides opportunities for people to hear, read and learn about a diverse range of cultures. The removal of ignorance is one of the greatest contributions that the library can make to social inclusion.

Twenty years ago, the sociologist Roszak (1987) was able to tell an American Library Association Conference that libraries recognize the 'art of thinking... librarians provide... a lively mind, a thinking presence'. However, there is much in the modern world that works against this. As a young respondent admitted to the RPK researchers: 'We have become lazy, as a generation. Information is in front of you with the TV and the media, so we tend not to look outside those resources...' (Yorkshire, 18–25 year olds). In truth it is not just the users who have become lazy, so too have some professionals. Instead of being inspired, and encouraged to develop, people who use library services are given the message that it is alright to simply stay as they are. At a professional conference attended by the present author, at least one contributor appeared to endorse a vision of the public library as a provider of services to bibliographic couch potatoes. *Sun* readers everyone, stuffing themselves on cheap crisps and their bibliographical equivalent. With the promotion of this kind of intellectual diet, it is not surprising that so many, particularly the young, now seek celebrity, fame and money rather than education.

Lessons from the Past

Observing this kind of phenomenon it is tempting to suggest that the public library might once again return to the golden age of the Finnish service and seek 'to edify'. At the very least public librarians might join Howard Jacobson (2007) and inform people that: 'You don't have to read Jordan's autobiography or take *The Sun*. You don't have to refuse to let your child eat polenta for school dinners and go on stuffing him with meat pie... knowing nothing is not your heritage.' In the words of a former UK Minister for Culture those who work in the cultural institutions, 'need to re-discover the energy, the connection with what people value, with their fervent hopes and the fierce ambition that so characterised public arts policy in 1945' (Lammy, 2006).

The Atlee administration of that time believed that culture mattered. It saw art and literature, not as luxuries but as essential components in the reconstruction of post-war Britain. It is fair to say that for an all too brief period this opinion was shared across the political divides. It is no coincidence that it was a time that gave birth to Penguin Classics, a number of literary and musical festivals, and the BBC Third Programme. This was a radio station that, in the words of *The Guardian* (1946) of the time produced 'programmes... for selective, not continuous, listening'. It introduced new voices such as Isaiah Berlin, Louis MacNeice and Dylan Thomas, and made the best of culture available to everybody. It was a time when the BBC was not afraid to make difficult material available to the public at large and was not governed by audience ratings.

In post-retirement mode, the present author must admit to occasionally 'looking back' and finding that some of the older publications reviewed as part of the research for the present text contain some valuable lessons regarding our current professional concerns. Certainly, they show that earlier generations have tried to solve problems similar to our own. Although it is necessary to be aware that people can and do learn the wrong lessons from history, the oft quoted, 'Those who cannot remember the past are condemned to repeat it' (Santayana, 1998), provides a sound reason for occasionally revisiting the past. Michael Gorman did this in an interview with *Update* (Hyams, 2005). Speaking about the public libraries in Britain in the 1950s and 1960s, he said, 'they were services of which a civilized country could be proud'. He was however, worried that modernizers would 'create a vast underclass of easily manipulated illiterates, semi-literates and a-literates' and that the use of libraries would be confined to 'an ever narrower sliver' of society. This he said was 'a bleak vision' that he was 'not prepared to accept', and neither should the present generation of public library professionals.

Intellectual curiosity does not depend on class, gender or ethnicity and well run public libraries make it easier for all people to access high quality material. They should provide access to accurate, trustworthy, and reflective sources of information, good literature and music. These are things that can often pass people by in their everyday lives. In fact it has been made easier for this to happen as the development of 'narrow casting' and the false promise of 'choice', makes it too easy for people to restrict themselves to a diet of mediocrity. 'Freedom of choice, as it is called,' says Winterson (2006), 'floods the market with trash, so that readers are genuinely bewildered about what is, and what isn't, worth the time... .' Rather than be part of this malaise there is an opportunity for public libraries to do something different and help people develop their critical capabilities. As a mass observation correspondent observed, if we are to 'see a re-emergence of interest in reading for intellectual stimulation, informational and cultural awareness, and self-improvement. Public libraries are indispensable' (Black and Crann, 2000).

The public library service should provide all people, irrespective of race, class, or gender with the opportunity to familiarize themselves with the seminal ideas, great art and literature of their own country and from the varied and fascinating cultures that lay beyond. In the words of a respondent, 'promoting culture is one of the essential things that libraries do and helps increase people's knowledge and understanding of the world around them' (PG). If the service will be able to continue and develop that role remains to be seen. Some contemporary writers fear that the onset of commercialism and its attendant evils will deny future generations these kinds of opportunity. In a frightening vision of a consumerist near future, J.G. Ballard (2006) recently wrote of, 'a place where it was impossible to borrow a book, attend a concert, say a prayer, consult a parish record or give to charity. In short, the town was an end state of consumerism.' In such a town, in such a state, public libraries will become victims of the commercial imperative and will find it much more difficult, if not impossible, to provide materials and services that contribute to self-improvement, complex culture, or the public good.

Chapter 5

Commercial Imperative?

Capitalism is based on aims and drives such as making profits for companies, creating markets, buying and exchanging commodities and money. Our public services, including our public libraries are based on a completely different set of principles.

Rikowski (2002)

Professional attitudes regarding the commercial imperative are an integral part of the debate about the true purpose of the public library and the services it provides. Are they to be regarded as fundamental rights of citizenship and public goods, or as commodities to be distributed according to the mechanics of the market place? In an earlier volume the present author (Usherwood, 1996) identified an increasing emphasis amongst public librarians on commercial as opposed to professional values. Ten years on that trend has grown. Less than half of those responding to the survey linked with this book thought that public libraries should counteract the negative effects of commercialism in the provision of cultural services (Chart 11). Perhaps even more telling than the figures are some of the comments that accompanied the responses. It was argued that: 'We live in a culture where the commercial sector [has] an important influence on individual expectations. In order for the public library to remain relevant and accessible to people, aspects of the commercial sector must be visible in the library' (HoS 21+). One respondent said that, 'we can't ignore commercial techniques – otherwise we won't reach people used to a sophisticated commercial world (HoS 31+). "Public libraries" said another have their own role, they do not exist as a foil to commercialism' (HoS 31+). Using the language as well as the ideas of the retail trade, a further respondent argued that: 'What we need is to offer a good product (and that includes what some librarians dismiss as "pap") attractively packaged' (SP 21+). Such views find further expression in a recent paper from the LASER Foundation (2004) which suggests that library services must follow retailing in being 'customer-led', and argues for more aggressive marketing and the introduction of premium services for those who are willing to pay.

Additional evidence gathered from various electronic discussion lists seems to indicate that some, but by no means all, librarians would like to be part of the commercial sector. Many now enthusiastically adopt the slogans and the values of commerce. In an electronic discussion about income generation, and audio visual material, one contributor commented, 'if you can't beat 'em, join 'em', and asked. 'How do we get a slice of the cake that's attractive to the PN [People's Network] users who are sat all day in our libraries not spending any premium-service cash [...]?' (Wallis, 2006). In slightly more measured terms, another revealed plans to:

implement a series of premium services to our members, whereby for a direct debit subscription they can borrow for free up to three DVDs, five music CDs and five audiobooks at any one time, and can exchange them as frequently as they wish. We hope that it will both provide us with a good, solid income stream, and enable us to afford to buy both AV and book stock in a more exciting way. We also are planning two other, cheaper, premium services – one to allow you to get free reservations and pre-notification of books being due back, and one for PN [People's Network] use (Nankivell, 2006).

Other contributors were concerned about how much they could charge for the rental of console games such as X-Box and PlayStation.

Thankfully, there are others in the profession who have perceived the dangers involved in taking such a commercial direction. Stainer (1997) considers that, 'librarians are being carried along, lending themselves unwillingly to the consumer culture because the profession lacks… the confidence to assert and implement its own vision'. From the United States, Sheppard (undated) argues that, 'As the marketplace moves to exploit the commercial opportunities of new information technologies, the nation's vital public needs for education and lifelong learning can easily be ignored.' A blog from another American colleague observes that, 'we forfeit our position at the center of our community when we choose to build on the shifting sands of market niches' (Keepers of the Flame…, 2002). A contributor to the UK discussion on audio-visual services pointed out that public librarians have problems in attempting 'to confront and successfully address the conflict between multimedia loans as a commercial operation (with income targets *et al.*) and as a way of increasing access to diverse cultural resources in the community' (Heywood, 2006). A compromise was suggested by a survey respondent who argued that while, 'we can't exclude current trends… we can contribute to people's ability to understand the trends and make their own minds up about their value' (HoS 31+).

The debate now taking place amongst librarians reflects the concerns of many of those who work with a variety of cultural institutions. The issues they raise have a real relevance for the library world, and members of the profession can learn from the 'commercial' experiences of those in other organizations concerned with the public provision of information and works of imagination. There are, of course, some positive lessons to be learnt, and there are many librarians who feel that the profession should quickly take them on board. A former President of Scottish CILIP has regularly articulated, 'the need for libraries to lose the traditional image, learn from the commercial sector, and be much more radical about selling themselves' (Methven, 2004). Likewise a respondent to the present study argued that: 'In an increasingly competitive world driven by market forces, in which there are competing services, libraries need to embrace initiatives in partnership with a range of services, that is publishers, local business. This will help raise the library's profile' (PG).

Other commentators have pointed to a reported decline in book borrowing and have suggested that librarians should adopt ideas and practices from their commercial competitors (Coates, 2004). The profession has been advised that 'in today's society, where people tend to be cash rich and time poor, the survival of the library service depends on its ability to compete with organisations in other market sectors, such as retail, leisure and hospitality' (McArthur and Nicholson, 2005). The people who hold these kinds of views are of the opinion that public libraries need to do more to meet the commercial competition. They believe that librarians should copy the retail sector and adopt the methods of aggressive bookstore chains, supermarkets and increasingly, the e-tailers who supply people with books and other material, albeit at a price.

It is a situation that was predicted to some extent by the *ASLIB Public Library Review*. The ASLIB team identified, 'the steady development of teleshopping' and 'significant developments taking place in the US retail book trade' as factors 'likely to have a substantial impact on libraries' (ASLIB, 1995). Cartwright (2001) in a well judged and award-winning dissertation suggested that, 'there may here be evidence of the beginnings of an income and age related split in use of the bookstore and the library'. She also, 'recommended that particular attention be paid in the library sector to the attitudes and behaviour of young people and middle-income earners, currently the groups most noticeably increasing their use of the bookstore'. A similar phenomenon has been observed in Australia from where it is reported that 'store managers have learnt their customers are the kind of consumers who expect good books and good coffee in the same neighbourhood. These are the book stores, in turn, that often produce reviews, magazines and support reading groups, that other booming phenomenon of the nineties' (Carter, 2001).

However, for others, 'the bookstore/coffee-shop model represents a near total denigration of the value of intelligent selection... ignoring the value of the investment in, and maintenance of, a collection (print, electronic or otherwise) available over time' (Buschman, 2003). The broadcaster and journalist, Libby Purves (2006) is another who doubts the value and values of some retail practices. Following reports of chain booksellers selling promotional space to publishers, she expressed the opinion that the true promotional message of retail bookshops to readers is, 'You are a fool pig, guaranteed to go for the shiniest swill-bucket.'

Commerce and the Book Trade

Views promoting the retail model have been widely disseminated and promoted in the library literature, and there is little need to go into further detail. The purpose here is to look outside the immediate profession and to review some of the possible consequences for the users of services that buy into the consumer culture. Broadcasters, booksellers, filmmakers and journalists have all expressed concerns about what they see as the harm caused to their areas of interest by an over emphasis on the commercial imperatives. Indeed as this is being written, someone is talking on the radio about the plight of booksellers, particularly those that are small and independent. They are unable to negotiate large discounts and face serious competition from supermarkets. Indeed, the position is such that some have bought supermarket copies of popular titles, such as Harry Potter to sell in their own shops. This is because the supermarket's discount to the public is larger that than the small independents can obtain from publishers.

Although supermarket discounts might appear to help consumers, in the long term they will reduce the number of booksellers and the range of material that is available. Figures show that a large number of independent booksellers and small chains have closed in the past year. This, in the words of Professor Thompson (2006):

should be of some concern to anyone who believes that good books are an essential part of a vibrant culture. It matters more because it further concentrates power in the hands of a small number of gatekeepers, whose decisions have far reaching consequences for the kinds of books likely to feature in our public life.

Thompson's opinion contradicts the stance of a group of economists who maintained, 'that many of the feared side effects [of the abolition of the Net Book Agreement] on independent bookstores, and title production, have been either ill founded, or have been smaller in magnitude than expected' (Davies *et al.*, 2004).

The same group also argued that, 'Consumers are spending more and more on books, which is comforting from a cultural and educational perspective.' However, a close look at the titles that are being published and bought in such great numbers reveals a educational and cultural picture that is far less comforting than the economists suggest. In the past, publishers' lists included potential best sellers, and the work of new writers. The booksellers were able to display, drama, poetry, new novels and serious non-fiction, because profits would come from the best sellers. This is no longer the case because they are now fighting for survival against the supermarkets chains and others who believe that books should be bought and sold as if they were merely a commodity. As a result booksellers have to reduce their stock to make more room for bestsellers. As Boyd Tonkin (2006), the literary editor of *The Independent*, has noted the chain booksellers, such as Waterstones, have 'made the cut-throat discounting of a few sure fire bestsellers the norm – with all of its risks to future diversity'.

We are facing a situation in which publishers forced to give generous terms to the supermarket giants are far more likely to publish the ghosted memoirs of laddish footballers than a literary work. Untutored, populist taste will tend to go for an easy read, and an illiterate 'celebrity' stands a better chance of being published than a new or experimental unknown writer of quality. However, 'if you dare suggest that the book trade should seek out and support literary ability… an assortment of wealthy populists will get very hot under their smartly tailored collars and call you "elitist"' (Tonkin, 2006a). There is a danger that, without an alternative outlet, good literature will be sacrificed on the altar of the commercial imperative. One writer argues that:

> The down-marketing of everything has meant that even though we have bigger and better bookshops than we've ever had before, in the main, they are stocking greater and greater trash. People like me have said for umpteen years, 'If only we had bookshops everywhere, just think what would happen to the population!', but when these bookshops came they sold Jeffrey Archer and Barbara Taylor Bradford. If these are the main type of things being sold in bookshops, the good that the book can do for society is being lessened (Norris, 1997).

As Franzen (1996) observes: 'There's never been much love lost between literature and the marketplace.' This is a view supported by D.J. Taylor (2006) who suggests that 'we inhabit a commercial marketplace almost deliberately designed to promote the interests of second rate books over really good ones'.

Placed outside of the marketplace, public libraries should be able to provide a wide range of materials and not just those that are commercially attractive. In addition

to high quality popular collections, they should supply that which is innovative and demanding, although it may initially have only a limited appeal. This ability to ensure equity of access to excellence distinguishes public sector organisations from those in the business world.

Broadcasting

Broadcasting is another area where the increasing priority of the market is seen as a cause for concern. Steven Barnett (in Gibson, 1999) and others have demonstrated how the constant pressure on finances and the need for profit has influenced the quality of programming, as broadcasters require, 'bright, safe, glossy, and formulaic guaranteed ratings successes'. The aims of the commercial sector were made very clear nearly 20 years ago by Schneider (1987) who admitted that, 'television's first mission is not to inform, educate or enlighten. It isn't even to entertain. Its first mission is to entice viewers to watch the commercials.' The impact of that statement is made even more alarming by the fact that Schneider was an executive with Nickelodeon, a children's television station. In the UK, there are reports that the commercially driven independent television has complained about the 'opportunity cost' of not showing more populist programmes and has asked to be relieved of its remaining public service obligation. Meanwhile, across the world media moguls and their producers spend their time calculating how they can titillate or push boundaries in order to deliver profits. Television critics, former presenters, academics, websites and various interest groups constantly comment on the deterioration in standards. For example, the Head of BBC News told a conference that:

> in this multi-channel age, I think there is more bad television than there has ever been. Some channels are devoted almost entirely to terrible programming – I've long had a belief that one day we'll have something called The Rubbish Channel – but the contagion has spread to some of the more mainstream offerings (Mosey, 2003).

However, despite such evidence and the increasing concern of scholars and social commentators very little happens. Partly this is because of, 'the long prevailing argument of the Murdoch Brigade of Guards – that the BBC is a State-controlled media rip-off, enjoying the protection denied to commercial television [and radio] and benefiting from a licence fee which they regard an outrage against The Market and the world of advertising' (Goodman, 2002).

Murdoch is another who constantly uses the elitism argument against anyone who dares to make the case for quality. For example, he told an Edinburgh audience, 'Much of what passes for quality on British television is really no more than a reflection of the values of the narrow élite which controls it' (1989). Dennis Potter in his marvellous 1993 MacTaggart lecture spoke for many when he told his audience to, 'Put Rupert Murdoch on public trial and televise every single second of it. Show us who is abusing us, and why. Ask your public library – if there is one left – to file those television franchise applications on the shelf hitherto kept for Fantasy, Astrology and Crime bracket Bizzare bracket' (Potter, 1994). Coincidently, or perhaps not, Murdoch's 'journos' rarely miss an opportunity to criticize those who support the values of public service broadcasting and challenge the Murdoch orthodoxy. Thus, the television critic of the *Times*, which is part of Murdoch's News International empire, categorized those who are critical of modern television as 'Grumpy Old Television Watchers who do not realize that life, fashions, humour [have] all moved on' (Joseph, 2006).

Practical and Philosophical Concerns

Indeed, many things have moved on, but we need to question the direction. 'Post-modern consumer capitalism' has transformed 'discourse into a private consumer product and as such reduces knowledge to mere information or entertainment' (D'Angelo, 2006). The emergence of the 'new public management', so called, in the UK, US and elsewhere, has led to an intentional 'shift away from supply-led services to demand-led services, no longer dominated by professional providers ...' (Farnham and Horton, 1996.) We have already seen how this can influence library collections, and can note in passing that professionals in the museum world are also concerned that such market led access policies have had a damaging effect on scholarship.

The result is that 'the less glamorous activities of conservation, cataloguing, education [are] all being drastically cut' (Moore, 1989). Gillian Tawadros, The Director of the Institute of International Visual Arts has described, 'our new museums' as 'culture's answer to the shopping mall – sleek, desirable and eminently forgettable' (in Gascoigne, 2000). In the United Kingdom, such developments have their roots in the Thatcher era when cultural institutions, 'had to repackage themselves and compete in the market place'. During this time museums were seen as a growth area but they 'redefined what we mean by the term museum and are as concerned with entertainment as they are with information' (Moore, 1989). This situation reflects the concerns of a Canadian colleague, who fears, 'the inexorable eclipsing of culture defined as conversation, social relations and community, by culture framed more as business' (Menzies, 1997).

Although the suggestion that libraries should adopt a more commercial approach, and focus on customer satisfaction, may have a superficial appeal, the experiences of those in related fields should give considerable cause for concern. Such concerns are both practical and philosophical. For example, the transformation of users or borrowers into 'customers' raises some fundamental questions about the function and purpose of public libraries and how they are carried out. The name we adopt to describe the people who use the library service says a great deal about our attitudes to them. The increasing use of the term 'customer' gets close to reducing a professional relationship to one of buying and selling. Adopting a 'customer focus' suggests that library activities are always to be seen through the eyes of the customer and that it is he or she who determines their value. At first glance, this concept has an apparent attraction but it takes just a little thought to realize the flaws in such a position. Users, for example do not always have the knowledge to judge every aspect of a service. In determining the value, values, and standards, of a service whose views should apply? Those of the individual user, the local community, the professional, or society at large? What should be the criteria for making such judgements? Are the demands of the majority always to be considered more important than the needs of an individual or minority group?

Retail Principles and Commercial Innovations

Despite such concerns, the idea of applying retail principles to public libraries is one that is now widely canvassed in different parts of the world. New Zealand librarians, in particular, have been influenced by a retailing consultant called John Stanley. In a breathless report of a visit to New Zealand two Australian librarians sing the praises of 'cutting edge retail techniques' such as 'branding', 'display' and 'mystery shopping' (Roberts and McIntosh, 2004). Despite what the protagonists claim, little of this is new to the public service. For example, nearly a quarter of a century ago, some of the present author's students were undertaking 'unobtrusive testing', now rebranded as 'mystery shopping' of library and information services in Sheffield. Even then it was not new. The Sheffield students' work was based on Childers' (for example 1972) earlier research while Hernon and McClure (1987) suggest that the technique began with the work of Webb and others as far back as the 1960s.

What is new, or at least newish, is the Australian authors' enthusiasm for: 'Another major retail principle, the need to make money!' In every library that they visited, 'Large areas of service are now seen as legitimate targets for fee for service with most libraries seeing it as an important way of demonstrating the value of services that they provide. Most popular were charges on loans for bestseller titles and DVDs, and charges for holds and renewals' (Roberts and McIntosh, 2004). The arguments for and against charging for public library services are too well known to need further repetition but even those who support the idea would find it difficult to claim that they contribute to equity of access or social inclusion. The public library service should not be dominated by those who can afford to pay. Everyone should be able to use what the library offers if they so wish. In the words of one of the *Checking the Books* respondents when using a free public library: '...it doesn't matter who you are, or what your background is, you are able to enjoy what the library has to offer. Everyone is treated the same. Everyone is given a chance' (Male 55−64, South East of England).

A further commercial inroad was made a little while ago in the United Kingdom when it was suggested that public libraries could be combined with supermarkets (Ball and Earl, 2002). This became a reality a few years later when Coventry council opened a new library inside a Tesco superstore. There were reported advantages from this new arrangement. The library was open for 60 hours/week and was said to have received 12,000 visitors and attracted over 7,000 new members within its first four weeks of opening (Managing Information, 2005). However, such an arrangement raises potential problems with regard to the neutrality of the service and the trust that users can place in it. Ball and Earl themselves raise the question as to 'what deals might be struck, involving the payment of rent and a volume-related activity fee by the public library, set off by access to the library's user base'. The same theme re-emerged recently when a contributor to the electronic discussion group on AV services quoted earlier floated the idea that, 'libraries could partner up with private sector operators to deliver a chart-driven, bestseller service delivered to home or office. Companies would value access to library customer databases, and possible reach to people who wouldn't have naturally taken up this offer, though of course there are huge DPA and trust issues' (Heywood, 2006).

The Tyranny of Numbers

Following the commercial model will also have an impact on what is bought by public library authorities. In the same way that the quality of television has been damaged by the continuous search for ratings and the marketplace promotes second-rate books, so the public library service will suffer if it bases stock management policies on the search for issues and other 'numbers'. In the United States, one library has been described as 'just a taxed funded recreation centre and not worthy of the dollars' (Long, 2001), and Berman (2001) complains that some American librarians 'fervently welcome and uncritically promote every piece of fluff or drivel their commercial mentors lay on them'. Despite research that has demonstrated the benefit of alternative forms of assessment too many librarians still feel that they have to justify the existence of their collections according to financial criteria and issue figures. The present author can recall this tyranny of numbers being demonstrated in student dissertations undertaken in the 1970s (for example Day, 1978). It is something of a disappointment to find the same lack of adventure or trust in professional judgement reported in more recent research. Thus, participants in Phillips' dissertation (2005) still regarded issue figures as a major factor. One told her, 'Sometimes I'll think "maybe I won't get many issues out of this" so I'll err on the side of caution.' The problem has been further exemplified in the management of AV collections where the close link between such 'collections and income generation has obscured the balanced selection of this material, so that the emphasis has historically been to purchase the popular mainstream titles that will generate income rather than looking to provide access to a broad range of titles' (Metcalfe, 2006). Surely, one of the roles of the public library is to provide specialist and other materials that commercial interests are unable or unwilling to supply.

Commercial imperatives are not only having an impact on what material is bought but also on the way it is bought. British librarians have been told that, 'the greatest efficiency gains could be made if all library services placed the same requirements on suppliers and negotiated through one mechanism with the suppliers of books' (PKF, 2005). The idea has been taken up in a current report (MLA, 2006) which advocates a new stock procurement model for public libraries. This report is mainly concerned with financial savings. One can have little argument with the recommendation to standardize servicing procedures, indeed to the author's knowledge they were suggested as long ago as the 1970s. More controversially the consultants want to remove the stock selection function from local library staff. They maintain that this will save 50 per cent on current selection costs but in making their argument they demonstrate little concern about loosing the value of librarians' professional knowledge and local expertise. There is a danger that British public libraries are moving to a position, observed in the US where 'libraries are increasingly utilizing the same technology to order books as chain bookstores, and doing away with librarians (those quiet folks who know about books) in the process' (D'Angelo, 2006). No doubt those who argue against the report's suggestions will be told that we cannot afford to support things that make a loss but as Raymond Williams once said, 'this is a nation not a firm'. If we view the public library simply as a commercial entity, it takes away the idea of commonality. In a true public library the user is a citizen rather than a customer. The commercial sector is not concerned with citizenship. Customers and consumers are viewed differently from citizens.

When libraries are part of a culture that places emphasis on profit and loss, and relies primarily on quantitative data it changes the ways in which libraries operate. In the recent past, it has influenced the way policy makers and others expect library services to be assessed. In common with many British institutions public libraries have faced an increasing number of inspection regimes. Many of the ideas of the former Conservative administration, if not always the names, were sustained by the Blair government. The concept of 'Best Value' in Local Government, for example, has had considerable implications for public libraries. 'Best value' represents a strategy for ensuring local government provides high quality services which meet users needs at the lowest cost. In the recent past adverse reports by Best Value inspectors have resulted in the 'early retirement' of some Chief Librarians and in one instance private consultants were called in, albeit on a temporary basis, to run a service which was described by the inspectors as 'poor [and] will not improve'.

Of course, those in receipt of public money must be accountable but many of the current regimes do appear to take this to needless extremes. Indeed, it has been argued that an over emphasis on inspection and accountability represents a lack of trust, and suggests a necessity to constantly check up on the behaviour of professional groups. As the philosopher, Christopher Frayling once put it: 'excess accountability is like pulling a plant out of its pot every day to check its roots and then being surprised when it withers and dies' (in Evans, 2001). At the time of writing, there are mixed signals regarding the extent to which the present UK Government wishes to reduce this bureaucratic overload of inspections. It seems likely that a central theme of the opposition Conservative Party's policy group on public services will be, 'trusting the professionals'. How far this would actually be implemented should that party form the next government is not clear, but at first glance, it is to be welcomed. However, if it is to work, library professionals must be less cautious than some of those quoted earlier and justify that trust, by demonstrating that they are prepared to make and defend judgements based on their knowledge and values.

The true value of public library services can not be measured in terms of statistics and inspections alone. There is a need to consider their public value, together with a range of other values; cultural, historical, social, symbolic, aesthetic, and spiritual (see Holden, 2004). In the social audit and related work undertaken by researchers at The University of Sheffield's Centre for the Public Library and Information (CEPLIS) an attempt has been made to evaluate the role of libraries in broader more qualitative ways. Through a range of projects they provided positive data regarding:

- The social role of the public library
- The sense of ownership that communities express for their library service

- The educational role of the library
- The economic impact of the library
- Its impact on reading and literacy
- The part played by the library in developing community identity and confidence.
- Equity in service delivery

The various research reports, many of which are available via the CEPLIS website (http://cplis.shef.ac.uk/), go into each of these in some detail, but suffice it to say that, based on the evidence from the different projects, it is reasonable to claim that public libraries enable individuals and communities to undertake a wide range of activities. In addition, sometimes with the help of other agencies, libraries help advance and maintain individual and community development. As might be expected the recognized and established functions of the public library in terms of education, information, culture, and leisure, remain important. In particular, the data suggest that the public library is a significant resource for school children and adult learners, and an important source of information on careers and training opportunities. The researchers were also able to demonstrate the importance of that most obvious library function: the lending of books. This was achieved through the *Checking the Books* project, which assessed the value and impact of public library book reading. As part of this project researchers addressed the question of what motivates adults to read imaginative literature and also assessed the benefits obtained from their use of the service (Toyne and Usherwood, 2001).

Political Pressures and Professional Confidence

Much of the work undertaken by CEPLIS and similar organizations was, in part at least, a response to the political and other pressures of the day. Indeed, in the case of Sheffield's early social audit work, it was a reaction to the quantitative reductionism of various Tory administrations. As such, it was and remains, important. The social, educational, and economic roles of the library are all essential but with hindsight, more could and should have been attempted which sought to examine and evaluate the cultural and educational function of the service. This did happen with the work on reading, but the overall direction of the research perhaps reflected a degree of pragmatism on the part of the research community, and a bias towards government policy. This may have resulted from a slight lack of professional confidence and/or an understandable desire to attract funding. One respondent echoed this view saying, 'We need to be confident in our core business of culture – books, literature, performance, and so on as well as our enhanced digital and community roles' (HoS 31+). Services that promote culture, education, and imagination are integral to the public library and need greater emphasis in any assessment of its value and values. There is hope in the fact that this is recognized by some of the coming generation of librarians. One of whom argued: 'Libraries are in a great position to precipitate the serendipitous pursuit of knowledge and the informal exploration of cultures and ideas past and present. To neglect this role would be a major failing' (Phillips, 2005).

Unlike commentators in some other related areas, librarians with some notable exceptions have been slow to question the growing commercialization of the public library service. Indeed, a number seem only too willing to accept it. A recent investigation into political and professional attitudes regarding commercialized models of service provision revealed a:

> strongly perceived pragmatic need, on the part of some participants, for the library to compete in the marketplace in order to survive in a consumer world. Others believed that there was little case to be argued for the future commercialisation of a library service, which existed to serve complex community needs rather than simple profit-making goals. It was thus found to be more likely that public library service provision in the future would be shaped by pragmatic partnership arrangements with a range of different services, rather than be moulded into any single commercialised model. A key conclusion to be drawn from this whole discussion is that no overall consensus about the feasibility or desirability of commercialised models of library service provision was found... (Fox, 2005).

As has been shown, a similarly confused pattern was found amongst those contacted for the purpose of the present book. Members of the profession need to heed the words of Frank Webster, a critical friend of libraries who has warned that, 'If libraries don't ask what it is they are about, then they meet the challenges of commercialisation unprepared, and incapable of doing more than adapting to a business agenda' (Webster, 1999).

An Alternative to the Market

Some others, the present writer included, would argue that it is a role of public libraries to provide an alternative to the many commercial institutions to be found in our society. Asked if public libraries should counter the negative effects of commercialism in the provision of cultural services, one respondent made the basic point that, 'libraries counteract commercialism just by existing and being used. The underlying trust implied by being able to borrow books for free is pretty radical [...]' (PG). Maria Moura (2004) one of Portugal's leading public library experts argues that: 'it's important for the development of everyone, to live and spend time in a space without any commercial pressure, in a safe and neutral environment, which offers the possibility of expanding knowledge, offering free, democratic access to information without any charge.' Buschman (2003) promotes a similar message when he talks of 'the need to provide alternatives and alternative spaces in a culture dominated by information capitalism and media image and spectacle'. The public library, says Ken Worpole (quoted in Black and Crann, 2002) should be a place where people 'can experience their identity as citizens rather than consumers'. It is a view that echoes a suggestion from Sweden that the library might be, 'civic society's unique space for free communication and critical reflection in contrast to the market's commercialisation of experiences' (Skot-Hansen, 2002).

It is a function of the public library to improve and enrich the overall cultural experience of the citizen. Those who favour the commercial approach argue that unless this experience is expressed via individual demands it is a waste of resources.

However, to take this view is to ignore the extent to which such demands are manipulated by the producers of low quality work. The marketeers maintain that the market gives people what they want. In reality the situation is rather different in that consumers are merely given an increasingly limited choice between what is on offer. The proponents of the market discount the possibility that people can be delighted and surprised by the creative brilliance of a work of imagination, piece of music, drama, or a comic creation that is new to them. To draw an analogy from television few people knew that they wanted a programme about dead parrots and the Spanish Inquisition but many were delighted by the genius that was *Monty Python*. In the same way a library should seek to surprise, challenge and delight its users by providing access to material that has not been filtered through the fingers of grad grind accountants. As Holden (2004) has written in another context, it should 'support experimental, edgy work undertaken by people who are not adept at filling in forms'.

In a world of formulaic celebrity, infotainment and the cheap exploitation of basic instincts, the library can be a balancing force that provides people with the opportunity to enjoy and engage with a richer cultural experience. It can also reflect, indeed record and restore the local community culture which does not depend on commercial gatekeepers but can be nurtured by word of mouth and the knowledge and experience of local librarians. To quote Moura (2004) again, 'Public Libraries are possibly the last cultural public space available to all without distinction. It is a public meeting and community space, where identity roots are sought and the future is accessed.'

On the other hand, the 'customer focus' and the associated mantra that 'the customer is always right', suggest that there is no difference between good or bad or right and wrong. There is a certain postmodernist logic about such a viewpoint but it is one that panders to the providers of populist material. Tessa Jowell's complex culture, high culture if you will, depends on judgement, expertise and a degree of professional authority. It is of course the kind of professional activity that is rejected by respondents who ask, 'Why should middle aged staff select material for 13 year olds?' (HoS 21+). This is similar to asking 'why should a 13 year old listen to a middle-aged teacher?' The answer is that it is part of the function of education and indeed the public library service to encourage discrimination between (say) good and bad writing, accurate and false information. To place an equal status on all kinds of material not only fails the individual but also society at large. This is a topic that is discussed further in the next chapter but it is worth emphasizing that populist material is also the subject of judgements. The difference is that these are, more often than not, concerned with the bottom line rather than the quality of the creative process. Such judgements are based on the question, 'Will it sell?' or, as we have seen in some libraries, 'Will it issue?'

These kinds of ideas, it is true, pervade much of the information industry but to quote an American colleague 'when markets become medicines for the exchange of information, they do so in order to satisfy consumer demand and generate profits, not to edify or educate the public' (D'Angelo, 2006). Markets are at odds with the service ethic of the public library. Public libraries are not simply parts of the retail book trade but complex public service organizations that have to balance the needs of the individual with those of society as a whole. They should be managed and assessed accordingly. Nearly half a century ago the authors of the Public Library Inquiry warned of the dangers of 'the attempt to engage popular favour and political support by competing with commercial cultural media' (Raber, 1997). As Buschman (2003) observes, 'The ability to research, read, and reflect... is non existent in an institution so conceived. It is like studying at the mall.'

The commercial model is not one to be followed if the public library service is to enable equality of access. It is a model that will exacerbate social exclusion because it is one that favours the rich over the poor. The commercial model values one part of the population differently to another. It makes the greatest efforts to provide for those who are likely to produce the greatest financial returns. For the world of commerce the critical factor is the bottom line, for the public library it is service. Professionals do things because they are important not just because they are profitable. Following the commercial road can sometimes cause librarians, and even library researchers, to chase funding associated with services and projects that are not consistent with the library's mission and purpose. It is a route that is to be avoided.

Chapter 6

Developing Critical Capacity and Creativity

> By prioritizing its cultural role the public library could reclaim its place as a centre of language -based culture and debate […] In doing so it would provide a space in which we might explore some of the critical issues which face our evolving society.
>
> Matarasso (2000a)

In the introduction to *Discrimination and Popular Culture*, a Pelican paperback published during the present author's time at library school, Thompson (1964) wrote that the 'individual must learn to discriminate if he is to grapple with the approaches of the mass media'. Thompson's collection was partly the result of a NUT (National Union of Teachers) conference that sought to examine the impact of mass communications. Then as now the development of critical skills was seen mainly as the concern of educational institutions but as Thompson observes, 'the schools can give no more than a start'.

Katz (1982) has argued that, 'the development of critical thought… must be encouraged throughout the cultural life of a democratic society'. As such it is a natural part of the public library's mission and purpose. This view is reflected in the fact that, when asked, over two-thirds of the librarians questioned for the purpose of the present book agreed that public libraries should help people develop a critical capacity (Chart 13). As one respondent argued, 'Why else do we give free access to information from a range of viewpoints? A critical capacity is vital for a full, positive and active engagement with society and the democratic process' (Dep 31+). Another seemed to suggest that it was almost an accidental function. He/she said, 'I don't know that we set out to do this, but by providing access to information, and to different or differing perspectives, we do allow people to make critical judgments between points of view, and so on' (HoS 31+).

Such a function has become more important as people attempt to come to terms with the products of a so-called information society. Many of those who work in the information industries of the twenty-first century appear to have rejected any idea of standards or public service. It is a world in which fewer people are encouraged to think critically about the issues of the day, or consider using information or imagination services other than those that are 'easily accessible' in all meanings of that term. In an article entitled, 'The end of imagination', Taylor (2004) observes that our society 'is based more or less on the glorification of stupidity. Five minutes in the company of a popular newspaper or primetime BBC 1, a few seconds spent examining one of the role models held up for the public's edification, is enough to demonstrate how little we value education and intelligence.'

Indeed, the few attempts to engage the intellect are derided in the columns of populist newspapers. For example, *The South Bank Show*, a rare commercial television programme dealing with culture was recently ridiculed by a journalist who mocked it as an 'invaluable public service for time pressed arty-farties, that is reading tricky modern books so we don't have to – and explaining what they're all about' (Ivan-Zadeh, 2006). A similar anti-intellectual tone can be found in the treatments of news and current affairs. For example, John Cole, the former, and much respected political editor for the BBC, has expressed concern that modern journalists have, 'created a public reluctance to make the effort needed for a worthwhile understanding of politics' (quoted in Allan, 2005).

It is a reluctance to understand or discriminate that can also be seen in many other areas of contemporary life. Roosevelt (1906), in a speech called, 'The man with the muck rake', which is a fitting description of much of what passes for current journalism, said that, 'The fool who has not sense to discriminate between what is good and what is bad, is well nigh as dangerous as the man who does discriminate and yet chooses the bad.' A century later, a number of people in the library profession have expressed similar ideas. As one respondent said, 'Opening up the world of knowledge and providing choice will only succeed if people can learn to evaluate between different options, otherwise confusion reigns' (HoS 31+). A good public library service has been described as one that reflects: 'The idea of the Enlightenment thinkers… to accumulate the knowledge generated by many individual creators and make it available to publics that… had been excluded from the privilege of knowledge and wisdom' (Vestheim, 1994). In a document on services for the poor, the American Library Association (2006) describes how libraries might help those 'excluded from privilege'. It argues that, 'it is crucial that libraries recognize their role in enabling poor people to participate fully in a democratic society, by utilizing a wide variety of available resources and strategies'.

Creating a Media Literate Society

It is, however, sometimes difficult to ascertain the precise strategies that libraries intend to use to undertake this function. There is for example, much professional discussion about information literacy and although this is a step, perhaps several steps, in the right direction it often seems to fall someway short of its target. If librarians want, as they should, to help create a media literate society then they could learn much from some of the pioneering work undertaken by those involved in mass media research. The publications of the Glasgow Media Group, now the Glasgow University Media Unit would make a good starting point. The Group comprises people employed in the unit at Glasgow University, plus some broadcasters and journalists. The aim of its work is, and was, to promote and develop methodologies and research in the area of media and communications. Members of the group feel that:

> Empirical work in the area has often been extraordinarily slight in its concerns or poor in its methods […] There has been an absence of will to address the real and often brutal power relationships which have transformed our cultural life. For many in cultural studies

a series of theoretical dead ends beckoned instead. Principal amongst these was what has become known as post-modernism (Philo and Miller, 2000).

Cultural power relationships were recognized as long ago as 1945 by some American librarians who feared that, a 'conservative group' that controlled library funding would not want a library service that encouraged 'the kind of reading that would create informed citizens who would then possess the understanding, tolerance, and willingness, to solve the international and domestic problems of war and social equality' (Raber, 1997). Such matters were to be found on Edward Dudley's curriculum at what in the 1960s was the North Western Polytechnic. Inspired by this the present author later included a variety of media topics on the Libraries Information and Society module at Sheffield University. This coverage encouraged a few students to produce some thoughtful dissertations which examined the media coverage of various events. These included a study of the treatment of the Brixton riots in a selection of British newspapers (Mackelvie, 1982), and a survey of privacy and the British Press with particular reference to the coverage of the Hillsborough disaster (Hutton, 1990). It is important that such subjects are included in professional education because, as Smidt (2005) told a recent IFLA conference, a 'librarian cannot be ignorant of the specific power executed by mass media'. Neither should the users of libraries, and it is interesting to note that at around the same time as Sheffield library students were being encouraged to examine the media Sheffield Public Library, in a separate initiative, was making 'a contribution to developing a culture where the opportunity to become media literate is open to every body' (Sheffield Media Unit, 1987). To quote the City Librarian of the time much of the work was about: 'helping people to be aware of, and able to analyse broadcasting and media techniques' (Coleman, 1987). Something similar would be of value today at a time when the public needs to understand the dangers of a range of new media, some of which have been adopted and promoted by librarians in a somewhat uncritical fashion.

In recent years, huge resources have been put into ICT. This in itself is not a bad thing but the Internet can be a dangerous place. In the words of the sociologist Roszak (1996), 'what passes through the medium is not bound by any significant regard for quality truth or taste'. Unfortunately, this is now increasingly true of much of the other media. The present author has been a lifelong supporter of the BBC but in recent times, even that organization has questions to answer with regard to quality, truth and taste. For instance, many British people were dismayed by the BBC's cavalier attitude to the truth in what became known the Gilligan affair. Gilligan, a tabloid journalist bought in to 'spice up' *Today,* a flagship radio news programme, produced an 'unreliable' and subsequently discredited report that made serious allegations against the British Government. An independent enquiry into the matter found that: 'The allegations reported by Mr Gilligan on the BBC programme... were unfounded', and that 'the editorial system that the BBC permitted was defective' (Hutton Inquiry, 2004). This was an occasion when the BBC fell well below the standards of accuracy one might expect from public service information professionals. It failed to make elementary checks on the accuracy of Gilligan's report, and jumped to too many conclusions in a search for a headline. In so doing, in the words of a lawyer in a related and tragic court case, 'they were making news and not reporting it'.

A lapse of judgement of another kind reflects some of the issues discussed in the previous chapter. In particular, it provides an illustration of how, even in a public service, quality can be effected by a market orientation. Thus:

> The embracing by the BBC of "laddish" culture is [an] example of... the Corporation's dive down market for ratings. Thus a programme such as *Top Gear* can become a celebration of the speed and sexual pulling power of cars. The values of the market celebrate a social and material world which is for sale and that is reduced to a mass of commodities. Human relationships and people are "commoditised" (Philo and Miller, 2000).

Just one example will serve to demonstrate the problems of quality arising from the uncritical use of the Internet. At the time of writing (September 2006) anybody typing Martin Luther King into the Google search engine will find that the second site to which they are directed [http://www.martinlutherking.org/] is in fact anything but an accurate historical examination of King's life and work. Rather it comprises far right propaganda and includes a discussion forum hosted by Stormfront. It is somewhat frightening to imagine how many children 'googling' a homework project on King have been misled by this, and what its effect has been on their attitudes and possibly their actions

Given this kind of situation, and it is by no means an isolated case, the public library needs to help children and indeed adults develop the critical skills required to assess the accuracy and possible bias of what they see on the Internet and elsewhere. The MLK site demonstrates only too well the need for Internet users to ask such questions as: What am I reading? Who wrote it? Why did they write it? Why do they want me to read it? Who paid for it? Am I being sold an idea or a product? Have I learnt anything? Indeed, these are just the kind of questions that Sheffield library school students were asked to address, when time permitted a consideration of such matters as the ownership and control of the mass media and other topics that now tend to be marginalized in the current LIS curriculum.

The need for the development of media literacy skills is perhaps even more important with regard to items on the Internet. It is unrealistic to expect the same standards of accuracy 'on-line' as one might expect in a book or even a newspaper. Items in a book or a journal will have gone through some form of editorial process or peer review but, in some ways, the Net is the electronic equivalent of the public bar and although these can be entertaining, few would unhesitatingly recommend them as a source of accurate information. Indeed, many information professionals, notably those dealing with welfare information, actively warn clients about the quality and accuracy of bar-room gossip, or indeed some of the information provided by generalized radio phone ins and the like.

For some Internet users, perhaps especially the general public, all information can appear to have equal weight. The medium of the screen may in fact give it a spurious authenticity. The Internet of itself does not select, evaluate, or authenticate the information provided, but to quote one writer, 'It conflates data and information with knowledge and wisdom, promising a paradisiacal state of happiness for all who plug in' (Karim, 2001). At the moment the bulk of the Internet traffic comes from the Developed World. It comes with Western values and a cultural baggage that take little account of the sensibilities of less developed countries. Developments, such as digital broadcasting, can provide immense opportunities for education, creativity, and development, but the information age will not fulfil its potential if the disadvantaged are excluded, or simply fed the populist crumbs, from the rich man's cable.

In such a situation, public access to a reliable and responsible range of material is more likely to be achieved if library services promote and recommend those sites that meet professional standards. Such intervention is to be preferred to the introduction of banning or filtering procedures, which may well be counter productive and are contrary to professional ethics. Older readers may recall the mantra, 'not censorship but selection' (Asheim, 1953) and it would be wrong to abdicate our responsibilities for accuracy *et al.* in a knee jerk reaction to the accusation of censorship. In many ways this is a reworking of earlier debates about wants, needs, and the malign impact of commercial models of service provision. With electronic resources, as with others, the need for professional skills of selection based on professional judgements remains. Indeed, some might argue that it becomes even more important.

There is a need to cultivate critical values amongst library staff and library users. The development of critical thinking skills is essential if the long term plans for the public library is to include, as promised in the USA, the promotion of enlightened citizenship. In the words of one respondent to the present study, 'we need to provide alternatives to the Internet and materials outside the mainstream – which challenge some 'accepted' thinking. So we lead by example – even if we cannot directly teach people how to think' (SP 21+). Rather than copying other communication organizations and aiming at the lowest common denominator, public libraries should try to inspire their users and raise their expectations of what the service can offer. Librarians should seek to enrich people, open their minds and provide equality of access to what is important. Some will complain that there is a degree of paternalism in this suggestion, but this is to be preferred to populism and the acceptance of the low expectations that many in the media appear to have of their audience.

Developing Public Taste

It is a subject that is also related to the difficult area of public taste. If, as suggested, public libraries should seek to educate their users about the quality of factual information should they not also undertake a similar role with regard to the arts and works of imagination? A note on the current (2006) BBC Proms. website provided a useful musical parallel for the library world. In presenting a brief history of the Promenade concerts it included a note on 'Developing public taste'. This reminded readers how:

> Wood and Newman were keen to introduce audiences to an ever wider range of music. In the first seasons, a tradition was established of a Wagner Night on Mondays and a Beethoven Night on Fridays. Wood continued to present an enterprising mixture of the familiar and the adventurous, programming new works each season (referred to as "novelties"). He also promoted young, talented performers, and he fought to raise orchestral standards, …

By 1920 Wood had introduced to the Proms many of the leading composers of the day, including Richard Strauss, Debussy, Rakhmaninov, Ravel and Vaughan Williams (BBC, 2006).

Providing people with new experiences and the opportunity to hear such great music was not an act of paternalism. It was and is a public service. The writer, Stephen McClarence (2006), in notes for a concert at Sheffield's City Hall recalls how: 'It was listening to Radio 3 that introduced me to "classical" music, and gave me the impetus to come to concerts in this hall... broadcast concerts... fast tracked me to "modern" music, by-passing prejudice.' This demonstrates how people can learn to acquire a taste for the best through having the opportunity to experience such material. Of course, it is true that education, their family and friends can also influence them but unfortunately, in many families today there is little emphasis on such activity. In addition, in some cases, a poor educational experience may discourage, rather than encourage people to try alternatives to the populist material that is readily and easily available elsewhere (Usherwood, Wilson and Bryson, 2005).

Part of the function of the public library service is to help develop public taste and to underpin cultural life. Indeed, many economists would argue that the universal nature of its funding implies such a function. A good library collection staffed by knowledgeable librarians can provide access to high quality material and make the great works available for people to use and experience. By supporting writers of quality, and through promoting a rich and diverse culture the library is providing a true public good. The alternative is to, 'pander to your public's every wish; flatter them; patronize them; but don't try to educate them. The lack of critical standards attests to the nihilism at the heart of postmodern consumer culture' (D'Angelo, 2006). Some feel that that point has been reached already. Michael Gorman (2000) bluntly states that 'The ethos of the modern public library seems to be in direct conflict with the ideas of discrimination selection and elevating taste.'

As has been shown the commercial sector tends to concentrate on supplying what people say they want but if public taste is to grow and develop, society also requires an institution that will actively support and promote literature and the arts. To encourage people to develop a critical capacity is not to turn them in to cultural snobs. In fact research shows that users expect and welcome professional help in navigating an increasingly complex world of ideas, information and works of imagination. As in other areas of their lives people want to be able to distinguish the significant from the superficial. To help them do so is a positive professional act. As Blake Morrison (1994) says, 'declaring that some books are better than others is not comparable with racial discrimination, social snobbery or moral disapprobation'. It can help demonstrate that reading good books is an enjoyable activity. Novels can help provide people with the emotional truth of everyday events and produce a greater understanding of them. Literature, 'helps to shape the personality, refine the sensibility, sharpen the critical intelligence...' (Beard quoted in Goulding, 2006).

Reader Development

As part of an exploration of reader development and the promotion of fiction reading, Glenn (2004) suggests that the public library should aim, 'to develop readers who are not only able to recognise their own fiction reading preferences and feel confident in their choices, but also to develop their tastes through an increased understanding of their own reading experiences... thus enhancing the quality of each reading encounter'. In addition, as Pearl (quoted in Ross, 2006) suggests: 'Libraries should introduce readers to books and authors they might not have read or found out about on their own.' This will require a selection strategy that encourages people to be more adventurous in their reading. 'The aim of the selector,' said Asheim (1953) 'is to promote reading, not inhibit it, to multiply points of view that will find expression not limit them... .'

In recent years, there has been a significant growth of reader development activities. In a way this returns the public library to its roots. At its best it can develop adult readers, widen their horizons and provide access to the great works of imagination. Interestingly, the RPK research also revealed the need to extend such activities to include social and political non-fiction genres. This made explicit the potential role of reading in helping people to understand contemporary social and political concerns. Some focus group respondents involved in the project, expressed the enjoyment they obtained from reading of this kind. One said, 'In terms of a general understanding of the political situation in terms of the Middle East and foreign policy, I've read around that... I mean that's quite easy to do... reading the likes of Pilger, which is quite popular journalism, really can help you do that...' (Midlands, MLA users). Another, 'was thinking specifically about the *Stupid White Men* book... that's a politically orientated title, I mean not particularly high-brow and academic' (Midlands, parents).

Proctor and Bartle's (2002) work on libraries and adult learners indicated that the library could often be an unexpected starting point for an interest in new topics. One of their respondents observed:

> It's not easy to put it succinctly, but browsing along bookshelves and being of an inquisitive nature you often find books that catch your interest, you open it up and read the flyleaf or you read one or two pages, thinking "What's this about?" and end thinking "I'll read that!' You've no intention of reading it before you went in the library. It hadn't crossed your mind, but it's there in front of you.

Others agreed stating that, 'What I like is finding information in books that you don't know about.' 'It's surprising what you're interested in if you read a new subject... .' 'I'm a browser. I love just going along the shelves not knowing what I'm going to find.' Similarly, Coughlan (2001) noted, that over a quarter of her respondents used the library for browsing – not necessarily connected to borrowing. Members of library staff were also considered instrumental in expanding users' interests: In the words of one respondent, 'I think it's nice to use the library in the capacity where someone, like the librarian, can very often say "have you read such-and-such!" And my first instinct would be, "I don't read that sort of thing" but then you do and it's great... .'

Creativity

Other library users want '...libraries to... provide everyone with the chance to relax and have access to creative experiences' (Binns, 2004). Certainly, creativity appears to be one of the current concerns of the MLA. In a book known to be revered by officials at that organization, Richard Florida (2002) argues that providing an environment that is attractive to the 'creative class' is a key to revitalizing cities (Florida, 2002). For this, and it is to be hoped other reasons, at both the national and local level the public library is being promoted as an agency, 'to improve people's lives by building knowledge, supporting learning [and] inspiring creativity' (MLA 2007). Such aims are shared by many UK library authorities. For instance, on the South coast libraries are 'Working to put culture and creativity at the heart of Brighton and Hove's success' (Brighton and Hove, 2006). There and in other places, it would seem that the public library is seen and promoted as a location where individuals and communities engage in and are stimulated by a diverse range of creative activities. On the other hand, some contemporary commentators, such as Holden (2004a) feel that public libraries are, 'the forgotten players in the creativity debate and their potential is vastly underrated'. Miranda McKearney (2004), also feels that, 'It is time for libraries to be much more fully recognized as part of the creative world', she maintains that 'their work to reach and inspire young readers injects creativity into the community in a big way, and deserves much greater attention. Its power to help achieve our national ambitions should not be underestimated.'

Responding to the government's Green Paper, *Culture and Creativity: the Next Ten Years* (DCMS, 2001), the then Library Association (2001) rightly argued that, 'Reading is itself a major creative experience.' However, the Association felt that it was 'not sufficiently recognised in the DCMS document'. More recently official attitudes to books and reading have been questioned following reports of a MLA announcement that library book budgets might be cut, and minimum standards for service would be reviewed. The press also reported that a MLA official had indicated books would be de-emphasized. He was quoted as saying. 'Public libraries have a vital role to play in helping local authorities achieve their communities' social, economic and environmental aspirations – they are much more than just places to borrow books' (in Ezard, 2006).

That last phrase is not in itself as damming as some of the headlines suggest. Indeed, variations on the theme of, 'Much more than books' have formed the basis of public library publicity for a large number of years. However, in the present climate when, to recall Etzioni's maxim, there are cracks in the public library institution, there is a need for strong professional and political reassurance regarding the continuing importance of reading and readers. Many still see this as the foundation of the service and resist any attempts to divert resources elsewhere. Some comfort was provided by John Dolan who, as Head of Library Policy at the MLA, told *The Bookseller* that contrary to the impression created by the previous statement the organization also loved books (Dolan, 2006).

Glenn (2004) has shown how Reader Development organizations such as 'Opening the Book', and the Reading Agency, have attempted to raise the status of the reader in the reading process. In particular they have promoted the concept of 'creative reading'. Those behind, 'Opening the Book' maintain that the reader does not simply passively absorb the original thoughts of the writer, but takes an active, creative role in the reading process. Ross (2006) is another who argues that new style 'readers advisory' or 'reader development' should put emphasis, 'not on the quality of the book but on the quality of the reading experience as determined by the reader'.

Some may feel that this ignores the integral relationship between the two and indeed there is much academic debate on this issue. This was reflected in the views of the readers quoted in Glenn's paper. She reports that for, 'a significant minority... the only way to link the concept of creativity to their own reading was to consider the ways in which it could stimulate the creation of new works of art'. Others, 'were confident that their intellectual input was synonymous with creativity, regardless of differences between reading and other recognised creative pursuits'. Glenn concludes that 'readers' experiences... could be divided into two basic categories: creative processes of reading, and creative outcomes. While her 'Participants are clearly divided in their views of the status of reading as a creative activity' her work, in common with the *Checking the Books* study, recognizes the contribution imaginative literature can play in developing an individual's imagination and how this affects the society in which they live.

An Arts and Cultural worker taking part in the *Checking the Books* project regarded developing the imagination as integral to personal welfare. She said,

> I think that is just as important, it's the feeding of the soul or it's a feeding of your mind, or it's a feeding of your senses and spirit that is every bit as important, well maybe not every bit as important, but is as important I think as having the roof over your head and other services... it's all part of individual growth or well-being and I think it's really important.

Respondents to *Checking the Books* felt that the imagination was fundamental to a developing society. Others pointed out how reading can help improve vocabulary and introduce people to new ideas. One person argued that a lack of libraries would, 'impact on the use of language'. He went on to argue that if people could not manage to get books:

> It would over a period of time impact on... the creativity in the use of language. A lot of poets need language to actually be able to do their business [...] You sort of almost pick up new language by reading, you're not consciously doing it but all the time you're looking you're unconsciously doing it (Male 30–40, N.W. England).

Creative Partnerships

The research indicates that public libraries can and do play an important role in promoting and developing reading although this can go unrecognized. John Holden (2004a) in a paper that aims to draw attention to the role of libraries as creative institutions argues that, 'The power of libraries should be harnessed; while maintaining their own sense of identity, they need to work in partnership with schools, youth services and social services to release young people's creativity.' He argues that libraries should be part of 'creative clusters' and, in line with government policy he advocates partnerships with other institutions such as museums, art centres, archives and theatres.

The literature provides examples of the benefits of such partnerships and perhaps more library practitioners should look at, and learn from the arts world and at their creative agenda. Nailer (2002) argues, 'The habit of creativity and the spirit of inquiry, the interest in and concern for others, which define civilized society, are relevant around the world.' This is shown to be true of the library world. In Australia the State Library of Victoria has developed a Creative Fellowships programme. This seeks to demonstrate the Library's strong commitment to original scholarship, writing, and creative endeavour, and aims to promote the library as a centre of scholarly activity and research, encourage scholarly, literary, and the creative use, of the Library's collections, and the production of publications/work based on them. As a result the library has been described as 'a hotbed of creativity, with writers and playwrights among those setting up house there' (Webb, 2003). Library Fellows have included historians, a playwright, a novelist and a poet.

An earlier Fellow had sought to study how Aborigines had been portrayed in photographs since European settlement. This example makes the link between creativity and social inclusion, and is in line with Robert Leigh's view that those who benefit from enlightenment should use their knowledge to solve the problems generated by social inequality (Raber, 1997). Culture and creativity can help communities and nations celebrate diversity. 'Libraries need to keep the cultural record in all its multiplicity, depth and richness... [and] prevent the cultural record from becoming fragmented' (Nailer, 2002). This is a view that is reflected in Singapore's plan for the future of its libraries. There, libraries 'will be places where individuals can find stimulation and self-development through a variety of offerings in content and programmes. Communities will be able to explore their own cultural heritage or that of others, and members will be able to engage in mutual support and self help' (Singapore National Library Board, 2005).

In the words of Jesse Shera, 'A library should be a place in which myriad schools of thought make contributions to knowledge, and the intellect may safely range and speculate.... It is a place where inquiry is pushed forward and the "discoveries" of the individuals verified and tested' (Shera, 1969). It is an organization that 'contributes to the creation of an educated, culturally aware group that can distinguish between ideas of lasting value and ephemera' (Raber, 1997). In his contribution to the *Public Library Inquiry*, Robert Leigh suggested that libraries may in fact only 'serve the group of adults whose interest, will and ability, lead them to seek personal enrichment and enlightenment...'. Of course, most librarians would want to increase the size of this group but now, as then, it is worth considering the Inquiry's conclusion that services to such a group of people will, 'have a social value much greater than the gross numbers involved' (Leigh, 1950).

For those who use it the public library, its staff and collections provide the kind of stimulating environment in which people can develop new ideas and reflect on, and increase their understanding of, old ones. It is says one commentator, 'a vital forum for intellectual stimulation, social concourse and serendipitous discovery'

(Spencer, 2005). Often such discoveries, and some that are more carefully planned, are of benefit to those who do not use the service. It is time for the public library to rediscover its founding principles and become 'a place where self discovery and self confidence can once again flourish' (Worpole, 2004). If it does, the thing that *is* society will gain from the creativity and critical capacity of those who choose to seek enrichment and enlightenment. It will gain from an institution that provides access to accurate information, the best ideas, and works of imagination.

Chapter 7

Providing Access to the Best

Libraries were set up a century and a half ago so that many more people could have access to the "best that has been thought and said".

Hoggart (1997)

Present government policies are aimed at increasing access to public libraries. This is a worthy objective but access, like patriotism, is not always enough. When considering the question of access, professionals and policy makers need to ask, 'access to what?' As we have already seen, government departments, and various other organizations in different parts of the cultural world and beyond, have sought to increase the size of the audience for cultural services. As a result of these siren calls to increase 'the numbers' some cultural organizations, be they museums, theatres, or libraries, have been changed beyond all recognition. At best some of the new and populist activities in which they engage may be regarded as a bit of fun that the core audience can take or leave. At worst, people can be driven away by the introduction of what they regard as an inappropriate, and an unwelcome ambience to a once loved institution. There are many users who do not want museums to become shopping malls, or libraries to be amusement arcades with a few books attached. Some rebranding activities may achieve their aim, but there is always the danger that any new found audience will desert as soon as the novelty wears off, or something it finds more interesting comes along.

Those responsible for public libraries have to devise access policies that strike a proper balance between the attraction of short term numbers, and the maintenance of long term values and distinct and valued experiences. In their wiser moments some policy makers have indicated that 'access alone is not enough [and that] Households must also have access to first rate content' (Department for Culture, Media and Sport, 2001). There is recognition that if we are to encourage a developed and informed citizenry, then those responsible for services need to be concerned about questions of quality. The aim should be to ensure that public libraries attract a diverse audience to what is a unique service that meets long term needs rather than simply satisfies quick fix demands for novelty and amusement that can be easily satisfied elsewhere.

Increasing use while striving for, and maintaining excellence, presents a major challenge to the public library service. Many social, economic, political and professional factors contribute to this challenge. These include demographic changes, growing demands to increase educational opportunities, and the needs of increasingly diverse populations. At the same time, the service is faced with budget and resource constraints, technological change, and the relativist attitudes of some professional staff and policy makers. There was a time, 'Four or five decades ago [when] most librarians saw themselves as offering, no matter what else they made available, a good selection of the best that has been thought and said [...] They made sure that they had well stocked shelves of the classics, good fiction, poetry and drama' (Hoggart, 1998). That is not always the case today.

Defining 'the Best'

Many of the professional librarians questioned for the present study were uneasy with the concept of 'the best'. A number adopted a relativist position many feeling the need to ask, 'What is "the best"? Who is the judge of this?' (Dep 10+). Others observed that, 'Everybody's "best" will be different' or suggested that, 'we [i.e. public librarians] are not wise enough to objectively state one "best" (nor should we), and our collections must reflect that' (Dep 31+). The *Checking the Books* study also found that, 'within some authorities the role of providing and recommending imaginative literature is still resisted' (Toyne and Usherwood, 2001). To be fair, this is no longer entirely a British viewpoint although it is perhaps surprising to find a Swedish colleague arguing that, 'the old view no longer works – namely, that the library knows what quality is and that visitors have to accept what we select for them' (Nilsson, undated).

How different from the situation some 50 years ago, when the librarians of Western Australia were confident enough to work to a book selection policy that maintained that, 'it is essential to ensure that there is ample supply of the best... it is better to duplicate heavily on titles of quality rather than to limit their numbers merely for the sake of a wider range of titles' (Library Board of Western Australia, 1966). Now, as then, public librarians need to address and not avoid the question, 'What is the best?' Not to do so is a dereliction of professional duty masquerading as democracy.

Moreover, professionals and others who work in related areas are not so reluctant to deal with the question. For example, although Grayling (2000) concedes that, 'It is hard to define what makes good books good, because good books come in so many different kinds', he goes on to say 'one thing in common to most of them is that they make readers think and feel, elevating or disturbing them, and making them see the world a little differently as a result'. Other commentators have approached the definition of quality, and quality literature in different ways. A judge for the Booker Prize argued that: 'Unlike popular or genre novels, literary novels cannot be prescribed by publishers [...] They create their own enclosed world, are inventive in terms of narrative and character, and have an inimitable voice, the personal signature of the author' (quoted in Dunn, 2005). The critic Magdalena Ball (undated) advises that quality literature comprises, 'books by the writers we call "great". Your list of names may differ from mine, but these are the writers who win prizes like the Booker, the Pulitzer, the Commonwealth Prize, and the National Book Award to name just a few.' She goes on to say that, 'the more great literature you read, the better able you will become at recognizing the elements which make a fiction literary'. Perhaps some public librarians would be better placed to make literary judgements if the once standard question, 'What do you read?' was asked by more staff selection panels.

Spiller (1991), a librarian who does read, and stock selection expert, also argues that, the 'Receipt of a literary prize is a clear indication of consensus approval for a writer, either from his/her own profession or from literary or cultural institutions.' Unfortunately, this kind of advice is unlikely to be taken by some who currently work in the library service. Hemsley (2003) found that some staff have:

> very negative views on literary fiction. One librarian canvassed opinion among her para-professional colleagues prior to being interviewed. "I can tell you what some of our staff think about literary fiction. A front-line library assistant of 20 years experience called literary fiction: 'elitist stock that does not issue. We need more best-sellers and books that people actually want to read, not what we think they should read'."

One can note with some amusement yet another example of the use of the misplaced elitist argument. As Franzen observes, 'Elitism is the Achilles' heel of every serious defense of art, an invitation to the poisoned arrows of populist rhetoric' (Franzen, 1996).

This is not to ignore the argument that certain kinds of material may reflect values and standards that can make some groups in society feel marginalized or excluded. Those responsible for the selection of material must be sensitive to such issues but also avoid the truly paternalistic assumption that quality material cannot be appreciated by people from ordinary or disadvantaged backgrounds. Making quality material available in public libraries does not force people to read good books, listen to fine music, or view great cinema but it does give them an opportunity to do so. For many people the public library may provide their only realistic opportunity of engaging in such activity. It is in such circumstances that to quote Hafner (1993) it becomes 'a place where the egalitarian political principles of democracy meet the elite claims of high culture'.

The reader development organization, Opening the Book declares that, 'The best book in the world is quite simply the one you like best.' However this apparently simple formulation continues, 'that is something you can discover for yourself, but we are here to help you find it'. For many years, the company has run training courses for library staff to help them, 'develop confidence in [their] reading and increase [their] ability to make judgements'. It attempts to enable librarians to 'to respond to the demand of library users, "What do I read next?"' (Critical Reading, 1994). Their approach is one that expects the librarian to intervene and not simply leave the choice of material to the users. They want library staff to, increase people's confidence and enjoyment of reading, and open up reading choices. They expect librarians to offer opportunities for people to share their reading experience, and raise the status of reading as a creative activity. Their approach is one that makes use of a reader centred definition of quality whereby instead of attempting to determine the quality of each individual title, they define a quality stock as one which represents a range of kinds of book in relation to a range of different audiences. They maintain that their 'approach is open and inclusive but not soft. There is a hard edge to our thinking' (Opening the Book, 2006).

Not everyone necessarily agrees with the reader centred approach but the Opening the Book initiative does something to address the question about what happens to users once a public library provides them with access to a range of material. In an earlier career the Director of Opening the Book worked as 'Community Arts Co-ordinator for Sheffield City Council which was based (unusually) in the library service'. It was there that she 'discovered libraries were the ideal place for the kind of audience development work she wanted to do' (Opening the Book, 2006). Today the UK library service provides numerous examples of this kind of activity. Dorset Libraries for instance suggest that, 'Reader development offers choices for the library service to become socially inclusive by offering wider reading to all individuals, groups and communities.' The social inclusion agenda can be met, 'by providing a core of literary fiction, first novels, world literature in translation, multicultural writing, poetry and small press publishing' (Dorset County Council, 2006). In this way a public library can provide for a diversity of interests, and ensure that people are given the opportunity to access the wealth of cultural capital be it in literature, music, the arts or current affairs. The public library has long been regarded as 'every person's' university and at its best, it provides equality of access to the classics and the canon, and also to new cultural opportunities and experiences. It may not always be used by everyone it but no one is ever excluded.

In their own way public libraries can provide access to small works of art, be they literature, drama, recorded sound, film or illustration. They provide material that can educate, entertain and enlighten. In order to undertake this function in a satisfactory way, a public library should include in its collection a reasonable high proportion of classics and high quality work. In the words of a former Secretary of State, 'great literature is, without question, our country's greatest gift to the world's cultural heritage, and libraries are the means by which we share and celebrate it' (Blackstone in Garrod, 2003). Material should be selected that contributes to the self-development and enrichment of the individual and the community. This attitude is reflected in David Spiller's (1991) text on stock selection, which suggests that a public library service should have a basic coverage of all subject fields and attempt to stock the standard works.

Library Policies

In recent years more public library authorities have attempted to articulate their policies on the selection of fiction material. Guides and selection criteria have always been readily available in the United States, and anyone with access to the Internet can find many contemporary examples. Many still reflect a concern for the quality of content. For example, in Orange County: 'Materials evaluators selecting fiction and literature, study professional review sources looking for stories with plausible plots, vitality and consistency in characterization, effectiveness in sustaining the reader's interest, and clarity of style' (Orange County, undated). In Tempe Library:

> Each novel will be judged on its own merits. Characterization and language will be evaluated in relation to the work as a whole and will not be judged out of context. Preferred fiction will be competently written, have constructive and plausible characterizations, and give an honest portrayal of the human experience with which it deals. Experimental novels, while often controversial, may be considered as they reflect new trends and styles

of expression. Novels in foreign language will be acquired according to demand' (Tempe Public Library, 2003).

The policy at Lawrence Library indicates that adult fiction should be selected:

> with reference to one or more of the following criteria: the materials should contribute to the individual's awareness of self, community and cultural heritage; it should contribute to the value of the Library's collection as a whole by representing all types and styles of literature; it should provide pleasurable reading for recreation and creative use of leisure time (Lawrence Public Library, 2001).

Other policies however, indicate a move to the kind of demand led selection that would have been an anathema to the authors of the Public Library Inquiry. Thus, the library in Dayton (Dayton and Montgomery County Public, undated) will often 'purchase fiction titles that are not notable for their literary quality or artistic merit but have substantial popular appeal. Popular titles are also duplicated as necessary to meet demand'. Kenton County Public Library (2005) adopts a similar philosophy. There, 'Public demand is the primary criteria in selection of fiction. It is selected to satisfy recreational reading needs of the adult public and the Library sets no arbitrary standard of literary quality.' At Memorial Hall Library in Andover, Massachusetts, 'Adult fiction titles in considerable demand because of extensive publicity, local interest, author popularity, or other factors are usually purchased, even if the title did not receive good reviews' (Memorial Hall Public Library, 2005).

Many UK policies appear in practice to be rather less prescriptive and tend to emphasize the importance of demand. That having been said, in their formal statements many do attempt to strike a balance between popular titles and those of literary quality. Thus, fiction selection at Slough public library will, 'fairly represent demand and issues. The bulk of our collections will therefore consist of popular genre fiction of all types. However, we also recognise the vital role of the public library service in supporting and promoting serious literary fiction and in ensuring the continued availability of classic works' (Slough Libraries and Information Service, 2005). Staff at Rotherham Library select fiction according to pragmatic criteria. They ask:

> Will it meet a need? Is it well produced and attractively presented? Is the format appropriate for public library use? Does the format support our services becoming more inclusive? Is the author/subject of local interest? Is it a sequel or in a series? Has it been reviewed and how was it received? Are there media links – television, film, video? Is it, or the author, an award winner? Will it offer a better choice in the library? Does it contribute to all cultures and lifestyles being represented? Is it value for money? (Rotherham Library and Information Service, 2004.)

At Knowsley Public Library: 'Some forms of genre fiction such as light romances, westerns and some crime stories, are bought when the author of the book may not be the most important factor in making a selection – the reputation and following for the series... might be the principal concern' (Knowsley Library Service, 2004). At Brighton and Hove Library it is recognized that, 'The provision of fiction is... a core function of the public library service.' There, unlike Knowsley, 'light romantic fiction such as Mills and Boon and Black Lace are not purchased because of their short life span' (Brighton and Hove City Council Library Service, 2005).

These policies reflect the fact that throughout the history of public libraries there has been a degree of tension involved when considering how services should respond to user demands for populist material. This is particularly true in the case of fiction. It is a situation that is recognized at Dorset Libraries where:

> The collection addresses the tension between popular and literary fiction. The drive to raise issues is tempered by the need to provide a wide range of imaginative literature. Reader development widens readers' expectations of contemporary literature. The collection meets those expectations by providing a core of literary fiction, first novels, world literature in translation, multi-cultural writing, poetry, small press publishing, and so on (Dorset County Council, 2006a).

The basic question remains, do you give the public what they want or do you concentrate on materials considered good? (Usherwood, 1996). The Carnegie Gold Medalist Aidan Chambers (2000) gave his answer when he argued that, 'browsing the stacks was only worthwhile because the librarians who stocked them believed their job was to make available a collection which was as representative as possible of all that was written in our language. They did not think they should provide only what their borrowers said they wanted'. This reflects the values of a time when, 'the role of the library in buying fiction and non-fiction of high quality but small distribution' was 'of especial significance' (Vakarri, 1989).

The debate regarding what was once known as the fiction question is likely to become even more relevant in the future because, the Sony Bookman notwithstanding, the provision of imaginative literature is likely to remain the one function of the public library that is least likely to be affected by developments in ICT. This is not to set up the book in opposition to ICT or *vice versa* but simply to reflect the fact that the full experience to be obtained from reading a novel, a poem, or a short story, is unlikely to be effectively replaced by the products of information technology. In terms of access, and in the words of the brochure for the Fourth International Conference on the book (2006), 'there is little doubt that people will always be taking that old printed and bound artifact to the beach or to bed, for the foreseeable future at least'. The public library is synonymous with books and seen as the natural place for readers, and those who wish to develop their reading. For many it is still the preferred provider of imaginative literature, although it cannot afford to remain complacent in the face of competition from the book superstores and a range of other organizations. However, by providing free public access to works of imagination the public library is offering additional benefits, real added values, which are rarely matched elsewhere.

Of course, and as numerous websites testify, ICT can be used to help develop the reading experience. As Bishoff (2000) observes: 'The development of the web and the application of scanning technology to library and museum collections offer unprecedented opportunities for increasing access to library and museum special collections and unique resources.' Increasingly it is being used to promote quality reading and no doubt many new sites will have appeared by the time this book is published. However it is unlikely that any will better Middletown Thrall Library's

(2006) electronically presented arguments for the inclusion of literature in library collections. It states:

> Literature represents the very best of human expression, and it's not by any accident that, long after bestsellers and sensationalized books have faded from memory, literature continues to thrive and remain relevant to our contemporary human condition. Literature has many purposes and opens doors to unique worlds, which are never wholly removed from our own, and characters, who almost always have much in common with us and the challenges we face in the modern world. Through literature we rediscover ourselves and our world time and time again.

Library Users are Anxious to Find Quality Writing

It should not come as a surprise to those public library professionals who are really in touch with their users that their clientele want, 'Classics and literary fiction [to] be available as they once were' (Libraries for life for Londoners, undated). Many in the general population recognize that some of our major achievements, be they as individuals or society, arise from a desire to be the best. Quality is appreciated and sought after in sporting performance, food, health care and many other human activities. In the same way, people are also conscious that excellence raises good literature above the mediocre. It is therefore reasonable to expect that the public library should provide everybody with the means to have access to such excellence. In the words of one Chief Librarian, 'Library users are on the whole anxious to find new quality writing and will thank the service for bringing it to their attention' (Froud, 1994). More recently, Shiraz Durrani has criticized those libraries that 'keep buying Mills & Boon and stupid fiction' (quoted in Goulding, 2006).

Rachel Van Riel spoke for many library users when she wrote:

> I can't be the only person to be reading titles short listed not for this year's Booker but for last year's or the year before that. My library could make me feel a whole lot better about this by offering a selection of Bookers, perhaps with a commentary suggesting why some look to become books of all time while others were books of the day (Van Riel, 1993).

Now there is much greater library interest in the prize. In 2006 all British public library authorities were sent a Man Booker Prize promotional pack, and regular email newsletters to keep them up to date. Library services and users in different parts of the UK took the opportunity to participate in the event. For example, on the day the prize was awarded the Lerwick Book Group linked to Shetland Libraries watched 'the winner being announced on a big screen and were delighted when the group's favourite – Kiran Desai's *The Inheritance of Loss* – won the prize' (Shetland Library, 2006).

Although most library stock selection policies do include a reference to serious literature it is not always evident that library practice reflects the philosophy suggested by such documents. In the majority of authorities examined for the *Checking the Books* study, the number of book issues still seemed to be the major criterion for assessing the success of fiction selection. Of course issue figures depend on what is made available in the first place and there is much evidence to suggest that some public librarians underestimate the needs and tastes of their readers. For example, one piece of research, undertaken in five local authority library services showed that while potential readers had a 50 per cent chance of finding John Grisham's *Brethren* in their library, they had less than 10 per cent chance of finding Ian McEwan's *Atonement* (quoted in Lister, 2002). In Camden readers have recently 'deplored the lack of a decent supply of classics, mourning the loss of complete collections of Shakespeare, Dickens and Chaucer' (Gadelrab, 2006). Similarly a correspondent to *The Times* wrote of his disappointment at the lack of good novels in his local library. He said:

> Taking a module in 20th Century American Literature, covering famous novels such as, *As I Lay Dying*, *Miss Lonelyhearts*, *The Crying of Lot 49*, and *Slaughterhouse-Five*, I decided to save some money and search for the books at my local library. Not only were none of them in stock, most were not even on their computer database (New 2006).

A possible reason for this state of affairs may be found in the way that library services are evaluated. For instance some of the librarians interviewed by Hemsley (2003) mentioned the pressure placed on them by targets that hold them to account for the amount of stock issued. They suggested that this prevented them from following a more adventurous policy when promoting books. The value of qualitative techniques for evaluating library services is becoming increasingly recognized, but there is still little evidence of official or managerial support for their general introduction. As indicated earlier the MLA decided not to fund any future development of the Stock Quality Health Check and it remains to be seen if what is left of the public library standards, after their current review, will have anything to say about the quality of material.

That having been said, there are some examples of professional initiatives designed to increase access to 'the best'. A Scottish Library Association promotion called *Now Read On* set out to identify and promote 'some of the best of recent fiction' through leaflets and book displays in Scottish libraries. It recognized that, 'as more and more titles join those already on the shelves the task of choosing a book becomes correspondingly difficult' and aimed 'to make selection a little easier by singling out some of the best of contemporary writing'. A Sheffield Masters student discovered that, 'In some libraries circulating collections have been introduced with the intention of providing wider access to literary fiction and minority interest books which would not be purchased for a large number of libraries individually' (Hemsley, 2003). In other places libraries have sought to bring books to minority audiences. For example, the annual Essex Book Festival, which is managed by the County Library Service, seeks to involve those in prisons and sheltered housing.

Providing Equality of Access

There are many sound reasons for providing equality of access to the best works of imagination and sources of high quality information. If the public library is not going to provide a superior selection of novels than that to be found in the local supermarket, or more accurate sources of information than the tabloid press, how can it justify public funding? The public library's justification for being considered a public good largely depends on its willingness and ability to take to the high ground and provide an intelligent and diverse alternative to the products of an increasingly abysmal mass media. In the words of one commentator the argument, 'is what we know perfectly well already – Dickens is not only better than Archer, he is doing something fundamentally different, something infinitely greater. Unless they are prepared to state and act upon that truth at whatever cost to their gross lending figures, libraries do not deserve a penny' (Appleyard, 1992).

In addition to, and in many ways more important than the economic argument, is the impact of good quality material on the individual and society. One Head of Service responding to the present study stated that, 'a library cannot socially engineer individuals to choose good over evil. High culture doesn't necessarily mean democracy is promoted' and advised the present author to, 'see George Steiner's words on high Nazi officials who spent evenings listening to music played by prisoner quartets while sanctioning gas chambers' (HoS 31+). This is of course true, and there is no guarantee that culture will always make us better people. However, it is equally true that the provision of high quality cultural material can have a positive value. It provides many people with richer and deeper experiences than they may have in their everyday lives. It helps people to understand other people and the world around them. For instance, by providing access to writers from the less Developed World, a library service can help the indigenous population learn about incomers, and the children of immigrants understand the past of their own society. By providing free and equal access the library gives all people the opportunity to share in the cultural heritage of a community.

When they are given such an opportunity most people will value and enjoy it. It may not always be appropriate to talk in terms of high and low culture but it is necessary for professionals to address the issue of quality. Sometimes it appears that public librarians' rightful concern with democratization, inclusion, and access, equates with a failure on the part of professionals to be prepared to say what is good or bad. Simply stocking libraries with material that reflects the assumed tastes of the public at large is a truly patronizing act. Moreover, it is one that reinforces the shallow values of the market and the media. The public library should aim to provide, 'a collection that opens the door to the endless possibilities inherent in books and reading' (Alabaster, 2002). To do otherwise is condescending and insulting to the intelligence of people from all kinds of backgrounds who are, as history shows, more than capable of enjoying works of excellence.

Providing Information

When it comes to providing information services, library professionals appear to have far less of a problem in recommending and advising on the quality of material. Those professionals who appear to be somewhat reticent at defining the best in terms of literature appear to have far fewer reservations in commenting on fashionable electronic resources. Their advice can be readily found and there is no need to go into detail here. Indeed, the then Library Association published two guides in one year alone (Chowdhury and Chowdhury, 2001; Cooke, 2001). Cooke, for example, produced a checklist for website users. She suggested that they: identify the purpose of a site and assess its coverage, authority and reputation, accuracy and currency. Users were also advised to consider the maintenance and the accessibility of the source and to evaluate the presentation and arrangements of information. In considering the overall quality of a site users are advised to make comparisons with other sources.

The RPK study demonstrated that information provided by public libraries is highly trusted. It is perceived to have higher levels of authenticity and neutrality; and a lack of editorial bias or manipulation. In addition, people value the professional assistance and standards offered by staff, and the provision of a variety of authoritative sources. One respondent to that study recalled how:

> as a boy from a working class family, I remember at 12 years old being given some information by a teacher which has stood me in good stead all my life, and has been very sensible. He said, 'So what happens with working class people? If they have got some problem they want to know the answer to, they ask around amongst themselves and they get all sorts of clouded information. If you want to know anything, go to a reference library. Ask them. They can more or less tell you any information you want' (Wales: focus group, 55+).

Overall, the study found that public libraries were the most trusted source and tabloid papers the least.

However, this sense of trust in the library service was not reflected in its level of use. Those seeking to satisfy their information needs in terms of contemporary social and political concerns tended to use sources associated with speed, immediacy and accessibility. Their information seeking behaviour often involved the use of convenient information sources that fit in with daily routines and responsibilities. Indeed, the national telephone survey undertaken for the RPK study revealed a worrying trend amongst the public to turn to some of the least trusted information sources when seeking information on social and political concerns. Immediately accessible sources of information such as newspapers, television and the Internet were seen as preferable despite the relatively low levels of trust and value placed in them. It is a fact that some of the information services provided by public libraries may appear less exciting than the infotainment served up by commercial organizations, but then that is often the way with the truth. In the end the provision of trusted information is what a public service should be about. As Virginia Woolf once observed: 'If truth is not to be found on the shelves of the British Museum, where I asked myself, picking up a notebook and pencil, is truth' (Woolf, 1929).

It would be wrong for public libraries to concentrate on the trivial, the tasteless and the titillating. The uninformed prejudices and commercial comparisons of contemporary society must not dissuade librarians from providing services that reflect their professional principles. The profession should recognize that one of the major ways in which people learn to acquire a taste for the best is through peer influence, education and frequent exposure to new experiences. The public library can be a source of such experiences. 'Libraries,' writes Bob (1982), 'have a responsibility to ideas, to nurturing, sustaining, preserving, and making readily available the intellectual capital of our society to anyone who may want or need it, now or in the future.' This does not mean that a public library has to be dull but it does have to be responsible. It is fine for the library service to be 'cool' at the edges but, it owes to society, to be solid at its core. The work to rediscover those basic tenets of the public library service rests on the shoulders of current library leaders and those being groomed for leadership positions. It is important for such leaders to be prepared to exercise judgement and to recognize that, in making such judgements, excellence should not be regarded as the enemy of equity. In short, when providing for a diverse public they must seek to provide all their users with access to the best.

Chapter 8

Information Is Not Enough

> There was a new library in the Civic Centre. It was so new it didn't even have
> librarians. It had Assistant Information Officers.
>
> Pratchett (1995)

There is a well-documented story that when Ted Hughes first wrote the poem,
Hear it Again as the introduction to *New Library: The People's Network*, he was
asked to delete a verse that offended against the report's enthusiasm for information
technology (Glaister, 1997). Unlike many of the technophiles in the government
and the library profession Hughes, the poet, recognized the limits of technology
and the much heralded information society. However, in professional circles and
beyond, the term 'information society', and related phrases such as 'information age'
and 'knowledge economy', are still used, sometimes interchangeably, to define the
emergence of the type of society, which is said to have developed in the late twentieth
century. Such expressions reflect a concept that has been enthusiastically adopted by
many academics, business leaders, governments, and information professionals.

Some writers have been less ready to accept the conventional wisdoms of 'the
information age'. For example, in his book, *Theories of the Information Society*,
Frank Webster (2002), after discussing the various paradigms, concludes that 'though
they appear at first glance robust [they] are in truth vague and imprecise, incapable
on their own of establishing whether or not an "information society" has arrived or
will arrive some time in the future'. Mullan (2000) has used Webster's conclusion to
generate what he calls frequently unasked questions about the so called information
society. In so doing, he asks:

> Why does the greater ability to process, store, and transfer, information translate into a
> qualitatively different society? Why does this represent a new era worthy of the label
> "information age"? Since the first Industrial Revolution 250 years ago there have been many
> technological breakthroughs in the means of production, of power, of communications and
> of transportation. Yet only in the past 20 to 30 years has the notion arisen that society is
> going beyond the industrial age into a post-industrial, information age. Why is information
> technology privileged over these earlier technological advances?

It is a good question and one that awaits an answer. There are several examples
of previous societies that have made significant use of information. In his 1982
Bowker Memorial Lecture Lowell Martin (1983) wondered, 'how the founding
fathers created a nation, and the founding scientists discovered the laws of nature
without information'. In the context of the UK, Black (2001) has written about the
increasing number of information workers operating in Victorian times and, from
outside the LIS professions, Tom Standage (1998) has described the nineteenth-

century telegraph as the Victorian Internet. In his book of that title he examined the impact the telegraph had on the ability to communicate information, and gives several examples of its uses, including the arrangement of what would now be called an 'on-line wedding'.

However, despite these historical precedents many working in the profession today seem to be obsessed with the 'new' technology. Moreover, some of these converts to the technological cause appear to have little patience with those who dare to question its high place on the professional agenda. In a memorable piece for *American Libraries*, Gorman (2006) wrote about 'the millenniarist librarians and pseudo-librarians who, intoxicated with self-indulgence and technology, will dismiss you as a "Luddite" or worse. They and their yips and yawps can safely be left to their acronymic backwaters and the dubious delights of clicking and surfing.' Their impact on the profession has been such that one commentator fears that: 'A nonprint, nonliterate bias in our resources and services is a limiting bias in our public sphere role of providing public information for a democratic culture' (Buschman, 2003). Such 'technological determinism' is not new. The present author recalls considering it as part of his Open University Studies of over three decades ago. However, at that time the idea that technology of and by itself could make a significant impact upon society was considered simplistic and misleading. The view then was that it was people, not just the products they make, that were important. In 1978, Antony Smith argued that it was social questions about information and its distribution that were likely to pose problems. These he said would be 'far more intractable than the primary technological invention of the new devices themselves'.

The truth of that prediction is to be seen today when so much of the information world is an essentially commercial environment. It is a world in which, for many, icons of all kinds are replacing ideas. It is a world in which, according to a recent Reith lecturer, 'we don't really give our children real education, but at best information ...' (Barenboim, 2006). Little value is placed on ideas as such. Television, which is for many people the main source of communication, is a prime example of this. To quote one observer, although:

> There is a considerable audience for exciting ideas discussed by top thinkers. The people, who run television today, except for the great, unwatched BBC4 and the occasional South Bank Show, do not have the same passion for ideas and for people who produce and create ideas. But you can be sure of one thing: they will not produce or commission programmes about the death of Socrates, the ideas of Foucault or the work of Walter Benjamin. That golden age is dead (Herman, 2003).

It is difficult, and beyond the scope of this book, to identify precisely when that golden age died but certainly these philistine attitudes were beginning to take root in the Britain of the 1980s. Oliver Letwin has been quoted as saying that Margaret Thatcher, the Prime Minister who characterized that dismal period, had 'absolutely no interests in ideas for their own sake' (quoted in Collini, 2006). That view appears to be reflected in many of her 'children' now working in the information industries.

Information 'has been prettified and made more fun, more entertaining and easier to digest than the real version. Information has been glamorized and beautified to make information, history, literature or reality easier to swallow, read or watch'

(McKenzie, 2000). Despite the high-minded claims of many of those in the industry, the new communications technology, like much of the old communications technology, is not over concerned with increasing human knowledge but with entertainment. This is often entertainment of the most trivial kind. One American commentator has expressed the situation as one where, 'All the cables will lead back to an enormous, leaking landfill of vicarious crap. Incredible sums of money will be made from this.' He concludes,

> every propagandist for the zillion channel environment talks piously about 'education'. Whenever a... entrepreneur invokes education in this context it behoves (sic) the citizen to smell a rat. Education is, or ought to be, about reality, and the dark star that lurks out there in cyberspace has less to do with reality than with the infinite replication of simulacrums, a hugely overscaled way... of amusing ourselves to death (Hughes, 1995).

As a result we find ourselves looking at, 'a new information landscape that often seems blemished and disappointingly dominated by pop culture, commercial entertainment values and billboard sensibility' (McKenzie, 2000).

The Limitations of Technology

Although there will be many occasions when ICT will provide an adequate answer public librarians, or for that matter library users, should not always go automatically to an Internet search engine when a book or other printed source might be more accurate and effective. Those who only rely on electronic sources would do well to note and heed the advice of MacArthur (2003), who described the differences between using a library and a computer in the following terms:

> Go to a library stack in search of a specific book and, thanks to the librarian you will likely find five related titles nearby that you'd also like to read, juxtaposition and contrast... being crucial to learning. Run a pseudo-authoritative search on the web and find a list, a very long list, that makes few distinctions and suggests nowhere to start.

As this description demonstrates, providing access to a vast range of information sources can be of limited value if people are unable to discriminate or obtain guidance as to what is reliable and what is not. In fact, more can often mean less, and the vast increase in the number of access points for information often means that people simply have access to more and more of the same. For example, many people in Great Britain now have over 400 different television channels available in their homes. However, the discriminating viewer will find numerous occasions when there is 'nothing on'. The simple provision of a large number of sources of information does not guarantee access to a comprehensive range of opinions and ideas. Nor does it ensure that people will retrieve high quality material. A large quantity of sources does not, by itself, secure an enriched or accurately informed population.

To suggest that a technical phenomenon should define our professional world is to turn reality upside down. Nevertheless, driven by the technological hyperbole, librarians have sought to place themselves at the centre of the so-called information society, and for many it is seen as the future, if not the saviour of the profession. In the words of Sallie Tisdale (1997) much of 'today's library literature [is] strangely infatuated, unquestioning, reflecting a kind of data panic, and filled with dire fantasies of patrons left behind – woebegone hitchhikers on the information superhighway'. That having been said, there are some from inside and outside the library world who have sought to question the central role of information in the future survival of the public library. A quarter of a century ago Martin (1983) observed that as 'an obscure node in a mighty and growing information complex', the public library may find its niche but it is unlikely 'that it will ever be as *the* information center'. More recently his near namesake argued that, 'We have… painted ourselves into a corner by convincing the public in general and our resource allocators in particular, that our primary *raison d'etre* is to provide information. And now that most… have direct access to the Internet on their desktop, we are paying the price for that misleading impression' (Martin, 2001).

This is a view that is supported by research evidence from different parts of the world. A recent survey undertaken in the Netherlands (quoted in Nijboer, 2006) indicates that the role of libraries in providing information will be marginalized. It showed that:

> 90 per cent of high school students used the Internet as the only source for writing assignments, and only 4 per cent also used sources obtained from the public library. Fast and easy were the most important criteria, and the reliability of the information seems to be of lesser concern (80 per cent did not check the information most of the time).

These findings reflect some of the attitudes found in the Sheffield RPK study quoted earlier. Similar comments are found in the Scandinavian literature from where it is reported that 'The [Finnish] public does not seem to use the library very frequently for finding specific factual information' (Vakkari, 1989). The Pullman Guidelines (2003) summarize the position in many countries. They indicate that, 'The increased availability of remotely-provided information services and Internet use for information-seeking could well lead to a decline in the number of physical visits to public libraries.' In addition they report, 'Many of Europe's children are now growing up with a well-developed and intuitive knowledge of the Internet and IST use.'

Providing Democratic Access

They add however, the important caveat that, 'there remain many excluded adults and children who have neither access nor skills to make use of these services'. In such circumstances they rightly argue, 'there remains an enormous need for friendly on-line services which meet user needs and which are accessible to all. Public libraries are well-placed to play an important role in their development and provision.' Despite the increasing private access to ICT there remains a significant number of citizens, who are in a very real sense excluded and handicapped, because they are not able to afford the new technology or because they have not developed the skills to use it. There is then a real role for public libraries in providing democratic access to electronic material. The gap between the communication haves and the communication have-nots is likely to remain an issue of concern for many years to come. It may apply especially to individuals and communities whose needs, for various reasons, are not the concern of those with commercial interests in the 'Information Society'.

There continue to be profound social divisions in access to information, ideas and works of imagination. These divisions can affect the life chances of millions and they are woven deeply into the fabric of many societies. The digital divide can take many forms, and the public library service needs to consider the needs, amongst others, of the elderly, the disabled, and those from the less Developed World. However, this role is under some threat. The concept of information as a right is now under attack, and charges for public library services are being advocated in many parts of the world and, in the case of some services introduced. If the library service is to retain its function of providing equity of access these kind of development will have to be resisted.

In the United Kingdom, the People's Network initiative has shown that the public library can also be instrumental in helping the general public to understand and use the new technologies. It also has an important role in conserving certain kinds of information for future generations. This can include local studies material and the indigenous knowledge of local people.

There are then many reasons why the public library service should continue as a major provider of information but, as Frank Webster (1999) warns, public librarians, in undertaking this role, need to be aware 'that they risk uncritically accepting the information that comes available on its own terms. And those terms are overwhelmingly commercial! One consequence is that a great deal of the information revolution manifests itself as information garbage.' The developments in ICT, the plethora of broadcast media and other sources, make it even more important to have a public institution with the financial and human resources to select, collect, maintain, organize and provide access to material of lasting value. Equity and excellence demands that the public library collection provides the opportunity for facts and ideas to be cross checked between different experts and different generations. Before the age of the Internet and the vacuous obsession with technology, this could almost be taken as a given in responsible library services. At that time: 'Most information used to come from authoritative sources… and was edited before being made available to the public' (Weise, 2000).

In the present 'information age' so called, there are many more sources of information but the true information professional, the true librarian, needs to be concerned about the quality of much of what is available. The lack of peer review and editorial standards, the ability to change the facts on sites such as Wikepedia, and many other factors make for a very volatile information scene. Dixon (2007), the Chief Revise Editor for *The Times*, while acknowledging the faults of newspapers, argues that, 'My default position is that every article on Wikipedia is rubbish.' He goes on to quote his colleague Rosemary Righter, who is of the opinion that it 'lacks accountability, authority, scholarly credentials, accuracy and scrupulousness'. As Choy (2007) suggests there is a need for librarians to 'play a role in "stabilizing" and maintaining the integrity and authenticity of documents in the digital environment'.

From Thinkers to 'Clickers'

Before the general introduction of digital technology, Postman (1986) in the introduction to *Amusing Ourselves to Death,* reminded his readers of Huxley's comment about 'man's almost infinite appetite for distractions'. He argued that *Brave New World* warns that 'people will come to love their oppression [and] adore the technologies that undo their capacities to think'. Nowadays, many people in the education world and elsewhere are worried about the similar effects of information technology. An American expert on learning fears that, 'The growing popularity of the World Wide Web is slowly but surely transforming the lives of human beings who are beginning to make the sad transition from being thinkers to becoming "clickers"' (Thirunarayanan, 2003). There are, in the words of Jesse Shera (1983), 'data, data everywhere but not a thought to think'. It is a danger that is increasing as the examples given in this book suggest. More recently, Lady Deech, a UK Higher Education expert, told a conference that while she was addicted to her computer, she believed that there came a time when students had to log out so that they could look at, and listen to, the world around them. She argued that taking down notes in longhand from a book in the library was better than cutting and pasting from the Internet, because it required students to 'digest' material (Frean, 2006).

In any case simply acquiring information is not enough. It is what people do with that information that matters. There are now many places where the public can simply access facts but facts on their own have a limited value. The real question is how people use them. Increasing technical skills amongst the general public may mean that many people know where to find factual answers, but at the same time some will lack the ability to ask intelligent questions. In the words of Jaron Lanier, we should 'Never treat information as being real on its own; its only meaning is in its use by people' (Lanier, 2000). Public librarians in addition to being concerned about issues such as accuracy and trust should also seek to provide opportunities for reflection and understanding. A good library, with properly selected material and the benefit of educated and professional staff, can improve people's capacity to think. It is a serious function that the profession should pursue. This is not to avoid the lighter side of library work, but to engage a sense of priorities and, to borrow and paraphrase the words of Carl Bernstein, (1992) to remind us that it's the role of libraries like journalists to challenge people, not merely to amuse them.

As Grayling (2006) has pointed out, such activities are integral to a society that seeks greater social cohesion and better mutual understanding. He argues that: 'This task requires not just an increase of factual knowledge, but reflective understanding of what it implies and why certain things matter so much to different community groups.' As those words are being written the British media are awash with sensationalist stories about the wearing, or not, of religious symbols be they a cross or veil. While many attempt to stoke the fire of controversy or worse, few try to reflect or analyse why such things matter to the people concerned.

A collection of well chosen material can provide a catalyst for change but it is not just factual material that increases people's understanding of the world around them. If we are to really understand other people it helps to read stories about them. Poets and novelists, as well as the authors on the non-fiction shelves, can help us achieve a deeper understanding than we can ourselves. For example, on the BBC radio programme *Poetry Please* a young man recently describe the impact of Auden's poem *Refugee Blues*. He emphasized the relevance of the poem to modern-day Britain, and the treatment of those who seek solace in our nation. How right he was. Auden's verse, his 'work of imagination', says more about, and gives a far deeper perception of the present situation facing asylum seekers, than all the sources of instant information and tabloid trivia put together. Readers are strongly recommended to read the complete work but just one verse will give a flavour of the benefits to be had by coming into contact with the work.

> Went to a committee; they offered me a chair;
> Asked me politely to return next year:
> But where shall we go to-day, my dear, but where shall we go to-day?

As this example indicates the shared experience and understanding of other people and communities gained through imaginative literature can be important to the democratic process. Putting good things in front of people is so much more productive than always going for the easy option. It is crucial that equality of access to such sources is maintained and encouraged, and that the public library service continues to provide for what Martin (1983) called 'that range of curiosity and aspiration and appreciation that characterized the alert, the sensitive, adventurous human being'.

Information Knowledge Wisdom

The philosopher Albert Borgmann (1999) links the rise of information with the decline of meaning. Moreover, he indicates that places such as libraries are much better sources of knowledge and experience than the computer from which, 'information, … comes endlessly and relentlessly pouring forth from one source to address an immobilized body via one sense. Or so it would if personal computers were a truly rich information source.' Likewise, Jenkins (1998) has observed that: 'A computer may gush torrents of information. A bookshelf gushes human experience.' D'Angelo makes a similar point when he argues that 'the post-modern information economy reduces meaning and knowledge to mere information' (D'Angelo, 2006).

Although some may argue that such writers demonstrate a degree of resistance to cultural change, their views do draw attention to a real and present danger. That is that the use of instant and accessible information sources can lead people away from the less glamorous sources of wisdom. They also serve to remind us that people need,'ideas, values, taste and judgement without which information is useless' (Roszak, 1996). 'Information is not knowledge and knowledge is not by itself understanding' (Grayling, 2006). It is then the role of the public library to provide much more than information. The Director of the American, Institute of Museum and Library Services, maintains that: 'The primary function of the public library is supporting and facilitating the transfer of knowledge' (Martin, 2001). Carl Sagan, the astronomer, and author, argued in an inspirational paragraph that:

The library connects us with the insight and knowledge painfully extracted from Nature, of the greatest minds that ever were, with the best teachers, drawn from the entire planet and from all our history, to instruct us without tiring, and to inspire us to make our own contribution to the collective knowledge of the human species (Sagan, 1983).

Looking for More than Information

That is a much more significant and complex function than the mere provision of information. However it remains the case that, 'In the current enthusiasm for the information superhighway, the larger purpose of public libraries risks being lost' (Gross and Borgman, 1995). Indeed, it is to limit professional horizons to see the public library service as primarily an information service. As Frank Gardner predicted, 'We are in danger of becoming too occupied... with information rather than reading' (quoted in White, 1971). 'When we read we are looking for more than information... A scholarly monograph is judged on its argument not just the number of facts in it; a literary novel is judged by the artistry of the writer' (Warwick, 2003). People should be encouraged to use libraries for these and many other reasons and 'our almost religious belief in the power of information deserves to be examined' (Levy, 2000).

It is, of course, true that the democratic process requires people to have access to information, but it is education that enables people to understand and reflect on that information and evaluate its quality. If, as is sometimes argued, information is the currency of democracy, a democracy based solely on information obtained from *The Sun*, *Daily Mail* or American talk radio is likely to be seriously devalued. In the words of James Billington, Librarian of Congress, 'For democracy to be dynamic, it has to be based on the dynamic use of knowledge.' 'The threat is that with the flood of new technologies has come a flood of infotainment, which degrades knowledge' (Library of Congress, 1996). The home computer can be used to help people find information about a great number of subjects but if they want to understand those subjects, they will be better off with the resources and ambience of the public library. Icons and pictures only have to be recognized but words are to be understood.

In considering the purpose of the public library, professionals should think less about its information role and rediscover the historic strengths and values of the service. Vestheim (1994) suggests that the 'approach might be to ask for more enlightenment, not more information' and argues that:

> the search for information is only one of many alternative means to enlightenment, to gain insight and understanding. It is not very interesting to talk about enlightenment in quantitative terms. Enlightenment is a question of quality – not a question of "how much" but rather a question of "what". It has very little to do with technical mediation of information – it deals with politics, culture – even with existential questions.

Readers will note the emphasis on quality in his statement. Batt (2003) the former Chief Executive of the Museums, Libraries and Archives Council, in a thoughtful but non prescriptive paper considering the future of what he calls 'a still unexplored landscape' has used the term 'Content Society'. He too emphasizes the importance of 'the scope, quality, accessibility and relevance of what the various channels will offer' and argues that public institutions should provide 'access to cultural assets, to new learning opportunities and to the services of government'. An aim that reminds one of the oft quoted comment of Toni Morrison (in Williams, 2006) that, providing, 'access to knowledge is the superb, the supreme act of truly great civilizations'. She added, as most readers will be aware that, 'Of all the institutions that purport to do this, free libraries stand virtually alone in accomplishing this mission.'

Chapter 9

Education, Education, Education

> Prejudices, it is well known, are most difficult to eradicate from the heart whose soil has never been loosened or fertilized by education; they grow there, firm as weeds among rocks.
>
> Charlotte Brontë

The increased number of information sources described in the previous chapter has created what one writer has called a *Data Smog* (Shenk, 1997). In this kind of climate people need something to give them a sense of direction. The public library can do this by providing educational opportunities that will develop the evaluative and other navigational skills that are necessary for a safe trip on the information highways. Of course in an age when celebrity ignorance is preferred to serious knowledge there can be no guarantee that everyone will take advantage of such facilities. Miller (2001) is not alone in wondering if, 'the dumber the population becomes, the more it will come to depend upon the educational resources of libraries? Or will people prefer to stay in their homes, isolated in the comfort of the limitless entertainment offerings of an interactive televised medium?' on the other hand Bundy (1999) is in no doubt that:

> Every library, and every librarian, has an educational role to play. If they do not, they deny their calling and responsibility. This responsibility has never loomed larger because information, writ large, is the currency of society... and there is no profession in the world better placed or able than librarians to reflect, comment, advise and educate on the rhetoric and reality of the Internet and information technology, or to challenge the assumptions of the techno lusts – assumptions which at best may be naive and at worst may be dangerous.

Policy makers from across the world have placed great emphasis on the value of education and literacy. Most famously, Nelson Mandela (2002) argued that, 'Education is the great engine of personal development. It is through education that the daughter of a peasant can become a doctor, that a son of a mineworker can become the head of the mine, that a child of farm workers can become the president of a great nation.' Although it is not always recognized by politicians there is, of course, a link between such educational outcomes and the provision of an adequately resourced public library service. Indeed, as the quote from Mandella suggests, education is one area of activity through which the public library can definitely make a great difference to the lives of individuals and communities.

At their best public libraries help to democratize knowledge, counter prejudice, and play an important part in promoting the values of a democratic and civilized society. Kelly (2003) exemplifies this in a review of a fascinating document called,

What Libraries Learned from the War. Written by the Secretary of the American Library Association in 1922, this document emphasizes the importance of 'Education of a broad liberal character' and argues that:

> The library has a part, and a very important part, in furnishing the means whereby every citizen may become an intelligent citizen. Libraries have the reputation of providing books on both sides of every important question. The radical and the extreme conservative meet in the library on an equal footing. The result is that the library makes for sane, intelligent development.

Although the language may have changed slightly over time this was the prevailing view in library circles for about the next 40 years. Long before the term was used by a UK politician Alvin Johnson described the public library as a 'people's university' (quoted in Raber, 1997). A little later Jesse Shera (1949) identified 'an enthusiasm for education for its own sake' as one of the factors linking the movements for universal schooling and tax supported public libraries. Edward Sydney, the Borough Librarian of Leyton between 1934 and 1950, argued that 'the public library was one of the major fundamental instruments in the continuous education and development of the adult citizen' (quoted in Muddiman, undated). For the librarians of Western Australia, education was 'the purpose of public libraries, not education in the narrow sense of "chalk" and "talk" but in the broad sense described by a distinguished American "That's what education means, to be able to do what you've never done before"' (Library Board of Western Australia, 1966). Likewise for Norwegian professionals: 'The aim of... libraries was to educate in order to create well-informed, independent and capable citizens. Behind the institutional face lay a humanistic, value-oriented and aesthetic cultural ideal' (Egeland, undated). However, as later parts of this chapter will demonstrate some of these cultural ideals started to be questioned in the late 1960s and 1970s.

The survey undertaken for this book revealed a variety of opinions among members of the current professional community, but it would appear, that for most of those questioned, 'Education will always be an essential feature of public library services, though not necessarily on the old "street corner university" model' (SP 31+) (Chart 5). It is argued that learning 'in museums, archives and libraries is different from that in formal education establishments' (Research Centre for Museums and Galleries, 2003). There are also differing views as to what librarians regard as education. A report from Insight Research (1998) concluded that while some public librarians do see themselves as having an educational role, others had become more cynical about what they might be able to achieve. In common with some earlier studies the Insight paper found a difference of opinion between those librarians dealing with adults and those primarily working with children. It concluded that, 'The majority feel that in the case of children the education aspect is more important, while with adults they should provide whatever is requested.'

Many respondents to the present study emphasized that, 'libraries offer opportunities for self development and gaining of knowledge which goes beyond formal education' (SDP 21+). It was argued that, 'Libraries do educate – perhaps not explicitly – but in an informal manner that can help citizens develop IT skills/

information literacy, and so on' (PG). Others stressed the 'Public library's role in life long learning and information literacy learning for the general public is pivotal' (PG). The public library is seen as a place that can help people prepare for school and other kinds of formal education. It is also thought of as an institution that can help people return to learning, and one that helps promote a positive home learning environment. Williams (1988) in his examination of, *The American Public Library and the Problem of Purpose*, describes the service 'as a source of informal self-education for children, students, and adults'. He argues that although it is only used as such by a minority that, 'minority consists of a great many individuals; and they use the library for something alone it offers'.

Libraries and Learning

For some however, the links between libraries and learning have become increasingly problematic. For example, 'In Norway, as elsewhere, the ideals of public education and the value it added were gradually seen by many as elitist, and the focus shifted from the library as an educator and arbiter of information supplied, to the individual's own right to information' (Egeland, undated). This view appears to be held by many of today's librarians. It is reflected in the comments of a number of respondents to the present study. One, when asked if libraries had an obligation to educate, decided to 'challenge the terminology [because] – I think a library has an obligation to support people to learn rather than to educate. Libraries are supportive organizations; they (and the staff) are not the upholders of what is right or wrong in terms of education' (HoS 21+). Another argued that, 'The public library should provide for people who want to use it for educational purpose, but it shouldn't be obliged to educate' (PG). One senior professional felt that it could be a disadvantage to be too closely associated with education and asked: 'Whatever happened to education, information and recreation? Libraries are seen as non-threatening so keep them that way and don't alienate people who don't want to be educated and only want the latest manga title' (SP 41+).

McCabe (2001), on the other hand warns that when 'public librarians move away from providing education to providing access, they move from the high professional calling of improving people's lives to the technical, material process of distributing materials and services without regard for the impact these materials and services might have...'. There appears to be far less emphasis on Shera's 'enthusiasm for education for its own sake' amongst many present day professionals. Indeed, it is now seen as an unfashionable view to hold. It seems that at the start of the twenty-first century, 'Learning for its own sake has foolishly become identified with snobbery and elitism' (*The Observer*, 2006). There was in the Thatcher era a definite antagonism to the concept and that view appears, to some extent, to have been carried over to parts of the more recent UK administrations. As a book reviewer recently asked, 'Where do libraries fit into [the then] Education Secretary Charles Clarke's concept that learning for its own sake is "a bit dodgy", and that medieval seekers after truth are an "adornment" to society?' (Prichard, 2003).

On the other hand, the library profession can take heart from the views of an earlier Education Secretary of the same political persuasion. In the foreword to *The Learning Age*, David Blunkett, argues that:

> Learning enables people to play a full part in their community and strengthens the family, the neighbourhood, and consequently the nation. It helps us fulfil our potential and opens doors to a love of music, art and literature. That is why we value learning for its own sake and are encouraging adults to enter and re-enter learning at every point of their lives as parents, at work and as citizens (Department for Education and Employment, 1998).

Participants in a workshop associated with the RPK project also suggested that museums, libraries, and archives embody the pleasure of learning. Members of the public maintain that there is, 'a role just for… acquiring knowledge and information not for any specific purpose but just for the sheer joy of acquiring it… there doesn't need to be a specific outcome, there is a role in there for libraries, archives and museums just to provide somewhere for people to acquire knowledge' (Usherwood, Wilson and Bryson, 2005).

Similarly, in their study Proctor and Bartle (2002) found that:

> one of the most effective ways of reaching and influencing low achieving and disadvantaged adults is through the public library service. Through providing facilities for people to learn in their own time and at their own pace, and through the encouragement of trained staff, the public library can make a significant impact on the self-confidence and self esteem of low achievers.

The data, from this and other research demonstrate that use of the public library improves the life chances of individuals, in terms of education and job opportunities. They show that public libraries can provide a 'ladder to learning and employment' (North East Museums, Libraries and Archives Council, 2005). Public libraries have the 'ability to recruit and re-engage adult learners, particularly those from hard-to-reach communities. As centres of learning, they support independent learning and provide adults with choice about how, and where, they learn. They offer real choices about learning, complementing mainstream provision and supporting regional targets' (North East Museums, Libraries and Archives Council, undated).

It has also been possible to demonstrate the educational importance of that most obvious of public library functions; the lending of fiction. Respondents participating in the *Checking the Books* study reflected on how works of imagination could be instrumental in providing instruction. That study clearly confirmed that recreational reading could have a variety of educational applications. It was seen to broaden linguistic skills generally, while fiction was also used as a learning tool for those developing English as a second language. Some readers described how they used their recreational reading to gain a wider education, obtaining insights into politics, history, anthropology, science, and geography via works of imagination. As Kendall (1998) indicates, 'Fiction reading for pleasure is the means by which many adults learn informally: about the experience of others, about life in other countries, about other periods of history.' In addition a quality library collection can help generate new learning interests. Many respondents to the Proctor and Bartle (2002) study recalled, 'how browsing the public library shelves had sparked their interest in a subject and this, in turn, had led to formal learning'. The researchers concluded that 'browsing in a public library has not been sufficiently recognised as a powerful tool for encouraging learning, both formal and informal'.

Supporting formal and informal education for young people according to Eyre (1996) has, always been 'central to the philosophy of library provision'. Indeed, it is argued that, 'When people talk about education, they tend to forget one fact of history: without a free public library service, the schooling of the so-called "common people" results in nothing more than the provision of factory fodder' (Chambers, 2000). Elkin (1996) also stresses the importance of public library services in the education of children, maintaining that for years they 'have freely supported inadequate school libraries and often substituted for non existent or inadequate school library services'. Augst (2003) takes the argument further by stressing the importance of what libraries contain and provide. He asks, 'What good was education if, in filling students with the equipment for learning, it left them without a "right of access" to the universe of knowledge.'

Framework for the Future (DCMS, 2003) emphasized the role of reader development work in improving literacy and encouraging reading. Evidence for this view can be found in a succession of evaluations of reader development and basic skills projects undertaken by Briony Train *et al.* at the University of Sheffield. (for example Train *et al.*, 2002; Train, 2003.) It is not an unproblematic area but from the first such evaluation the researchers were able to report that, 'the data revealed many examples of ways in which reader development could be used to enhance basic skills education, for example in encouraging self-direction and self-confidence. It was also felt that reader development could become part of the infrastructure of basic skills education' (Train *et al.*, 2002). Many of these projects involved partnerships with other agencies, and it is apparent that, in recent years, in educational provision as elsewhere, the public library service has entered into numerous partnerships for the benefits of its users.

Public library services and professional associations across the world have been involved in various projects to promote the basic skill of literacy. At the start of the new millennium one UK expert was able to conclude that, 'the public library has been perceived as a major component in the movement to promote literacy' (Lonsdale, 2000). Five years later IFLA created a Literacy Working Group. This, in its final report, made six major recommendations, outlining a number of areas in which public library services could aid literacy programmes. As the present text is being written, another international venture,'Public Libraries in the Learning Society' (PuLLS) is reaching its final stages. This is an EU project managed by the University of Brighton and a marketing agency in the Netherlands. It involves the public libraries of Aarhus, Barcelona, Helsinki, Ljubljana, Sutton, and Würzburg. The group maintains, 'that education is the key to active citizenship and general well being' and aims, 'to develop a new library concept that is applicable all over Europe' (PuLLS, 2006). The final report on this work is expected shortly.

Education, Equality, and Democracy

Arguably, it is through its involvement with education that the public library can do most to contribute to social equality and democracy. A senior professional involved in the present study observed that, 'The public library is a place where a new start is always possible. It can support learners, introduce people to learning, and introduce other learning providers to new audiences they might otherwise never reach. It is the bedrock of a literate and democratic society' (SP 31+). As Battles (2003) reminds us in his unquiet history of libraries, the 'Chartists recognized the importance of education in fulfilling the aspirations of those excluded from power and position'. In a later manifesto Anthony Crossland (1956) observed that, 'the idea of social equality requires the first priority to be given to educational reform'.

In *The Learning Age* David Blunkett, a politician from the present time described the benefits of these reforms. He writes:

> Men and women, frequently living in desperate poverty, were determined to improve themselves and their families. They did so through the creation of libraries, study at workers' institutes, through the pioneering efforts of the early trade unions, at evening classes, through public lectures and by correspondence courses. Learning enriched their lives and they, in turn, enriched the whole of society (Department for Education and Employment (1998).

Some library historians, it should be said, consider this a rather rose tinted view of the past. They argue, 'that the focus of public libraries on social inequality and division has been patchy and ambivalent and that action in this field has been hampered by a legacy of universal but passive service provision which has favoured the middle class' (Muddiman, 1999a). The American historian Harris (1973) far from celebrating the public library's educational function views it as an instrument of social control. Such views have been the subject of considerable debate but it is a matter of fact that for many the library has been, through accident or design, a positive and valuable educational resource. A Scandinavian writer who, although tending to support the social control argument admits that, 'the very provision of the library itself served as a means of emancipation, contributing to the cultural and "political" development of the town. The library was an important resource of enlightenment […] ' (Haugen, 2006).

From outside the library world some contemporary commentators suggest that the emphasis on education reflects the view of an educated liberal elite who are out of touch with the values, aspirations and beliefs of the poor white working class. For example, in the UK, Collins (2004a) the author of a polemic about the white working class entitled *The Likes of Us*? defends 'chavs who have been branded because they have made it into the lower-middle class via money instead of education' (2004). In his book, those who endeavoured to improve physical and or intellectual conditions are dismissed as 'missionaries', and efforts to encourage reading, the opening of a library, and other educational initiatives are all written off as the work of those adopting 'the missionary position'. Lord Reith in his, 'bid to educate, inform and entertain, in that order' is described as 'the voice of the patrician class nannying the nation'. The novelists and others who did so much to draw attention to working class poverty are accused of producing little more than 'slum fiction'. Without any note of regret, indeed almost as a badge of class solidarity, Collins reveals that: 'Like most of the neighbours we lived in a home where no one bothered with books.'

Collins and those who think like him present a view that restricts the horizons of the working class. He writes about library users who have been given the opportunity to experience delight but only sees fit to portray them as, 'downcast, confused, and apparently redundant, in a world of Tate Modern and multiculturalism'. In so doing he dismisses their potential, and the role of critical friends who may yet persuade them that education has benefits and that there is a more fulfilling life to be had beyond the shopping mall and the fantasy of reality television. It is a view that ignores the fact that many working-class people, such as the schoolboys depicted in Alan Bennett's (2004) play *The History Boys*, have found the basic truth in Ruskin's belief in the ability of a beautiful picture, a good book or a beautiful piece of music to transform a person.

As one who grew up as a member of the white working class in the East End of the 1950s, the present author, unlike Collins, is grateful for the 'missionaries' in the local public libraries and to the post-war BBC. Indeed, he is still grateful to them and is currently using the informed presenters of BBC Radio Three and the resources of the music section of Sheffield City Library to increase a limited knowledge of classical music. 'Education, education, education' in its various forms can enable people to escape from a limited and materialistic world, and if the present writer has made it into the lower middle class or anywhere else then, in common with many from a similar background and contrary to Collins' mantra, he owes it to education rather than money. To missionaries rather than mercenaries.

Another group to benefit from the educational role of the public library have been the immigrants to a country. In the words of a recent report: 'Public libraries in the United States have a long history of providing resources and education to immigrants. This tradition may be traced to Andrew Carnegie's support for public libraries as a place for immigrant self-education, enlightenment, and the study of democracy and English' (Office of Citizenship, 2006). In the United Kingdom, the 'Libraries Change Lives Award' provides several excellent examples of projects designed to meet the needs of black communities, travellers and asylum seekers. Indeed, here, as in America, libraries have always played a major role in helping newcomers. A BBC radio programme *Voices from the Reading Room*, broadcast a few years ago documented how the former Whitechapel Library served the needs of the Jewish, Bengali, and other communities who passed through that part of East London. Among the early users of that East End library were, Dr Jacob Bronowski, Bernard Kops and Isaac Rosenberg. Their visits were of benefit not just to themselves but also to many others who gained from the knowledge and skills that they acquired.

Education at the Heart of the Public Library Service

Traditionally, education has been at the heart of the public library service. The founders of Boston public library considered 'that a large public library is of the utmost importance as the means of completing our system of public education'

(Boston, 1852). In the words of one respondent to the present study, 'it remains one of our core purposes – but there are many ways of educating' (Dep 31+). It involves informal and formal support for the school curriculum, life long learning, instruction in the use of ICT, and increasingly the concept of information literacy to help create a more engaged and media literate public. The role of educator is far more complex and important than that of a simple information provider. Indeed, as Roszak (1996) has observed: 'People who think education equals information have no idea what either information or education is.' Several generations earlier, Tawney (1964) eloquently argued that:

> The purpose of an adult education worthy of the name is not merely to impart reliable information… it is still more to foster the intellectual vitality to master and use it, so that knowledge becomes, not a burden to be born, or a possession to be prized, but a stimulus to constructive thought and an inspiration to action.

Libraries need to be seen as an integral and essential part of education. In so doing they will of course serve an instrumental purpose, and help people gain employment, but as public services 'we also provide the education we do, because it is believed that it both civilises the individual and better equips the person to understand at least enough of matters in general to make basic participation in the democratic process meaningful' (Henderson, 2006). Although it is true that the democratic process requires people to have access to information, it is education, which in the end enables them to understand and reflect on the facts they have found.

A major function of education, and as already indicated public libraries, is to encourage and enable people to develop discriminatory skills; skills that facilitate discrimination between good writing and bad writing, and make possible an informed choice between different sources of information and ideas. Public libraries provide for those who wish to acquire knowledge about matters that are important for themselves and their communities. With so many players in the information world, it is important that public librarians focus on what they are good at. Despite the clarion calls to adopt a populist agenda, and to use their skills elsewhere, they need to rediscover their established role supporting learners of all kinds. Such an undertaking does not mean that other concerns, such as information and recreation have to be ignored but rather that librarians should see themselves as professionals who serve the public good by sorting the good from the bad.

If judged solely by the rules of the market place such a strategy may be deemed a failure. 'Education is unlikely ever to win an "open market" competition with entertainment because "easy" and "hard" can never compete on equal ground…' (Barber, 1995). 'The aim of… education is to inculcate a rational, critical intelligence…' (Fernández-Armesto, 2006), and that can take time. It is a function that requires libraries to provide a range of sources, and space and facilities for reflection. 'Libraries', says McKee (quoted in Erickson, 2000) 'are, above all, intellectual retreats, full of curious, subtle discourses. It seems cynical to have to bait children with trendy imagery to excite their supposedly flaccid gray (sic) matter.' Indeed populist policies and the use of trendy imagery and retail style branding techniques designed to attract new users should be used with care. They can be detrimental to public libraries educational activity. The public library service should have the confidence to promote itself via well-presented and intelligently chosen collections. Collections of quality, together with the professional skills and values of librarians, act as a multiplier and enhancer of a myriad of small-scale experiences that will benefit the individual, and society. They show that public libraries are an educational resource and in, Tawney's words, 'a stimulus to constructive thought and an inspiration to action'.

Chapter 10

Through Excellence to Inclusion

No one on the left should… think that a taste for high culture which means in short, a taste for the best things in all arts – is anything but as conducive to the general good as it is to their own.

(Grayling, 2002)

For the past decade public libraries, in common with many other institutions, have been affected by government policies which are designed to bring excluded members of society into the mainstream. In the United Kingdom, this has been a major aim of the New Labour administrations, and strategies concerned with equality and diversity look set to continue for the foreseeable future. Moreover, government Ministers have made it clear that public libraries are to be included in future policy initiatives designed to 'combat social exclusion and promote neighbourhood renewal across the country' (Woolas in CILIP News 2006). It is now widely accepted that: 'Public libraries have an excellent record in tackling social exclusion by reaching out to marginalised communities and offering a huge range of valuable services. Libraries are integral to every community in Britain and provide a neutral environment where people can access resources which might otherwise remain out-of-reach' (Brown in CILIP News 2006). The library is seen as a democratic institution which 'succeeds in reaching groups in the poorest social position' (Vakkari, 1989).

Although one respondent taking part in the present study felt that, 'egalitarian aspirations have either not existed, or have not been actively pursued, by elitist and exclusive library managers' (HoS 21+), expressions of concern about the needs and demands of minority groups are now part of the professional and political mainstream. For example, Britain's Conservative Party is now presenting a caring face to the electorate and its leader proclaims that it is now the party for working people and seeks to recruit and support a range of minority groups. More specifically one of its prominent members recently, 'pledged to bring together Conservative Councils to develop a deliverable vision for libraries' (Swire, 2006). The precise nature of that vision is unclear at the time of writing, but it seems unlikely that the new Tory Lite leadership will endorse the kind of hard line monetarist policies favoured by the party in 1986. That having been said, the right wing Adam Smith Institute (undated) still talks about 'liberating' (its word for privatizing) libraries, and encourages readers of its website to 'read more about library commercialization'.

David Lammy, when he was the minister with responsibility for public libraries argued that 'we're on a journey' (Rushton, 2006). Although few doubted his energy and commitment, some, including the author, harbour reservations about the precise route that the government is planning. To express unease at the direction of some government policies is not necessarily to disapprove of its chosen destination, although there are those in the profession who are apprehensive about the political perception of the service. One librarian told Newman (2007):

> I think at heart we are viewed as rather old Labour – the idea of the public library has a resonance that New Labour are not comfortable with. The idea of everyone paying into a common pot so everyone else can have access to a public resource is no longer popular. It's a bit like public broadcasting except that libraries are weaker. For all they [government] talk about social investment and social inclusion, they view libraries as somewhat old fashioned and irrelevant to what they are interested in (respondent 3).

There are a number of concerns, but the present author has no wish to join those who constantly talk down the considerable achievements of the library service. For him the argument is between those who want to maintain professional values and believe that 'we have a responsibility to widen horizons and present the opportunities and services available, not to be solely demand led' (HoS 31+), and people who no longer see the relevance of this approach. Professionals who take the latter view do not see it as part of their role to support, and explain, the provision of high quality material. They tend to accept that, 'People's cultural tastes are now accepted as a democratic given, and the idea that a cultural elite... could impose "higher" tastes is no longer accepted, as it was quite widely accepted 30 years ago' (Coveney, 2005). On the other hand, there are those who feel that when librarians start to lower their standards in the name of social inclusion and improving access, they demonstrate a professional pessimism about the intellectual abilities of the people they seek to serve. As one user argues in a related context, 'It is actually insulting to intelligent working – class people to suppose they will only enter museums and art galleries specially geered (sic) to attract them' (Brady, 2003).

The Waste of Human Potential

However, it is an unpalatable fact that some people, raised in contemporary society, do not appear to have any desire to use public libraries, and will not do so however far the service is changed to meet their perceived requirements. A group quoted by Muddiman (MVA 1998 in Muddiman, 1999) told researchers, 'I think you're flogging a dead horse here, because people in this room don't really use a library and I don't think whatever you call it you're not gonna get us through the door. It's because we don't read the fact that we don't go really (sic).' This reflects a poverty of aspiration and is in the words of Tessa Jowell, 'a terrible waste of human potential' (Jowell, 2004a). Of course, some library services have worked successfully with 'excluded' groups. For instance, Islington's New Horizons Estate Reading Project involved socially excluded residents and set out:

> to provide an opportunity for people to discover the pleasure and enjoyment of books, and to get people who have got out of the reading habit back into reading. Supporting the development of reading skills and learning, the project is specifically targeted at teenagers, reluctant readers especially men, people who do not have English as a first language and family learners.

This kind of project did not mean that the library service had to be altered beyond recognition and it avoided the process of dumbing down which can, according to Furedi (2004) be 'a direct consequence of public policy that promotes inclusion at any costs'.

That having been said, it needs to be recognized Britain is now subject to the behaviour of the members of an amoral and apolitical section in society who are neither deserving nor poor. It is a group that is against learning, anti intellectual and, in the words of one commentator, 'despise [s] browns and blacks (especially if they are making something of their lives) and also education, enlightenment and internationalism' (Alibhai-Brown, 2007). Sometimes identified by the inelegant label 'chav' members of this group raise issues that are uncomfortable to address. However, their attitudes are contrary to all the public library stands for and the profession must be prepared to confront them. Because they are often, if wrongly, equated with the white working class they have received some support from writers on the Left (for example Hari, 2004; Harris, 2006). In truth however, their way of life owes more to the consumerist and meritocratic attitudes of the Thatcher era than to the traditional values of working people.

The sub group decried by Alibhai-Brown and defended by Hari and Harris are part of a culture that often provides a negative role model. As such, they can bring peer group pressure, or worse, to bear and thus dissuade young people, in particular, from investigating the opportunities provided by the library world. A head teacher illustrates this danger writing that in Britain, 'among the young, of all classes, it seems, the highbrow or intellectual pursuit has to be a closet affair, to avoid the lacerating sneer' (Williams, 2000). More recently, the broadcaster and author Bettany Hughes (2007) told *The Independent* how, at her Primary school she 'used to be beaten up for reading'. A quick tour of some electronic discussion groups reveals the intimidating nature of such behaviour. On one, a teenager reports: 'They [chavs] also like to give anyone going into either the next door health food shop, or library dirty looks. Literacy? Health? Don't be such a twat mate!' While another tells how he, 'was once smacked by a chav in the xxxx xxxx Library'. Another contributor states that his 'local library got burnt down a couple of years back' and blames 'Damn chavs and their fires!' A teacher observes that in his town:

> The only building that causes confusion is the library. Red-brick and modern, its purpose clearly mystifies and actually evades most Chavs. Occasionally, they can be spotted muttering and pointing in its direction whilst wheeling little Courtney Dakota back home for some Tartrazine flavoured juice and unsupervised play. Consequently, the library remains unvisited, un-graffittied and untouched. Because no-one knows what the fuck it is.

In library terms, that sad litany raises a number of issues. The teacher's final cry of despair provides further evidence, if it were needed, that 'low awareness of available services [is] sometimes the key issue' for young people (Define Research and Insight, 2006). However, in times of limited resources we need to ask if the profession should attempt to provide specifically for people who choose to exclude themselves and, all the evidence suggests, are never likely to use what the service can legitimately offer. Obviously, they should be given every chance to engage with the service but not at the expense of people who can and want to benefit from what a library provides. As one commentator observes 'there are plenty of vibrant people in the working class who aspire to something better than chav life without being what these writers seem to see as class traitors. There is nothing middle class about having books in the house and a degree [...]' (Cruise, 2006).

As one professional observes, 'we cannot please everyone all of the time. Trying to do this has led to services not delivering the quality expected' (SP 21+). Another quoted in Phillips (2005) was 'all for social inclusion' but also 'concerned that the educational role of the library is being overlooked in the drive towards widening access'. The question we have to ask, according to one of the respondents to Phillips' (2005) study, is 'what are we including people in?' ...if you turn a library into a nursery or a play centre, is that the main function of the library?

Competing Interests

This is but one of a number of questions with which the twenty-first century librarian is faced. She or he will have to make judgements regarding the competing interests of different groups. It is unrealistic to expect any service to be able to afford to do everything, and policy makers and professionals will have to take decisions about what they will, and will not, provide. This will mean that some types of service, and some interests, will be better provided for than others. Respondents to the present study were keen to emphasize the need for balance when providing different aspects of the service. It was argued, for example, that in general terms, 'a balance has to be kept – but [it is] still very important to attract as wide a range of people as possible and expose them to all that libraries can offer' (SP 21+). Another stated, 'I feel there needs to be an appropriate balance between the two ends of the spectrum in order to broaden the appeal of the service but also to provide the most sustainable service' (SP 31+).

In terms of stock it was felt that the public library service, 'Should aim to have a balanced and representative range of material available.' And that, 'within that context [it] should aim to ensure the "best" is represented, and where "best" is attributed through peer evaluation (for example award winning, or academically authoritative, this should be clear to [the] customer)' (HoS 31+). Respondents emphasized that there must be a 'role for the minority interest – libraries must take a balanced view... the primary stock should be popular, but we also need to offer other stock' (SP 21+). It was felt that, 'customer needs should be reflected and have a high priority – but it's important to get the range of stock too, including the more challenging stock and that which caters for the minorities' (SP 21+). Some considered that, 'we must aim to spend [a] bulk of [the] money on what local people want to use – we don't have enough money to do anything else', but at the same time stressed that 'we do have a duty to buy some resources that will gain lower levels of use but that will be of great value to individuals' (Dep 31+).

One respondent spoke of the importance of 'some leadership on our part' (HoS 31+) and another, of the need for there to 'be a balance between customer-expressed choice and professional judgment based on knowledge of the community' (SP 21+).

It was observed that, 'We need to reflect popular culture and encourage mass use, but also maintain a balanced long-term approach to collection content and service provision' (Dep 31+). However, a balanced approach does not necessarily mean that the same level of consideration should be given to all demands. Professional leadership and judgements are required. The equation for the public library service professional has to include questions of needs and benefits both for the individual and for society at large. In fact it may be better to think in terms of a response that reflects an informed judgement on the role of the library in meeting the needs of different populations. For instance, the current professional emphasis on the needs of young people may be thought to be somewhat disproportionate at a time when more people in Britain are over 60 than under 16. Similarly in the United States it is expected that the senior adult population will consist of more than 54 million people (see Kleiman, 1995).

There are many other sections of the population that deserve the attention of the profession. Many groups that can also claim to be victims of social exclusion. It is not our purpose to discuss each group in detail but rather to provide some examples as illustrations of the challenges facing professionals who have to promote social inclusion and establish service priorities. The reality is that no public library service can afford to supply everything and library professionals are faced with the dilemma that, 'Excellence is not necessarily exclusivity, but neither is it trying to offer everything everywhere and diluting scarce resources' (Dep 31+). Another respondent observes, 'we have tried to be all things to all people, and lost confidence in our core business of books, and even in the word Library in some places. This was with the intention of "staying relevant". Big mistake' (HoS 31+).

It is assumed that most readers will be aware of some of the major social inclusion/exclusion initiatives that have taken place in recent years. For those who are not, 'The Network' website and its associated archive of Newsletters is a good place for UK readers to start. The site reflects the activities of 'a network of public libraries, museums, archives, other organisations and individuals committed to tackling social exclusion'. Its mission is, 'To assist the cultural sector, including libraries, museums, archives and galleries, heritage and other organisations, to work towards social justice' (The Network, 2007).

Suffice it to say that those experiencing social exclusion are not all the same and the library service may not always be able to provide the most relevant solution. As Opening the Book (undated) argues, we must avoid making 'absurd claims for the power of reading (no, reading a book will not get you off heroin, it won't stop you nicking cars, it won't prevent your cancer spreading, it won't even make you a nicer person)'. In dealing with the requirements of any one section of the population the question of need, and the benefits that the library can be expected to provide should be taken into account. For example, the LASER Foundation report (Define Research and Insight, 2006) on young people and libraries unsurprisingly discovered that they wanted, 'material and services that fitted with their particular current "lifestyle" interests. For boys this tended to be sports focused. For girls, this included fashion, health and beauty, celebrity and shopping and café culture.' However this kind of material is readily available elsewhere and there seems relatively little benefit in the public library simply replicating such provision. Instead, public librarians should, 'spare a thought for the adolescent, male or female, who nurtures a passion for Mahler rather than Manu, for Austen rather than Austin Powers' (Williams, 2000). The library can be a valuable refuge for this excluded group.

In the words of one respondent we must 'ensure we don't forget those who are not so vocal or don't have the ability to express their views so easily' (HoS 31+). They are less often served by commercial providers, but a good library should have the ability to meet their needs and in so doing provide a valuable and unique service both to the individuals themselves and to the wider society. They are often the modern day equivalents of, 'a heroic army of men and women who refused the state of ignorance, and by self-cultivation put themselves in a position to help the rest of the educationally and culturally disenfranchised from whose ranks they had come, at last thereby winning the argument that no one should be discriminated against in this most fundamental of ways' (Grayling, 2002).

Promoting and prioritizing high aesthetic and other standards does not make public libraries culturally exclusive. On the contrary, for a public library to provide what is an inferior product is to exclude people from high quality material that they may not be able to afford or to obtain elsewhere. Chambers (2000) illustrates this clearly when he recalls:

> It is only because of a brilliant teacher, Jim Osborn at Darlington Grammar School in the late 1940s and 1950s, that I could write the book that won the Carnegie Medal, and it was mainly because of public libraries that I was able to make full use of what he taught me… Given my family background, I could not have become an independent reader without the aid of a free public library. There I navigated my way through the stacks and sniffed out the books I didn't know I wanted until I found them.

He goes on to note that the librarians who did so much to help him 'were not populists. They were democrats. They knew populism is perfidious. It pretends to be democratic when in reality it is brutally undemocratic.' Providing people with the opportunity to experience and examine the range of material described by Chambers is an attempt to open doors rather than close them.

As the former Secretary of State suggested, 'Complex cultural activity… is at the heart of what it means to be a fully developed human being' (Jowell, 2004a). Moreover, people who are not given the opportunity to experience great literature, or the works of great artists, writers and thinkers, are in danger of being deprived of the basic knowledge that will enable them to function in contemporary society. Such people may lack what has been termed 'cultural literacy'; that is knowledge of the background information that communicators in a society expect people to have. It is a term most often linked to the controversial American educationalist Hirsch (2002) who argues that. 'We help people in the underclass rise economically by teaching them how to communicate effectively beyond a narrow social sphere, and that can only be accomplished by teaching them shared, traditional literate culture.' Although it is obvious to anyone who reads his work that Hirsch clearly acknowledges the needs and contributions of a multicultural population he has, perhaps unfairly, often been portrayed as a purely conservative figure.

There are political and other arguments in this area, but they are not a simple matter of the Left *versus* the Right. For librarians it is a question of artistic and literary judgements, public taste and perhaps above all their view regarding the purpose of the public library. As Phillips (2005) observes, 'It may not always be possible to balance the entertainment and educational roles of the public library and sometimes priorities must be decided.' A respondent told her:

> As a chief librarian what you have to say if I've got a finite amount of money what is my major role? ... if you have a choice between buying another 1000 copies of *The Da Vinci Code* or a few copies of a Booker Prize-winning novel, I think at some point we have to say 'What is the role of the library?'

It should go without saying that in addressing such questions, every effort should be made to take note of the needs, experiences and backgrounds of people in a multicultural and diverse society. However, there is little evidence to suggest that introducing people to excellence *per se* leads to exclusion. On the contrary there is much in the literature and elsewhere to show that public libraries, in so doing, have had a positive impact on many individuals and groups across the world. As Mäkinen (2001) points out 'the universalism of services was an essential feature of the public library long before the birth of the welfare state'. In Finland the library, 'has to a certain extent succeeded in levelling out the differences which existed between various social groups in getting to the sources of reading' (Vakkari (1989). In Poland, 'the drive for the unification of the culture of the elite with that of the masses, found its expression... not only in the form of the opening of a large number of libraries... but also in that of personal contacts with contemporary writers ...' (Kolodziejska, 1971.)

Testimonies from Library Users

Similarly, there are many individual testimonies from a wide range of library users. These include the anonymous contributor to an online debate who wrote:

> As a youngster in a northern English slum more than 50 years ago, the local library was my first contact with civilization − more so than my schools which, although they taught me to read, had few or no bookshelves. Put simply, I owe my rescue from barbarism to the library (Anon, 2006).

There is praise too from sports stars who 'spent many, many hours in public and school libraries' and found 'the current definite answer to almost any question... within the four walls of most libraries' (Ashe in IFLANET, undated), and from writers who found that for a 'child whose family could not afford to buy books, the library was the open door to wonder and achievement' (Asimov in Williams, 2006), or view it as a place that says 'touch me, use me, my hush is not indifference, my space is not barrier. If I inspire awe, it is because I am in awe of you and the possibilities that dwell in you' (Morrison in Williams, 2006). In addition, there is a multitude of others who, over the years, have provided evidence of the difference public libraries have made to their lives (see for example Usherwood, 1993; Bundy, 2002).

Besides the weight of individual testimony there are also numerous examples of public library projects that seek to deal with the problems of exclusion. In the UK 'The CILIP Libraries Change Lives awards scheme is proof of the role libraries play to lift people out of social exclusion and regenerate neighbourhoods' (Molloy quoted in *Managing Information News*, 2006). In America:

> The library was also a haven for the waves of immigrants arriving after 1890 and, equally importantly, for their children. Storytelling was used to socialize immigrants and teach the customs and expectations of U.S. society. Libraries came to resemble community centers, waging a war for "Americanization". By the 1920s the term "adult education" had entered the library vocabulary (Straight, 2006).

In addition, there is a substantial body of research that demonstrates the overall value of public libraries to disadvantaged groups. The various social audit studies undertaken at the University of Sheffield (for example Linley and Usherwood, 1998; Toyne and Usherwood, 2001, Bryson, Usherwood and Streatfield, 2002) found that, libraries enriched the lives of many people and enabled individuals and communities. Yet more evidence is to be found in studies such as those undertaken by Comedia (1993); Proctor *et al.* (1996), and Matassaro (1998). Such work demonstrates that across the world public libraries are used and greatly appreciated by many people from erstwhile excluded groups.

The large quantity of academic research and the personal testimony of users do not convince everyone within the profession. Pateman (2004) for example believes that libraries:

> do not deserve their reputation as "street corner universities". The common assumption – which has become an enduring myth – is that public libraries were established to provide informal education for working people. The reality is that they were set up and run by the Victorian establishment to control the reading habits and idle time of the "deserving poor".

Harris (1973) has made similar comments about American public libraries accusing their early library leaders of 'authoritarianism and elitism'. McCabe (2001), on the other hand, considers this 'dour assessment of the founders of the public library and their successors' to be the work of 'revisionist historians'.

Muddiman (1999) acknowledges that the working class use public libraries, but argues that only a small section is benefiting: 'The numerical evidence suggests that it is a minority of the working class who are socially, educationally, or intellectually aspirational who particularly value and use public library services.' At this point, it is worth noting that the argument that libraries only serve the middle class is one that has also been frequently used by those on the Right. As Blacker (2005) observes: 'During the dark years of Tory rule... smooth types from the Adam Smith Institute would appear on *Newsnight* to argue that libraries were only used by the middle class.' It is an argument that ignores the fact that: 'The search for enlightenment has characterised the advance of the working population over the years. Despite the considerable limitations imposed by apathy, illiteracy, and ignorance in our midst, many working men and women fashioned ideas and built movements which transformed the living and working conditions of their fellows' (Jones, 1990). The beneficial impact of those who did use library services on their colleagues and their communities is substantial and should not be underestimated.

Existence Value

It is now recognized that many who do not physically use public libraries also profit from their existence. There is a need to take account of what has been termed 'existence value'. Arrow *et al.* (1993) argue that 'for at least twenty five years, economists have recognized that individuals who make no active use of a particular beach, river, bay or other such natural resource might, nevertheless, derive satisfaction from its mere existence, even if they never intend to make active use of it'. They refer to Contingent Valuation, a tool, that until recently has largely been used in the environmental sector. There remains a debate as to whether this is a totally appropriate form of evaluation for public libraries, but many argue that there are important similarities between environmental and cultural goods, and it is interesting to note that the method was used by the British Library (2004) in its recent exercise, 'Measuring our Value'.

Other recent research shows that 76 per cent of those questioned who had not visited a museum or gallery during the past 12 months thought it important for their local town or city to have its own museum or art gallery (MLA, 'Visitors to Museums and Galleries' (2004). Similarly in the Sheffield RPK study (Usherwood, Wilson and Bryson, 2005) when focus group respondents were asked how they would feel if museums, libraries and archives suddenly ceased to exist, their responses reflected what the researchers described as a sense of 'moral obligation to preserve and obtain such institutions irrespective of individual use and patronage'. They conclude that: 'Respondents across the sample showed that there are high levels of "existence value" placed in our traditional repositories of public knowledge.'

On the surface, this chapter has revealed strong differences in professional opinion regarding the effectiveness of the public library service. Although the current emphasis on social inclusion has had a significant impact on the public library world, how far, and with what result it has been reflected in practice is the subject of some debate. The professional and research literature provides a variety of sometimes contradictory views. Recent publications have revived some of the 1970s' professional arguments about class. At that time, *The Assistant Librarian* carried articles that asked librarians to consider important questions about, 'social class, race relations and the public library' (Jordan, 1972). It was argued then that 'a library in a working class area... must be reader centred, and must reflect in as many ways as possible the abilities, interests and aspirations of the community' (Devereux, 1972). More recently the profession has been accused of 'institutional classism' (Pateman, 2000) and, reflecting 'a white, middle class, academic culture which alienates many disadvantaged people' (Muddiman, 1999). However, an investigation into how far public libraries are meeting the needs of working class individuals and communities concluded that, 'In many ways, the evidence seems to contradict... arguments that libraries are not serving working class people. [And that] while there were some complaints, the overall response from users was generally positive' (Bentley, 2002).

The study did identify 'low user expectations in disadvantaged communities [and] that, whatever the reality, the library is perceived as a middle class place'. The researcher observed, '...that some changes could be made', and this is a conclusion with which the present author would agree. However, there is little to suggest that members of disadvantaged communities want librarians to purge their services of poetry, classics, literary fiction and other material dismissed as elitist. As has been shown in earlier chapters most complaints are not about libraries having too much high quality material on offer but rather about its lack. Contemporary users, similar to the working class autodidacts who read Homer, Milton and Shakespeare knew that 'the politics of equality must begin by redistributing... knowledge to the governed classes' (Rose, 2001).

Others question the purpose of the institution in the twenty-first century. Indeed, as Matarasso observed at the turn of the millennium, 'The changing needs and values of the public library's owners have pushed it this way and that until it's really quite hard... to see what it's actually for' (Matarasso, 2000). The question of *who* the service is actually for is easily answered at the theoretical level. Libraries are for and open to all, and the concept of fairness is inherent in their public provision. As indicated above, in practice the service has to meet the needs of many worthy and sometimes competing groups, and no library professional worthy of the name, least of all the present author, would wish to exclude any group from the use of the library. However there are, as Furedi (2004) indicates, dangers in inclusion at any cost. To advocate social inclusion without being concerned about the standards of the inclusive experience is dishonest. Evidence suggests that, given the chance many people will enjoy, and benefit from, the opportunity to access more demanding material. Professionals and policy makers who are willing to lower the quality of the library experience in the name of inclusion are in fact demonstrating a patronizing pessimism about the ability of their clientele. Of course, a quantity of philistines will always be present in any society. It would be quite wrong to assign these to any group or class but, whatever their background, they should not be the people who define our professional policies.

Forty plus years ago at the start of his career the present author believed that public libraries could contribute to establishing a fairer and more civilized society. That view has not changed. Libraries have provided an avenue of social mobility for many populations across the world and there is ample academic, anecdotal and arithmetical evidence to demonstrate that they can be a force for good and that, in contemporary language, they contribute to social inclusion. In a democracy, the public library's role is to provide all people with quality services. These should be services that support the vulnerable while satisfying and extending the able. Many examples of populism are essentially undemocratic. We live in a society where highly educated people often give people what they (that is the highly educated) say the people want. Think, for example, of those responsible for *Big Brother*, *Wife Swap* and other such televised trash. In the words of the playwright Jimmy McGovern, 'They have utter contempt for their audience. These executives don't sit around and say, what kind of intelligent, informative thought provoking programmes would we like to watch? They think, what will the ignorant plebs that watch our channel want to see?' (in Martin, L. 2006).

The experience of the writer Jeanette Winterson provides a more positive scenario. She describes how through the arts she, 'escaped from a life of poverty, got myself to Oxford, become a writer, and all because of the power of art. My text was simple; if art can do that for a working class girl whose father could not read, art is neither remote nor a luxury.' It would of course be misleading to suggest that, in practice, the route through excellence to inclusion is always easily available to all. In public libraries as in other institutions there are clearly some barriers for some people to overcome, and these will be examined in the next chapter together with the political, professional, financial, and managerial implications of a public library service that seeks to provide equity and excellence.

Chapter 11

Professionals, Practice and Policy

> Critical to the future success of the public library service will be a clear sense of purpose and value shared by policymakers, service managers and staff, communities and stakeholders of every variety.
>
> Dolan (2007)

According to staff in the Congressional Reading Room at the Library of Congress, the quotation for which they receive most requests is a statement made by Senator Hubert Humphrey some 30 years ago. In this he argued, 'that the moral test of government is how that government treats those who are in the dawn of life, the children; those who are in the twilight of life, the elderly; and those who are in the shadows of life – the sick, the needy and the handicapped' (Humphrey, 1977). It is not surprising that these words still have resonance today as policy makers and professionals from a wide range of disciplines seek to improve the life chances of the most disadvantaged in society. As the previous chapter indicated, the British government believes that library services can and should play a significant role in combating disadvantage, and what is now called 'social exclusion'. When it first came to power in 1997, it established a Social Exclusion Unit as part of a cross-government approach to the issue. In 2006, that unit was replaced by 'a new Taskforce that will put social exclusion at the heart of government' (Cabinet Office, 2006).

David Miliband (2005), who is regarded as one of Britain's leading political thinkers, has described social exclusion as, 'an extreme consequence of what happens when people don't get a fair deal throughout their lives, often because of disadvantage they face at birth, and this disadvantage can be transmitted from one generation to the next'. He expects cultural organizations in common with other bodies, to 'bring different people together and bridge divides. This will involve these institutions become (sic) more porous, participatory and interactive – being not just in the community but of the community.' In so doing they can 'contribute significantly to the more tangible dimensions of inclusion – better education, better health, higher employment, and lower crime'.

The extent to which the public library service can contribute to this agenda and, at the same time, meet professional requirements for excellence and equity depends on a number of factors. These include how the service and the parent organization are managed, government policies, and a range of matters outside the immediate control of professional staff. As discussed in the previous chapter, it is unrealistic to suggest that public libraries will always be able to have a direct impact on every social problem, although it should be emphasized that literacy skills are an essential prerequisite to a full participation in most societies. Clearly, those who are unable to use and access the traditional and/or new forms of communication are in danger of being excluded from significant parts of economic and social activity. Illiteracy is a form of information poverty that has come to be regarded as a key indicator of social exclusion, and one that policy makers can look to the public library to help combat. As McCook (2001) observes, 'What better service can librarians provide to poor people than to develop support for them at the beginning of a journey to full participation in democracy? The first step in this journey is, of course, literacy.'

A public library service that is free at the point of use can help to remove many of the economic barriers that deny the disadvantaged access to information and ideas. A library, said Tessa Blackstone (2004) is, 'one of the few free community spaces available. Anyone can go into a library; they can come off the street and benefit from what libraries have to offer'. Research shows that free access is still seen as crucial. Respondents, for example, in the Checking the Books study felt that,

> if they could only buy books their reading would be far more limited. Purchasing books was simply beyond their budget.... Even some of those in rather better economic circumstances admitted that they could not afford to buy at the rate at which they read, and that without the library their reading experience would be greatly restricted (Toyne and Usherwood, 2001).

For those suffering the physical consequences of poverty the library performs many functions. For example, children living in overcrowded housing can use it as a place to study, while for parents who simply want to take their children or themselves to new surroundings, it is one of the few interesting places they can visit that does not charge an entrance fee. Moreover, many libraries are open when schools are closed and during the long holidays, they can be used to support, supply, and sustain, the reading habit.

Serving Excluded Groups

The library literature from different parts of the globe is full of examples that demonstrate how diverse excluded groups have been served by general and quite specific services. For example, the Radio Prague website carries the story of a project through which book titles with multi cultural themes were sent to 500 public libraries throughout the country. The aim, in the words of the organizer was, 'to influence people's thinking and teach them to be more tolerant towards ethnic minorities... to offer people a way how to learn more and to remove prejudices'. One of the most successful titles was an autobiographical story, which describes the way the Romanies live. The project is said to have been very successful, especially with children who, in the words of the report, 'are not burdened with prejudice or racist thinking' (Skodova, 2002). Such thinking of course reflects a poverty of thought, and can be as damaging to society as the physical poverty described earlier.

On a different continent and concerned with the other end of the age range American colleagues are aware that, 'The public library is exceptionally well positioned to help realize the aging opportunity. As a source of information, ideas, and community connections, the library has inherent qualities that make it a powerful asset for older adult learning and community engagement.' In its report the Americans for Libraries

Council (2005) also discusses how, 'public libraries are preparing to offer creative alternatives to retirement to a generation notorious for their idealism and activism'.

In Norway, three public libraries have been transformed so as to become 'a well-adapted arena of knowledge, a meeting place and a working place for people with disabilities'. These include 'people with asthma or allergy, and vision, hearing, motor, cognitive disabilities' (Olsen and Andersen, undated). This is part of 'The Accessible Library Project' which recognizes that, 'buildings are often inaccessible for people in wheelchairs and computers lack the equipment for visually impaired users. In addition, most books and material need special adaptations to be available for users with writing and reading problems'. People with learning disabilities are among some of the most vulnerable in society and often their needs are overlooked by commercial organizations. However, the MLA has recently drawn attention to the importance of providing facilities for this group. One librarian reports how her service, has been 'encouraging anyone and everyone to join. If they have trouble with the form we will help them, or their carers will help them, but they'll all go away with their library card and sometimes the look on people's faces to get this library ticket is a joy' (Roberts, 2006).

In the United States, the Roads to learning project, seeks to encourage 'linkages among libraries, community organizations, and service providers to improve service to learning disabled people, their families, professionals, and other interested people. The initiative's goal is to bring information about learning disabilities to the general public through libraries while increasing libraries' capacity to serve their communities in this area' (American Library Association, undated). Prentaki (2002) in her study emphasized how assistive technology could be of particular help observing that, 'the variety in new technological tools is as broad as the diversity of learning disabilities themselves. There are tools that address the needs of people with organizational problems, auditory processing problems, writing skills problems, and so on'. Providing free access to such technology is particularly important in this instance because people with learning disabilities often have limited financial resources.

This chapter, indeed the book, could have been filled with many similar examples of what the public library service can and has achieved. It has enhanced and enriched the lives of many and those from within and without the profession who are critical of the public library service need to be reminded of its contribution. The distinguished library historian, Alistair Black (2006), who can never be accused of seeing the professional past through rose tinted spectacles, acknowledges 'the diversity of... usership, past and present' and concludes that public libraries: 'have proved their relevance to the needs of a wide variety of client groups, including children and the disadvantaged, as well as the many ethnic minority populations that have made use of them.'

Barriers to Participation

That having been said, like any service that aims for inclusivity the public library has to deal with barriers, real or imagined, that prevent full participation and or lead to the exclusion of those who can benefit from what it has to offer. Yvette Cooper

(2004) identifies 'the root causes of exclusion [as] unemployment, poverty and early childhood opportunities'. A number of these barriers are outside the immediate remit of library services although, as indicated above the service can help ameliorate many.

Some barriers are very much the responsibility of library managers and policy makers. There are for instance still in existence some library policies and procedures that ignore the needs of poor people. Fees and fines, whether real or imagined feature high on this list. Further evidence of this can be found in The Vital Link Toolkit, which lists a number of other administrative measures that can inhibit library use. These include the fact that 'New learners may be unaware that joining and using the library is free of charge.' It adds that 'Even if they know that using the library is free, they may fear high overdue charges if they forget to return books, or worry about charges for damage to books by children or pets' (Vital Link, undated). This view is supported by the evidence of people interviewed as part of the Checking the Books project. This research found that:

> All of the respondents commented on the value of the free service but many felt that the introduction of charges into other parts of the service was a prohibitive factor. For instance, there was widespread agreement that fines could have a negative impact. Some felt that they restricted their reading experience. The fear of returning books late, and subsequently being made to pay, made them reluctant to borrow. For others, the cost of the fine was psychological rather than economic. Respondents felt that the introduction of fines meant that they were being punished by the service. This was viewed very negatively (Toyne and Usherwood, 2001).

Bureaucracy whether in the form of rules and regulations, or inappropriate language can also create barriers to use. Issues raised by the literature, research and practice include the 'problem' of homeless people who can not supply a home address and library authorities that follow the kind of procedures used in benefit agencies, and ask for proof of disability, because they do not want to run the risk of abuse by dishonest applicants. In addition, reduced or restricted opening hours are an obstacle for many. This is particularly the case for those in full-time work (Proctor, Lee and Reilly, 1998). The location of the library can also have an impact. Respondents to a number of projects have described how the fact that a library was nearby had helped to establish their reading habit. Older members of the community, in particular, need access to local service points for physical reasons. This is a factor that is sometimes forgotten in the administrative rush to rationalize service points.

Library design can also be a crucial factor in determining if the library is used or not. Often, this is discussed in relation to physical access into the building. A Sheffield research project noted how a library taster course on the enjoyment of literature which had been specifically designed for people with disabilities, was spoilt by the fact that out of the eleven people who took it, seven experienced difficulties getting into libraries and had been unable to access books (Toyne and Usherwood, 2001). The Disability Equality Duty, which came into force in December 2006, now requires UK public libraries and other public bodies to look actively at ways of ensuring that disabled people are treated equally.

The various needs of different disabled groups need to be considered when planning library services. Research by Prentaki (2002) for example has shown that public libraries can be very confusing places for some people with learning disabilities. To help overcome this, it is suggested that library managers should take steps to ensure that the library environment is made more user friendly for people who have difficulty in recognizing numerical and letter characters. Members of Mencap, a UK charity that campaigns for equal rights for children and adults with a learning disability, suggested that this could be achieved by combining classification numbers with pictorial signs and providing illustrations for the various categories of material.

Personal and Professional Attitudes

There is no excuse for overbearing and thoughtless administrative procedures and it is to be hoped that library authorities would have long ago rid themselves of rules and regulations designed to catch the few who abuse their systems, and replaced them with procedures that help the large majority who wish to use them. At the same time, members of staff may also need to consider or reconsider some of their own attitudes to members of disadvantaged groups. From the United States, Sanford Berman (2005) observes the need for librarians and others to:

> recognize their own attitudinal hang-ups, understanding what makes them view welfare mothers and homeless people, for example, unfavorably, and ultimately grasping that poverty – not poor people – is the problem, that poverty can be reduced if not ended, and that the most vulnerable and dispossessed among us are citizens & neighbors who deserve compassion, support, and respect.

Such considerations are important. People from new user groups will not stay if they have negative experiences when using the service. A respondent to the UK report *Libraries must also be buildings* echoed Berman's concerns saying that, 'You're asking for fairly traditional librarians to become more adventurous. And they have to deal with more social problems. For example encouraging teenagers into a library as a group in an after-school club creates its own social problem' (Bryson, Usherwood and Proctor, 2003).

If the service is successful in attracting new users it is likely that some of these will come into public libraries without the prior knowledge or experience that it is required to benefit fully from the materials and services on offer. However, as has often been demonstrated in the world of children's' libraries, high quality work by well trained and dedicated professionals can do much to help people develop such skills. Following a visit to a library the author, Terence Blacker (2006), described how: 'With the help of conscientious and heroically patient librarians… children received encouragement and interest that they got neither at home nor at school and largely through their own free will and enthusiasm often develop an interest in books and the world of possibility and escape that they contain.' These are attributes that will benefit them for the rest of their lives and can do much to help include them in society. Older members of the public also need the active help of librarians. As

Jennings and Sear (1986) discovered, 'The assumption that the reader knows what he or she wants, and needs nothing more than to browse among the A-Z shelves or the returned section, was certainly not true.'

When undertaking this kind of work public librarians have to be prepared to make judgements, maintain values and confront the culture of ignorance. Such work requires that an appreciation of high quality and standards is combined with a sensitivity to the needs of users. However, there is some evidence to suggest that too few librarians are able or willing to put these values into practice. Indeed, as this is being written there is an interesting spat on one of the electronic mailing lists about the idea of running 'customer appreciation days'. It is suggested that these might include, 'sponsored soft drinks/biscuits/cake for customers, and... a free voucher for DVD/video rental'. One cannot help thinking that rather than behaving like anxious shopkeepers, it would be more appropriate for librarians to offer their users a good books appreciation day, a good poetry day, an information awareness day, or at least something, that reflects their professional skills and the value and values of the public library service.

In an entertaining article discussing anti-intellectualism in American librarianship Michael Winter (1998) argues that 'populism and instrumentalism are... closely-related to developments in contemporary librarianship'. In so doing he identifies in the profession, 'The populists [who] want to serve the tyrannical majority', and those, 'which we may refer to here as CWS, or Corporate Wannabee Syndrome'. One respondent to the present study, if not exactly demonstrating the populist position, indicated a skepticism about the value of educational qualifications observing that: 'our experience has been that highly qualified library people do not necessarily have the right skills to deal with communities and the challenges of delivering a responsive community based library service. We are looking for highly qualified people in other senses' (HoS 21+).

Some might argue that these kinds of attitudes together with a lack of book knowledge, or the unwillingness to use it are some of the causes for the much-publicized decline in book issues. As Katz (1980) argues, 'the whole concept of professionalism is tested on the selection battle line'. Bob (1982) also raises the question 'do taxpayers want to pay a professional salary... to a librarian to do whatever a page could do just as well'. Indeed, at a time when one of the UK's leading library authorities is considering cutting its professional staff by 40 per cent there is evidence to suggest that we are beginning to suffer the consequences of all those in the public library ranks who described professional qualifications as elitist, and said they wanted people with the skills of shop assistants, etcetera. If we constantly talk the profession down eventually politicians will act on what we say. A respondent to the present study made a related point observing, '...there is a danger of not being taken seriously by the decision makers at all levels if libraries are seen purely as popular institutions with no real value. It's important to get the right balance between popularity and credibility' (SP 21+). There is a danger, as Garceau (1949) observed over half a century ago, 'that the public must be given what it wants, has been too readily accepted by librarians for them to command the public respect accorded to learning. In the equation of politics, the policy chosen may well be a source of weakness not of strength.'

Other writers have linked the contemporary librarian's rejection of an educational role, to the problems that have been identified regarding the recruitment and retention of good public library staff. For instance McCabe (2001) asks: 'Why would anyone want to dedicate their efforts to an educational institution that does not seek to educate? ... If the public library is not actively trying to strengthen communities through education, why should a highly qualified person be interested in this work?' Such concerns are not entirely new. Nearly 50 years earlier the ALA Council heard that, 'the profession was unable to recruit quality personnel due to the "superficial conception" that the public had of librarianship and its work' (Raber, 1997). One member wondered 'just what challenge there is for the young person who has some social vision, when he goes into a public library and sees the per cent of books being circulated which really are absolutely inconsequential' (Amy Winslow quoted in Raber, 1997).

The majority of respondents to the present study did not feel that the lack of an overt educational role stopped people from seeking careers in public libraries [Table 21]. However, most thought that staff gained satisfaction from contributing to people's life chances, learning and development. As one said, 'Why bother with a qualification if you are not going to help people develop and grow?' (Dep 31+). Present-day staff find it satisfying 'to make a change in someone's life however small, when that change is achieved by someone written off by the academic world – or someone who has been led to believe they had no chance to develop' (HoS 31+). Another respondent found that:

> Our highly qualified staff – at all levels – relish seeing the library service used and enjoyed – and they are most moved when they see it making a difference – enabling people to develop or move on – enhancing people's lives – empowering them – enabling learning – enabling community engagement, and so on. Some of this will fall under the label of education (HoS 31+).

A newer member of the profession was, 'driven by a desire to ensure people aren't socially excluded... education is a bonus. But "seeking to educate" is loaded [...]. Letting people learn or discover that society does have a place for them is pretty educational in my book' (PG).

Attracting Users

As publicly funded organizations, public libraries should seek to attract a diverse set of users. However, in seeking to attract users emphasis should be given to the quality of collections and services. That does not mean that the service should not undertake promotional and other activities designed to increase the different public's knowledge of what is on offer. Research has shown that there are many excluded groups who could benefit from a quality library service but that they are simply unaware of what is available. For example, cultural barriers, both real and imaginary, can stop some adult learner groups from using library services. In the same way, some immigrant groups may not have such services in their home countries, and may not know how a library can meet their needs. Following her research, Prentaki (2002) argued that, 'people with learning disabilities must be informed of the potentials of using the library'. She suggested that libraries host organized group visits by people with learning disabilities in order to demonstrate the sources available.

Such promotion should not merely copy or adapt the methods used by commercial organizations, but demonstrate that libraries can and do offer something different from that available in the market place. It should be the kind of promotion that helps widen people's horizons. Stimulating books are still published and library professionals should promote these. As Alabaster (2002) reminds us, 'the public library must continuously assist in eradicating ignorance and intolerance by integrating cultural diversity into its collections'. As a whole, the profession must be more ready to affirm, and use, its expertise. In the words of respondents to the present study, 'we need to be confident in what we do and telling people about it. We need to be confident in our core business of culture – books, literature, performance, and so on as well as our enhanced digital and community roles' (HoS 31+). 'Libraries should cease to afraid of what they provide and the values they hold. The word "library" is an honourable one' (HoS 21+). Public libraries like other 'cultural institutions have to argue their case in their own terms and show, for example, how they distinguish themselves from theme parks or social agencies, while not reverting to exhausted snobbery' (Pachter and Landry, 2001).

A library audience should also be attracted by providing appropriate and welcoming accommodation. A Sheffield research project on library buildings (Bryson, Usherwood and Proctor, 2003) revealed that the best of Britain's new library buildings were regarded as physical spaces to see people and be seen and to carry on a conversation. They were perceived as comfortable places providing a sense of security and safety. In addition, the traditional, contemplative spaces within the buildings were appreciated by many. Respondents valued the opportunity to get away from a busy and hectic lifestyle.

The study also revealed the need to be sympathetic to the requirements of different groups. The data suggested that in some cases, older library users feel 'marginalized' by the emphasis on the young. Some of this results from what one respondent called, 'hoodlum-ism'. At the time of the research, staff at one of the libraries in the study were beginning to focus their efforts on recovering the lost 'elders' demographic. The Head of Services explained:

> We're still anxious that we don't loose all of our older people. And we need to be a bit careful and think about what we're going to do to keep them on-board, because we still want them to keep coming as well, but it is difficult to serve two groups in very close proximity to each other because of the different expectations… .

Although different audiences will have different expectations and requirements, there are many aspects of a public library service that can transcend such differences. A great piece of literature, an insightful item of non-fiction, and/or a trusted source of information can appeal as much to a 'minority' user as to anybody else. 'A difference in social or religious significance does not affect, still less negate, differences in quality' (Grayling, 2002) and 'a reader of serious or scholarly books is as likely to be found way out in the bush as in the big city' (Library Board of Western Australia,

1966). That last sentiment is exemplified, albeit in a very different context, by the experience of Will Crooks. Growing up in poverty in the East End of London, he read *The Iliad* and found:

> Pictures of romance and beauty I had never dreamed of suddenly opened up before my eyes. I was transported from the East End to an enchanted land. It was a rare luxury for a working lad like me just home from work to find myself suddenly among the heroes and nymphs of ancient Greece (quoted in Rose, 2001).

As we have seen, a high quality public library service can be an important source of ideas, information, recreation, and education for people from many different backgrounds. They are public spaces, which belong to everyone, and those responsible for their management have a duty to encourage their use, and to ascertain why some groups use the library while others do not. Academic research and professional experience suggest various reasons for non-use. These include unnecessary rules and regulations, a lack of knowledge of the full range of services provided and how these can benefit different groups, difficulties of physical and or psychological access. It could also be a simple case of the potential user not being able to read and believing the library is unable to help.

The latter is an example of where the public library may be able to provide help as the result of partnerships with other agencies. As Miliband's remarks quoted earlier suggest, social exclusion is often the result of a number of connected social problems. Moreover, the difficulties are made that much greater for an individual when these linked issues start to act on each other and become mutually reinforcing. It is argued that many such matters can not be adequately handled by a single agency working alone and that, by working together, public services 'can ensure that even the most excluded have a stake in the society and economy of tomorrow by seizing the opportunities that life in Britain offers today' (Cabinet Office Social Exclusion Task Force, 2006).

This applies as much to cultural as to other organizations and increasingly library services are working with other agencies such as galleries, museums, schools, public service broadcasters and universities in an attempt to find new ways of engaging with disadvantaged groups. A number of research projects have shown how combining services can help to combat many areas of exclusion through promoting community cohesion and developing the confidence of individuals and groups. A report on services in the South West of England concluded that:

> The theme of community identity and social cohesion was detected in all eight services and they are clearly making an impact in this respect. If the idea of visual consumerism is applied to the understanding of community identity, then museums, archives, and libraries each have something to contribute. They are repositories of public knowledge, holding resources of shared identity and creating factors that bind society together and build social capital (Bryson, Usherwood and Streatfield, 2002).

These are important and valuable functions, and ones that are enhanced by the stewardship of staff with a concern for professional standards and values.

From the public library perspective, it is clear that any final evaluation of the organization needs to take account of the quality of a library's collection and services and the nature of its engagement with the community. If policy makers and professionals are to achieve the kind of balance described in earlier chapters then they have to be clear about what they want the service to achieve. If a public library is to successfully serve a diverse population, then the management must have a clear vision of who the library serves and their needs. More generally, the library profession needs to consider the function and purpose of the library in contemporary society. Is the public library to be just one of many information and cultural organizations or is it to have a distinctive role? The view of the author is that it should be the latter, and in the final chapter, he will argue that this should be achieved through an authentic professionalism that counters the deceptive paternalism of those who dismiss the potential of the people that the public library service seeks to serve.

Chapter 12

Equity and Excellence –
A Value Judgement

In their ease of access, their freedom and their ubiquity, public libraries are the British institution that comes closest to truly embody the values of egalitarianism and democracy.

Self (1997)

The view of the public library that is expressed in this chapter is a value judgement. That judgement is based, in part, on a critical assessment of the literature and research reviewed in the course of writing the present text. It also incorporates an analysis of the views of those who contributed to the survey of current professionals. That survey made use of statements taken from the professional literature and elsewhere. It was designed to encourage respondents to comment on the challenges and opportunities involved in providing public libraries which prioritize equity and social inclusion while at the same time, attempting to promote and maintain excellence in collections and services. The full statistical response to this is shown in Appendix 2 but as is often the case greater insight into the current professional mind-set is provided by the comments that accompanied, and sometimes appeared to contradict the numbers. For this reason, the appendix also includes a selection of indicative quotes taken from respondents' comments.

In the event, the combined data reflect a diversity of views. In particular, there is a difference of opinion regarding the kind of strategy that is required for the public library service in the twenty-first century. The survey asked respondents to prioritize three options. The full wording of these can be found in Appendix 1 Question 34 but essentially, the choice was between, 'lifestyle libraries', 'libraries promoting access to and use of ICT', and libraries 'where quality is seen as being universal'. Although as Chart 34 indicates most feel that a strategy based on information technology is not the long-term answer, members of the profession appear to be almost equally divided between a service based on lifestyle and one that emphasizes quality. Unsurprisingly many respondents felt that it was impossible to choose between the options offered. They argued that public libraries should provide 'a combination of the three [suggested strategies], where people can relax in a welcoming, comfortable environment, with access to free ICT and a quality service in all that we do. It's not really an either/or situation!' (HoS 21+). In many ways, that is a reasonable response and, in practice, many libraries attempt to achieve that and more. On the other hand, the reluctance to state a preference could be seen to reflect a worrying lack of any underlying philosophy and an uncertainty about the prime purpose of the service.

Moreover, in a world of limited resources and competing local government agendas the 'all purpose' strategy may not always be possible.

The model that is suggested by the present author is that everyone should be enabled and encouraged, to take advantage of the opportunities provided by public library services that are sensitive to difference and seek to provide access to the best. On the surface, that is not a controversial aim although it may be difficult to achieve in practice. It is, as many respondents mentioned, one that assumes it is appropriate for professionals to make judgements about what is 'the best'. It is acknowledged that that is almost certainly a minority view. However, it is hoped that readers will recognize that it is not presented as a justification for professional self-importance but rather as a requirement for a public librarians who want to fulfil the potential of the people and communities they serve.

Earlier chapters have demonstrated how in cultural and other organizations an increase in use has often been obtained by adopting a populist approach. It is argued here that the public library should seek to avoid that fate. In the preceding chapters, an attempt has been made to provide a foundation for that argument and to demonstrate its relevance to the different elements of a service designed to meet the twin objectives of equity and excellence. The author does not claim that the conclusions set out here are beyond discussion or the need for any further justification. The reader may, indeed should, ask how the author came to his value judgement and how far it can, or should be, translated into contemporary practice.

Almost by definition, a value judgement includes a large element of belief and the present judgement is rooted in a longstanding belief that the public library has to be much more than a simple retail service. Moreover, it should be prepared to do things that commercial organizations will not do and seek to counteract the ignorance and prejudice engendered by a society that cultivates celebrity, cash and trash. In so doing, it needs to provide equality of access to excellent, socially beneficial, material and services. Often these will be materials and services that are not provided elsewhere, or not immediately accessible to those without the ability to pay. As a public service, the library exists, in large part, to provide what the market will not. In the words of an American commentator, 'the library should identify what makes it unique and make a virtue of that necessary uniqueness' (Scrogham, 2006).

Policy Professionals and Purpose

Policy makers and professionals responsible for the service, must agree on its purpose and be committed to it. It is now time for the library profession to move on from the position of addressing agendas that have been suggested by others, to one where *it* argues what is necessary and valuable. This is a suggestion that has something in common with the contemporary concept of public value. In discussing this theory Holden (2004) makes the point that, 'organizations must determine, and be committed to their own purposes rather than being given them by others', Given that, economic, social, political and other circumstances prevent the public library service from being all things to all people, 'it must decide what things it will be to whom' (Berelson, 1949). This means that those responsible for the organizations we call public libraries will have to articulate the values that they wish to encourage, and align their practices, policies, and services, to meet those aspirations.

As a result, those in professional leadership will have to face the fact that their exercise of professional judgement may not always produce solutions that coincide with short-term political and/or public priorities. The perils of populism have been argued and demonstrated throughout this text. The experiences of similar organizations, some of which have been described in earlier chapters, suggest that the more a service places emphasis on populist appeal the greater the risk of sacrificing its integrity and losing sight of its original purpose. For what might appear to be the right reasons, professionals working in museums, broadcasting, publishing and similar arenas have been urged to popularize what they provide so as to attract people who are not currently using what the service offers. In some circumstances this has simply lead to somewhat bizarre provision, which is all too often a poor replication of a commercial environment that is readily available elsewhere. At worst, it has deprived people of an experience they value. It is the result of a form of elitism whereby educated professionals give people what they have decided people want while, at the same time, denying them the opportunity to benefit from what they themselves have enjoyed in the past.

Populism as a policy may work in the short term, but over time regular library users may, indeed as the figures suggest will, become unhappy with second rate material while the new users, temporarily attracted by *MTV* screens *et al.*, will quickly move on to new delights elsewhere. In the end the library loses both ways. More importantly the people who stand to lose most from this kind of approach are the immigrants, the poor, and other disadvantaged groups who need, use, and value established library services. If the profession really wants to help less advantaged people, and reach out to others in similar circumstances, it should perhaps look back at some of the original arguments made for public libraries. Perhaps it is time to see them one again as a place for education, for self-improvement, learning and creativity. Places where people can be transformed as the result of access to good books, scholarship, and diverse cultural activities. Rather than embracing an easy populism the library needs to be a public space where excellence moves to centre stage and 'the idea of learning infuses every issue and where individuals and organizations are encouraged to learn' (Pachter and Landry, 2001).

The Price of Ignorance

Providing access to learning is one of the greatest contributions that the library can make. It is one that benefits individuals and society at large. Far from being bliss, ignorance excludes people from much that is important and valuable. Moreover, as a society, we are beginning to pay the price for the fashionable celebration of ignorance, and the modish dismissal of the value of education. This price can be high. For example, 'Racism – the fear and dislike of people alien to you – is slumberingly integral to all ignorance, … not all racists are stupid, but all stupid people are at some level racists, cowed into resentment and mistrust by the enormity of their incomprehension' (Jacobson, 2007).

Ignorance and intolerance go hand in hand and the library profession should set its face against both. Of course, as is indicated in Chapter 11 public librarians must do everything they can to encourage and support people with learning difficulties and others who, 'are in the shadows of life'. Indeed, the library service should concentrate on services for these people rather than diverting resources from them in order to provide diversions for what one commentator has called, 'a growing band of feckless, greedy envious British natives whose crude, loud prejudiced moans increasingly dominate the public space' (Alibhai-Brown, 2007). Such people are not by any means genuine representatives of the disadvantaged, and public librarians have to be very wary of the siren voices of some policy makers, and others who mistakenly seek to promote their interests in the name of inclusion and equity. If the profession takes the populist route there is a real danger that the bad will drive out the good, and that many people will be denied the opportunity to experience the joy and benefits that access to a high quality library service can provide. Serious attempts to reflect cultural diversity and promote social inclusion do not have to lead to the 'Macdonaldization' of the service.

In finding a way to marry equity and excellence the public library must embrace services for the educated and those ambitious to be educated. This does not mean that its services have to be narrowly academic or unrelentingly serious, but all should be excellent of their kind. Library policies should not be dominated by a class or ideology. The widest range of cultural voices should be heard, and diversity respected. All the community, regardless of background or circumstances should be given opportunities to share the benefits of the service. Such provision can help counteract the defects in our society that come from such factors as, commercialization, social exclusion, dumbing down, and the fashionable 'philosophy, that what is low is high' (Jacobson, 2007). The public library service should be a service that is built on a belief in excellence, education, social justice and the public good.

Enhancing the Individual and Public Life

Many of those responding to the present study expressed a dislike at the suggestion that the public library had an obligation to educate. They found the language, 'very old fashioned' (HoS 31+) and decided that, while 'learning is implicit in what we do. education is not our remit' (Dep 10+). There is however, a need to ask if it is the concept of education that is perceived as old fashioned or simply the language that is used to describe it? While not wishing to underestimate the importance of language used to describe what public libraries do, it is not unreasonable to suggest that they should provide diverse opportunities for people to search for knowledge. It is in a library that people can make the connection between the value of education, in its widest sense, and the enhancement of their day-to-day lives.

Just 10 years ago Stainer (1997) found that:

> All the evidence suggests a broad agreement that the purpose of library stock in the context of a public service is the enhancement of individual and public life by the use of recorded works. Stock is information; communication; equipment for citizenship; the unbiased representation of all recorded culture; a tool for self-education; a developer of

critical thought and judgement; the source of recreation and pleasure through the record in any format of fiction, music, drama, comedy, sport and more.

High quality materials such as literary novels, serious non-fiction, music, *et al.* have always been the staple stock of excellent public library services. For an earlier generation of professionals they were seen as a self-evident good thing. Some of today's librarians, as we have seen, often question if they should now be given this kind of emphasis. One argues that such material should only be kept if it 'is used and meets local needs – not just because it is "worthy" or "important" or "best" of its kind' (HoS 21+). Another felt that, 'to sink millions of pounds into minority interest areas is neither democratic nor value for money – rather it becomes a public subsidy of an activity patronized by people who could probably afford to pay for it' (SP 21+). On the other hand it was pointed out that:

> Reference material and specialist material which may not be frequently used would not be available for the general public if not stocked in libraries. This material provides alternative sources of information and viewpoints, which would be lost if we stuck to popular material only. We need a range of literary styles to develop readers' reading habits (SP 21+).

Another respondent observed that, 'Material that would be of value to the collection because of their significance... should still be bought. We should keep in mind that the reasons for not using some material may lay within the library's lack of appropriate promotion' (PG).

In the words of one commentator, the public library is 'at a crossroads. The choice is one of resistance or conversion to a model of service that has its principles grounded in the private sphere. It is a choice of the public library maintaining its traditional uniqueness or, through its loss, inviting fragility into its future' (Scrogham, 2006). As part of the public sphere, public libraries should be able to operate without reference to the profit motive. As such, they have a duty to provide not just mainstream material, but also the experimental and unfamiliar. In addition they:

> precipitate the serendipitous pursuit of knowledge and the informal exploration of cultures and ideas past and present. To neglect this role would be a major failing. While public libraries do have an important role to play in literacy and social inclusion they must not lose sight of their role as protectors, and perhaps promoters, of culture. By this is meant "high culture" in which "quality literature" is included (Phillips, 2005).

ICT: Simply Another Format

For many readers it may seem rather anachronistic to emphasize this kind of activity at a time when so much prominence is given to the new, and not so new, technology. As a distinguished academic librarian argues:

> networked information technology... has acquired an unprecedented prestige. For many, it supplies a fundamental cultural and ethical framework increasingly embraced by a

wide variety of professionals who once looked to independent intellectual and critical models of our high culture. Intellectuals, and many writers as well, eagerly try to become businessmen, and many librarians seem bent on joining them (Winter, 2001).

However, there are, as we have illustrated, limits as to what the technology can achieve. It remains something of a paradox that, as Brown and Duguid (2000) observe, 'despite all the rhetoric about the Internet "killing" the book and tailoring information, the first great flagship of Internet enterprise was a book retailer'. By itself, information is not a substitute for knowledge and ideas. However not everyone appears to be aware of this and, in the library profession as elsewhere, there is a danger that, 'the devotees of information technology seem totally brainwashed, confusing a delivery system with culture' (Drummond, 2000).

Moreover, in the same way that populist material is readily available elsewhere so in the future will be the products of information technology. That having been said, the public library will, for some time, have an important role to play in protecting and providing for those on the wrong side of the digital divide. It will continue to help citizens use the technology and navigate the information highways. However, it is likely that, in part at least the importance of these functions will decrease. As time passes, the electronic equipment will come down in price and become even more commonplace in domestic settings. In addition, people will become more familiar with the use of ICT and require less technological guidance. As one respondent argued, 'in the future most will have access in the home to IT, but they will still need the expert staff and collections' (HoS 31+).

It is interesting to note that despite the best efforts of the profession the public have never been as gung ho about the role of ICT in public libraries as some professional leaders would wish. Rather, 'the evidence is that the public library user does not see the routing of the information superhighway into libraries as a "saviour" technology, but simply regards it as another, albeit important format' (Black and Crann, 2000). This rather more balanced perspective means that information technology will be seen, and used, as but one aspect of a public library service which is, above all, expected to be a unique storehouse of intellectual stimulation providing free and equal access to information, ideas, and works of imagination.

The Public Library Workforce

Of course, if this is to happen the library has to be 'a place with a collection staffed by knowledgeable professionals who build, preserve, and promote that collection. The public should know what to expect from the library, and the library should ensure that those expectations are met' (Scrogham, 2006). In recent years there has been much concern expressed about the future of the public library workforce. Recruitment, retention and leadership have been the subject of numerous reports and projects (for example Usherwood *et al.*, 2001, *Leading Modern Public Libraries*, 2005), and it has been argued that a personnel time bomb is already ticking away in the UK public library sector (Usherwood *et al.*, 2001).

Less than a third of the chief librarians interviewed for the Sheffield Workforce Study were confident that they had staff who were equipped to succeed to senior posts. If their views are a true reflection of the profession then the quality of the services provided is in serious danger. To some extent, the whole workforce question is coloured by a developing debate about de-professionalization. The data suggest a steadily declining number of professional librarians per head of population in the UK. In addition, almost half of the respondents in the Sheffield study said they would appoint a person without a professional qualification to a professional post (Usherwood *et al.*, 2001). Furthermore, library authorities are reducing the number of posts that are designated for professionally qualified librarians. All this would seem to work against the provision of an excellent library service. Similar worries are raised by the research by Cookman and Streatfield (2001) which indicated that the use of volunteers is now a common practice in UK public libraries. Volunteering has a place and is encouraged by the present government. However, although some American colleagues claim that 'volunteers... enable libraries to reflect community diversity in a very visible way' (Reed, 1994), it can never be a replacement for a high quality professional service.

Many of these arguments are for another place, but specifically there is a need for public libraries to employ staff whom:

> welcome the opportunity to discriminate between the good and the bad, the timeless and the ephemeral, as librarians traditionally have done. They ought to regard themselves as not just experts in the arcane ways of the Dewey Decimal System, but as teachers, advisers and guardians of an intellectual inheritance.

> The alternative is for them to morph into clerks who fill their shelves with whatever their "customers" want, much as stock boys at grocery stores do. Both libraries and the public, however, would be ill-served by such a Faustian bargain (Miller, 2007).

Some authorities appear to have made that pact with the devil and, 'the admission from a public library administrator that she is an entertainer but not an educator [is] a sign of a debased civilization' (D'Angelo, 2006).

This attitude amongst some librarians is reflected elsewhere in society. The late Sir John Drummond, who was responsible at various times for the Edinburgh Festival, BBC Radio 3, and the Promenade concerts, complained in his autobiography about the:

> anti-intellectual laziness of so many of today's leaders – not only in politics, but also in education and the arts – is for me a form of appeasement. Failing to differentiate between the good and the indifferent, while sheltering under a cloak of spurious democracy, is simply not good enough. It is a betrayal of all our civilization has stood for (Drummond, 2000).

It is significant that both D'Angelo and Drummond regard some prevailing attitudes as a challenge to civilization. If nothing else it indicates the importance they place on cultural institutions.

Although some contemporary practitioners express concerns about the next generation of library professionals, arguing that they, 'don't seem as interested in collection development or acquisitions, or find things without a computer' (quoted in Gordon, 2006) many are rather more prosaic in their attitudes. In the recent past, as we have seen, the quality of library materials, particularly imaginative literature, was regarded as an accessory to public library management rather than as an integral part of the process. Despite the fact that, 'Managing the fiction service effectively is the most visible sign to a critical public of the success of a library' (Kinnell, 1991), it was with notable exceptions, not a major concern of writers contributing to the professional literature. In the late eighties it seemed that books and other library material were hardly considered save perhaps as a way of boosting issues or cutting costs. At that time, Labdon (1991) observed that, 'As a specialism, the art of selecting novels for adults is virtually dead in public libraries.' Evidence of the priorities of that period can be found in the comment of senior librarian interviewed as part of a joint Sheffield/Loughborough project on Total Quality Management. When asked if Quality Management had had an impact on candidates selected for employment the person replied, 'we have moved away from requiring any knowledge of books for one thing'.

It is good to see that in the last decade books and reading have returned to practitioner and academic agendas. For instance in the mid nineties, with the financial support of the Arts Council, the University of Central England and the University of Sheffield introduced modules on the promotion of literature in libraries. These were offered not just to students but also to the wider library community. In addition, for many years, public library students at Sheffield participated in the practical stock selection exercise mentioned earlier whereby they 'selected' books for local community libraries or a special service. Books and reading also feature in the research programmes of universities on both sides of the Atlantic. In Canada, Ross *et al.* (2006) have worked to show that *Reading Matters* whilst in the UK, Train and others have undertaken important studies in the area of reader development.

It is clear from the literature, and the world of practice, that new skills will be required from staff working in future library organizations. In addition, our discussion has also shown that established skills will be needed in new circumstances. There are implications here for those involved in professional education. In terms of the curriculum, the present author is attracted to the Scandinavian model in which: 'Cultural consciousness, communicative ability and literary competence [are] seen as the three main building stones of the cultural dimension in library education' (Smidt, 2005).

If public libraries are to achieve equity and excellence the people who work in the service, need not only to have the appropriate knowledge, skills, and personal qualities but also respect for professional values and the confidence to defend them. However some argue that 'staff have lost confidence in giving people advice about books and offering ... borrowers the chance to try something new to read' (Prescott 2006?) If, as some predict, libraries fade away in the next 20 years, it will be the final victory of the 'rival values' identified by Finks (1989) all those years ago. It will be partly the fault of the bureaucrats who cannot see beyond their spreadsheets, but above all, it will be a result of an anti-intellectualism that argues that all things are to be judged equal in the library world, and fails to distinguish between the good and the bad. Such are the consequences of a relativism which 'leads to populism which then leads to levelling; and so to reductionism, to quality-reductionism of all kinds – from food to moral judgments' (Hoggart, 1995). If the public library is to survive, the librarians of this and future generations must reject this philosophy and return to the values and beliefs that used to underpin professional practice.

Assessment

The lack of confidence in the intrinsic value of libraries is often demonstrated in the way that services are judged and evaluated. The success or otherwise of a public library should be assessed, 'in terms of the quality of, and need for, the product rather than the volume of use' (Raber, 1997). In a target driven world there is a danger that library services will not be judged on the quality of material and services and the unique experience they can offer, but simplistically on how many people come through the doors. It is essential to go beyond the numbers and assess the value of the library experience once people are inside. As suggested in earlier chapters, the profession has perhaps been too ready to assess libraries primarily in terms of their contribution to other people's agendas. Public libraries can and do contribute to the government's seven shared priorities for local government but they also provide much more. There is a need to consider what they actually do, in and for themselves. Just because the service performs important social and economic functions it does not mean that its wider cultural and educational activities should be ignored.

Indeed, there are those who feel that these activities should be given greater attention. For instance, the Demos think tank in its publication, *Capturing Cultural Value* (Holden, 2004) asks:

> Having lost both a critical language, and also the Arnoldian, and indeed Fabian, idea that Culture improves people, how can we find a way of justifying state spending on the arts, museums, libraries and historic buildings? Can the idea of "intrinsic value" be articulated in a new way that avoids the taint of either patrician judgement, or mystification, and yet allows us to take account of factors beyond the easily quantifiable?

The report goes on to argue that: 'Reference to cultural values is commonplace in the literature of anthropology and material culture studies, but is rarely applied explicitly in discussions of the cultural context in which we currently exist.' It then identifies different kinds of value; historical, social, symbolic, aesthetic, and spiritual. All of which could be as easily applied to public libraries as to other cultural organizations. Demos also discuses the concept of public value in terms that reflect a number of matters raised in the present text. In particular, it emphasizes that: 'Professional judgement is placed at the heart of public administration, and that raises many questions about how confident and competent professional judgement can be nurtured and recognised.'

In a presentation to the Arts and Humanities Research Council, Horner and Bevan (2006) described an approach to Public Value that suggests that the goal of organizations should be to engage with, and shape, what the public want. They maintain that whilst services and institutions have to be responsive to what is valued by the public that does not mean pandering to ill-informed preferences. It is argued that the orientation to greater engagement with the public means more than merely collecting consumer-like preferences. It includes deliberation and education. This is a process of refinement of preferences (adapted from PowerPoint® presentation).

A fuller discussion of the application of these ideas to the public library service is beyond the scope of the present text but it is interesting to note that the concept of public value is said to have been inspired by an observation of a library service. According to Crabtree (2004), Professor Mark Moore who first developed the idea used the following example of a librarian:

> She works in a library for adults that are open only at certain times of the day. She realises that, with minimal extra funding, the library could open at different times to let in children before and after school. Instead of letting the thought pass, she develops a plan, convinces her political superiors, finds the money, promotes the plan to local newspapers and makes it happen. She delivers a new service that pleases the public, improves levels of education, and increases public faith in government. In short, she builds public value.

Clearly, such ideas need to be worked through in greater detail, but public librarians should at least see their introduction to the evaluation debate as a welcome move away from the tired use of number crunching, customer satisfaction surveys, and market mechanisms, as indicators of value and impact.

Equity and Excellence

Equity and excellence can co exist but for this to happen, those responsible for the public library service have to have a clear sense of purpose, and must believe and ensure that they have the capability and capacity to be, and provide, the best. The best services are those that appeal simultaneously to many different interest groups without compromising the needs of any of them. The politicians and professionals involved will need to be committed to the integration of equity and excellence in the library service, and implement policies that balance the various needs. As Professor Stewart (1995) argues 'One of the key roles of local authorities is to reconcile or to balance the aspirations, demands and the needs of communities.... .'

That role involves deciding how and where resources are to be spent. In coming to these decisions, policy makers and library professionals must focus on the issue of excellence. Increasingly librarians are going to have to deal with conflicting, and sometimes contradictory demands. In an imperfect world of restricted resources, professional leaders taking account of community needs will be required to set priorities and make some difficult judgements. These may well include decisions to stop doing some things, before they arrive at a final portfolio of services.

Such judgements will need to be based on an assessment of the impact of different aspects of the service on individuals and the community as a whole. The content of collections, and the services provided by the library, must take account of the cultures and needs of a diverse range of users. Library policies and procedures should encourage participation by all groups and individuals who will benefit from the service, and seek to remove any barriers that may prevent them from using it. Wide participation in library activities does not have to be at odds with the maintenance of excellence in services and collections. At its best the public 'library is a place of books and reading, of research, of librarians, of free thought, and of balance – balance between education and recreation, between print and electronic, between quiet and noise, and between parental concern and civil liberties' (Scrogham, 2006). High quality public libraries can transform the lives of individuals and groups. They are one of a decreasing number of institutions that provide access to material that enables people to fully engage with their society, participate in democracy and enjoy new experiences. Accurate information and well-written works of imagination can help counter prejudice. Libraries are educational institutions that broaden minds and help people overcome the ignominy of ignorance. They provide an arena in which different cultures can be celebrated, debated and discussed.

No public library can appeal to everybody all of the time but, if it is to help people make the journey from exclusion to inclusion, it has to provide a service founded on the idea of excellence. It should go without saying that access to this service should be available for everybody irrespective of ability, age, gender race, sexual orientation or any other diversity of the human race. The library must be open to anyone who is willing to use it. However, equality of access is different from equality of use. The audience for the public library that provides for excellence and equity will be drawn from all those who feel that they can benefit and gain enjoyment from the services offered. The service should seek to maximize the number of people who feel they can benefit. However, it is a waste of public funds, an insult to those with genuine needs, and a denial of the public good, to use scarce resources in order to provide trivial pursuits for those who, in the words of Howard Jacobson (2007a) subscribe to 'a culture of wilfully embracing ignorance'. It is difficult to see how the public library can be enhanced by providing for people who do not appreciate the kind of services it offers.

The public library should emphasize, encourage and embrace excellence. Excellence is not about elitism, neither is it restricted to what is sometimes characterized as literary fiction or high culture. It can be found in a popular novel and on the shelves of a small community library. However, it is important to be able to recognize the difference between excellence and the populist appeal of mass produced pap. This is a judgement that public librarians must be prepared to make. In the words of the first person to respond to our questionnaire, 'if quality and excellence is at the heart of services then the rest will follow as a matter of course' (HoS 31+). Equity is at the heart of this approach because everyone can freely access and use public library services if they so choose. As Lord Reith (quoted in Grayling, 2002) once said, many horses taken to water might actually enjoy the drink. The mission of the public library should be to provide for those, from whatever background, who want to combat ignorance and intolerance and quench their thirst for knowledge.

Postscript

I began my career with Devon County Libraries, and it was on an early summer day in Devon that I discovered a wonderful account of the power and relevance of cultural activities. It was contained in a document[1] displayed in an exhibition at High Cross House in Dartington. This splendid international modernist style building contains the artefacts, archives and bibliographic collections belonging to the Dartington Hall Trust. This is an organization that aims to change people's lives, 'by providing a place where inspired ideas can be realised through imagination, exploration, reflection and practice'.

In words that resonate today the paper states:

> In a pessimistic and defeatist world, where beliefs have been destroyed and replaced by a spiritless, material and coldly destructive approach to life, it is the responsibility of all the arts to lift for a moment or for longer the hearts of everyone and through a picture, a symphony, a dance or a performance, to show the greatness of life, the frailty but real beauty of human beings and their problems, and to touch at the mystery of the forces working around and through all of us.

It was written in 1937 by the actor Beatrice Straight who in the same year appeared with the Dartington Hall Players as Viola in *Twelfth Night* and Goneril in *King Lear*. Much later, she won an Academy Award for her 1976 performance in *Network*, a film that prophesized the media world of today where serious programmes are discarded, the audience is patronized and the ratings drive everything. In 1937, she was writing about the function of theatre but her sentiments, like the aims of the Dartington Trust and the message of *Network* are clearly relevant to our library world.

---

1   For the record, the document belongs to the Dartington Hall Trust Archive and is from folder: MC/S4/14/S.

Appendix 1

Questionnaire:
Equity and Excellence in
the Public Library

UNIVERSITY OF SHEFFIELD
DEPARTMENT OF INFORMATION STUDIES
Postal address: Western Bank, Sheffield S10 2TN
Location: Regent Court, 211 Portobello Street, Sheffield S1 4DP

As from:
xx xxxxxxxx
Millhouses
Sheffield
xx xxxx
Tel xxxx xxxxxx

Dear Colleague,

I am undertaking research about 'Equity and excellence in the public library'. In this I plan to examine the challenges and opportunities involved in providing a public library service which prioritizes equity and social inclusion and, at the same time, attempts to promote and maintain high intellectual and literary standards. The objective is to analyse and assess how professionals, such as yourself, perceive this issue and deal with it in their day-to-day work. I would be most grateful if you would help me by completing the attached questionnaire.

The questionnaire is in four parts and, in pre-tests, has taken about 30 minutes to complete. It is expected that a book making use of this research will be published in 2007, but I can assure you that your answers will be treated in confidence and that no individual will be identified in the final publication without her or his expressed permission.

It would be greatly appreciated if you would return the completed questionnaire by **Friday 30 June 2006.** It can be sent by post to my home address as shown above or via email to <r.usherwood@sheffield.ac.uk>.

I should of course be happy to talk to you or your staff about this project at any time.

Thank you for taking part in this research,

Yours sincerely,

Bob Usherwood
Emeritus Professor of Librarianship

EQUITY AND EXCELLENCE IN THE PUBLIC LIBRARY

Section A

You will find below some statements about public libraries. Please indicate your strength of agreement or disagreement with these statements by marking / boxing or otherwise identifying one of the following categories:

STRONGLY AGREE
AGREE
NEITHER AGREE NOR DISAGREE
DISAGREE
STRONGLY DISAGREE

Thus, if you agree with the first statement, you should mark it as follows:

1. **There are basic principles that are inherent in the very nature of the public library.**

STRONGLY AGREE | AGREE | NEITHER AGREE OR DISAGREE   DISAGREE
STRONGLY DISAGREE

Please also give brief reasons for your response, or make any additional comments in the space provided

****

1. **There are basic principles that are inherent in the very nature of the public library.**

STRONGLY AGREE   AGREE   NEITHER AGREE OR DISAGREE   DISAGREE
STRONGLY DISAGREE

Please give reasons for your response, or make any additional comments, in the space below

2. The proper business of the public library is with the serious user.

STRONGLY AGREE   AGREE   NEITHER AGREE OR DISAGREE   DISAGREE
STRONGLY DISAGREE

Please give reasons for your response, or make any additional comments, in the space below

3. Public libraries should not be "dumbed down" in order to attract people who are not interested in them.

STRONGLY AGREE   AGREE   NEITHER AGREE OR DISAGREE   DISAGREE
STRONGLY DISAGREE

Please give reasons for your response, or make any additional comments, in the space below

4. The public library should be judged on its ability to satisfy public demand.

STRONGLY AGREE   AGREE   NEITHER AGREE OR DISAGREE   DISAGREE
STRONGLY DISAGREE

Please give reasons for your response, or make any additional comments, in the space below

5. The public library has an obligation to educate.

STRONGLY AGREE   AGREE   NEITHER AGREE OR DISAGREE   DISAGREE
STRONGLY DISAGREE

Please give reasons for your response, or make any additional comments, in the space below

6. Public libraries should aim to make the best material available.

STRONGLY AGREE   AGREE   NEITHER AGREE OR DISAGREE   DISAGREE
STRONGLY DISAGREE

Please give reasons for your response, or make any additional comments, in the space below

7. It is a waste of public money buying material that is not frequently used.

STRONGLY AGREE   AGREE   NEITHER AGREE OR DISAGREE   DISAGREE
STRONGLY DISAGREE

Please give reasons for your response, or make any additional comments, in the space below

8. Public libraries should provide equality of access to the best.

STRONGLY AGREE   AGREE   NEITHER AGREE OR DISAGREE   DISAGREE
STRONGLY DISAGREE

Please give reasons for your response, or make any additional comments, in the space below

9. The culture of self improvement is a thing of the past.

STRONGLY AGREE   AGREE   NEITHER AGREE OR DISAGREE   DISAGREE
STRONGLY DISAGREE

Please give reasons for your response, or make any additional comments, in the space below

10. When libraries promote culture they contribute to the public good.

STRONGLY AGREE   AGREE   NEITHER AGREE OR DISAGREE   DISAGREE
STRONGLY DISAGREE

Please give reasons for your response, or make any additional comments, in the space below

11. Public libraries should counteract the negative effects of commercialism in the provision of cultural services.

STRONGLY AGREE   AGREE   NEITHER AGREE OR DISAGREE   DISAGREE
STRONGLY DISAGREE

Please give reasons for your response, or make any additional comments, in the space below

12. Public library services must be 'customer-led'.

STRONGLY AGREE   AGREE   NEITHER AGREE OR DISAGREE   DISAGREE
STRONGLY DISAGREE

Please give reasons for your response, or make any additional comments, in the space below

13. Public libraries should help people develop a critical capacity.

STRONGLY AGREE   AGREE   NEITHER AGREE OR DISAGREE   DISAGREE
STRONGLY DISAGREE

Please give reasons for your response, or make any additional comments, in the space below

14. The public library is where citizens should be able to find challenging material that may never make the best seller lists.

STRONGLY AGREE   AGREE   NEITHER AGREE OR DISAGREE   DISAGREE
STRONGLY DISAGREE

Please give reasons for your response, or make any additional comments, in the space below

15. The professional librarian who knows what quality is should be mainly responsible for what is selected for the library.

STRONGLY AGREE   AGREE   NEITHER AGREE OR DISAGREE   DISAGREE
STRONGLY DISAGREE

Please give reasons for your response, or make any additional comments, in the space below

16. The professional librarian should, 'Let the customer select'.

STRONGLY AGREE   AGREE   NEITHER AGREE OR DISAGREE   DISAGREE
STRONGLY DISAGREE

Please give reasons for your response, or make any additional comments, in the space below

17. All but a very small amount of materials should be selected by library suppliers.

STRONGLY AGREE   AGREE   NEITHER AGREE OR DISAGREE   DISAGREE
STRONGLY DISAGREE

Please give reasons for your response, or make any additional comments, in the space below

18. The public service ethic provides people with the opportunity to grow and develop.

STRONGLY AGREE   AGREE   NEITHER AGREE OR DISAGREE   DISAGREE
STRONGLY DISAGREE

Please give reasons for your response, or make any additional comments, in the space below

19. The public library should provide people with the opportunity for reflection and understanding.

STRONGLY AGREE   AGREE   NEITHER AGREE OR DISAGREE   DISAGREE
STRONGLY DISAGREE

Please give reasons for your response, or make any additional comments, in the space below

20. Promoting and prioritizing high aesthetic standards would make public libraries culturally exclusive.

STRONGLY AGREE   AGREE   NEITHER AGREE OR DISAGREE   DISAGREE
STRONGLY DISAGREE

Please give reasons for your response, or make any additional comments, in the space below

21. Highly qualified personnel will not want to dedicate their working lives to a public library service that does not seek to educate.

STRONGLY AGREE   AGREE   NEITHER AGREE OR DISAGREE   DISAGREE
STRONGLY DISAGREE

Please give reasons for your response, or make any additional comments, in the space below

22. The public library should actively try to strengthen communities through education.

STRONGLY AGREE   AGREE   NEITHER AGREE OR DISAGREE   DISAGREE
STRONGLY DISAGREE

Please give reasons for your response, or make any additional comments, in the space below

23. Public library services should seek to renew themselves as cultural institutions.

STRONGLY AGREE   AGREE   NEITHER AGREE OR DISAGREE   DISAGREE
STRONGLY DISAGREE

Please give reasons for your response, or make any additional comments, in the space below

24. The public library should be a centre of intellectual life of the area it serves.

STRONGLY AGREE   AGREE   NEITHER AGREE OR DISAGREE   DISAGREE
STRONGLY DISAGREE

Please give reasons for your response, or make any additional comments, in the space below

25. The public library is a place where the egalitarian principles of democracy meet the elite claims of high culture.

STRONGLY AGREE   AGREE   NEITHER AGREE OR DISAGREE   DISAGREE
STRONGLY DISAGREE

Please give reasons for your response, or make any additional comments, in the space below

26. Local authority support for the arts improves residents' quality of life.

STRONGLY AGREE   AGREE   NEITHER AGREE OR DISAGREE   DISAGREE
STRONGLY DISAGREE

Please give reasons for your response, or make any additional comments, in the space below

27. It is undemocratic to promote high culture at the public expense.

STRONGLY AGREE   AGREE   NEITHER AGREE OR DISAGREE   DISAGREE
STRONGLY DISAGREE

Please give reasons for your response, or make any additional comments, in the space below

28. Egalitarian aspirations have hindered attempts to create public libraries as centres of excellence.

STRONGLY AGREE   AGREE   NEITHER AGREE OR DISAGREE   DISAGREE
STRONGLY DISAGREE

Please give reasons for your response, or make any additional comments, in the space below

29. Some social inclusion policies can be detrimental to public libraries' educational activities.

STRONGLY AGREE   AGREE   NEITHER AGREE OR DISAGREE   DISAGREE
STRONGLY DISAGREE

Please give reasons for your response, or make any additional comments, in the space below

30. It is insulting to working class people to suppose they will only use libraries specifically designed to meet their perceived demands.

STRONGLY AGREE   AGREE   NEITHER AGREE OR DISAGREE   DISAGREE
STRONGLY DISAGREE

Please give reasons for your response, or make any additional comments, in the space below

31. In the public library populism is perfidious.

STRONGLY AGREE   AGREE   NEITHER AGREE OR DISAGREE   DISAGREE
STRONGLY DISAGREE

Please give reasons for your response, or make any additional comments, in the space below

32. Opening up public libraries as requested by policy makers will destroy the quality of the service.

STRONGLY AGREE   AGREE   NEITHER AGREE OR DISAGREE   DISAGREE
STRONGLY DISAGREE

Please give reasons for your response, or make any additional comments, in the space below

33. The public library should promote an unashamedly popular image.

STRONGLY AGREE   AGREE   NEITHER AGREE OR DISAGREE   DISAGREE
STRONGLY DISAGREE

Please give reasons for your response, or make any additional comments, in the space below

Section B

34. Writers have suggested different strategies to make the public library viable in the twenty first century. They argue that each could give the service a kind of distinction and individual profile. Please mark the suggested strategies listed below with a 1, 2, or 3 where 1 = your first preference, 2 your second and 3 your least favorite. It is recognized that a service might involve aspects of all three strategies. You are asked to indicate where you think the greatest emphasis should be placed.

- Public libraries become 'lifestyle libraries' with a café environment, books, videos, coffee and magazines.

- Public libraries play a central role in creating access to and use of information technology.

- Public libraries become places where quality is seen as being universal and something which is, to a great extent, inherent in their collections.

Please give reasons for your response, or make any additional comments, in the space below (Use an extra sheet if required)

Section C

35. Do you believe that public libraries SHOULD be managed and organized so as to ensure that excellence and equality are given equal importance?

YESNO

Please give brief reasons for your answer (Use an extra sheet if required)

36. How does your library service attempt to balance the concerns of excellence and equality, and who is responsible for maintaining that balance?

Section D

Please state the type of local authority for which you work (e.g. English county, English Metropolitan district, London Borough., NI Education and Lib. Board, Scottish district, Welsh county, etc.)

....

Please indicate the political control of your local authority

CONSERVATIVE LABOURLIBERAL/DEMOCRATNO OVERALL CONTROLOTHER (PLEASE SPECIFY)

Please give some details about yourself below: (This will help me compare your answers with those of other respondents and to contact you if required. However please leave all or some of this section blank if you prefer)

Name: ....

Academic / Professional qualifications...

How long have you been in the library profession?   ....years

Job Title...

Organization:...

Address:...

....

....

Telephone...

Email...

Thank you for your co-operation

Your reply will be treated in strictest confidence, however if you are willing for your comments to be identified in the final publication please indicate this by writing YES in the space below.

....

Please return the questionnaire by Friday 30 June 2006 to:
Professor Bob Usherwood
xx xxxxxxxxxxxxxxx
Millhouses
Sheffield
xx xxx
Or by email to: r.usherwood@sheffield.ac.uk

Appendix 2

Summary of Responses to Survey

Chart 1 (There are basic principles that are inherent in the very nature of the public library)

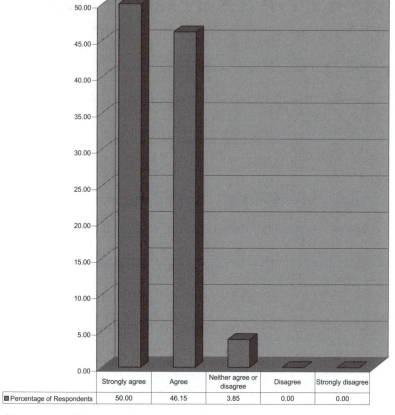

	Strongly agree	Agree	Neither agree or disagree	Disagree	Strongly disagree
■ Percentage of Respondents	50.00	46.15	3.85	0.00	0.00

Chart 1   There are basic principles that are inherent in the very nature of the public library

Summary

There is clear support for the idea of basic principles, of these; free access received the most mentions. The majority of respondents appeared to be critical, or at least wary, of making value judgements. However, there was strong minority support for maintaining standards and the founding principles of the service.

Indicative quotes

The Library Service should seek to offer the very best service to everyone in the local community – regardless of age, gender, ethnic, cultural or social background, disability, etc. (HoS 31+).

Without basic principles it would be very difficult to provide a coherent service (PG).

The service is there to make information and "literature" available to all, without value judgments about the individual, or the work. It's one of the greatest bastions of equality (SP 21+).

We have a history stretching back over a long period, and the founding principles of providing ready access to "learning materials and enrichment materials" for all remain sound today – albeit in a modern context (HoS 31+).

It must be free, people of all ages and ethnic origins must feel safe and welcome and it must be a neutral space. It supports reading and learning, and gives people from the whole community an opportunity to discover and learn. It is a part of the community (HoS 21+).

It is a democratic institution that provides a range of service to people of all ages and backgrounds in a non discriminating and non-judgmental manner (PG).

Chart 2 (The proper business of the public library is with the serious user)

Summary

The vast majority of respondents disagreed with this statement. Many were reluctant to define what is meant by 'serious use', although interestingly Mills and Boon was often used as an example of something that might not be regarded as serious.

Indicative quotes

Definitions of seriousness are notoriously difficult. A service funded by and for the entire community should attempt to serve the whole community – which is not to suggest an abandonment of standards or a denial of the need to prioritize (SP 31+).

The Library Service is for everyone. We should not judge what is "serious" and what not. Who is to judge that the elderly person borrowing Mills & Boon does not actually get more personal benefit from that loan then the researcher or academic – or the young person playing a game on the computer, and thereby learning mouse skills and the PC's potential alongside the person doing homework? There is learning potential in everything (HoS 31+).

One man's Mills & Boon is another's Shakespeare – it all depends on their standard of literacy, education etc. Our job is to give the same opportunities to the erudite and the illiterate (SP 21+).

Whose place is it to judge what "serious use" is. A parent attending a baby rhyme time, and gaining confidence to share nursery rhymes and books with a child, or a group of children gathered round a terminal doing their homework is just as valid as the scholar (HoS 21+).

"Serious" does not necessarily mean highbrow, or in possession of advanced formal education. Anyone using library facilities to further their knowledge or learning in whatever relevant way is a serious user (HoS 31+).

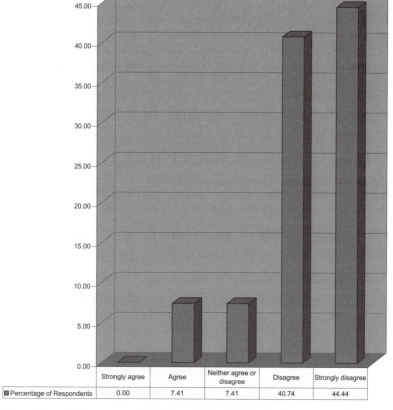

	Strongly agree	Agree	Neither agree or disagree	Disagree	Strongly disagree
■ Percentage of Respondents	0.00	7.41	7.41	40.74	44.44

Chart 2   The proper business of the public library is with the serious user

The proper business of the public library is to provide a service that everyone can find useful – as and when they need it. The implication of the statement is that some "users" aren't "serious" which is surely wrong (PG).

Depends on definition of "serious". Public libraries shouldn't just be for academic or scholarly use – users should be able to use libraries for leisure/recreation but they should be "serious" about their use of the library – i.e. respectful and take it seriously (PG).

Chart 3 (Public libraries should not be 'dumbed down' in order to attract people who are not interested in them)

Summary

Opinions were divided on this statement although a large number of respondents disliked the phrase 'dumbed down'. Once again, respondents were also uncomfortable with what some felt to be an implied 'value judgement'.

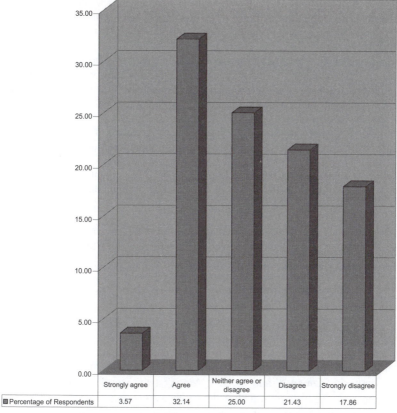

Percentage of Respondents	Strongly agree	Agree	Neither agree or disagree	Disagree	Strongly disagree
	3.57	32.14	25.00	21.43	17.86

Chart 3   Public libraries should not be 'dumbed down' in order to attract people who are not interested in them

Indicative quotes

We need to meet people's needs. Dumbing down may get people in, but what for…? Getting more users is not the point of our service; it is getting more users benefiting from the outcomes of engaging with the service. What is the point of *Big Brother*? It might get high audience numbers, but so what? (HoS 31+)

We should make libraries as popular as possible to attract the widest possible audience. We should do this "by any means necessary" (HoS 21+).

No point in maintaining a library just for small elite (SP 31+).

It's possible to design and provide a modern service which attracts non-users and hard-to-reach groups without having to necessarily dumb down. Having said that, it has to be acknowledged that hard-to-reach groups are just that: hard to reach (SP 31+).

Whilst we should attract a wide cross section of society, we should still retain quality and high standards (HoS 21+).

The library must be a "broad church", where the popular and the specific co-exist and no one feels either patronized or excluded. Provision of popular material, alongside a wide range of other resources, is not "dumbing down" (Dep 31+).

We live in a changing society and people access information and leisure or culture through various mediums and in a "quick fix" instant way. There is nothing wrong with libraries making themselves more accessible to the non-traditional user. It is not dumbing down, rather opening more points of access (Dep 10+).

While libraries should aim to make themselves more accessible to non users, this can surely be achieved without "dumbing down" and undermining their own purpose (PG).

This again is a value judgment on the learning potential of the more "trivial" stock or activity. Creatively used anything can become a tool for learning and new experiences (HoS 31+).

"Dumbed down" is a value judgement and is unhelpful. We cater for all tastes and levels of use, so leisure use is equally valid as working towards an exam (HoS 31+).

Chart 4 (The public library should be judged on its ability to satisfy public demand)

Summary

A substantial majority favoured this statement although some comments reflected confusion between 'demands' and 'needs'. Amongst the significant minority who disagreed there was a recognition that demands were often created, and that to simply reflect demand was to limit the library's potential.

Indicative quotes

Public libraries are used voluntarily. If libraries cease to satisfy public demand then they have failed (HoS 21+).

It would seem nonsensical to me to defend a service that was clearly unable to satisfy public demand (SP 31+).

A library that does not seek to satisfy demand will not secure a strong base of community support; but there is also a role for the library in raising expectations and achievement, challenging received wisdom and charting a path through competing demands and priorities (SP 31+).

We have to be customer focused and if we do not satisfy customer demand, we will be failing. However, alongside this we should seek to influence the nature of public demand by explaining what we have to offer and its value. If we cannot persuade the public of our merit, then we do not deserve support (HoS 31+).

The library should be judged by this, but not exclusively, there are other roles we fulfil. Public demand must also be reasonable and informed (Dep 31+).

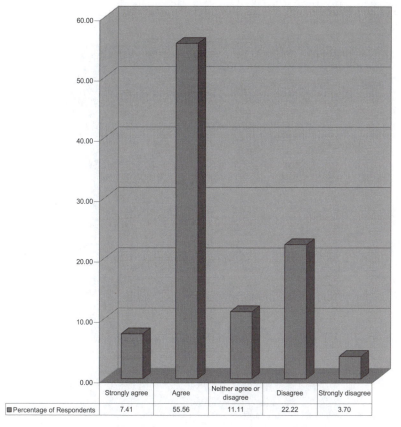

Percentage of Respondents	Strongly agree	Agree	Neither agree or disagree	Disagree	Strongly disagree
	7.41	55.56	11.11	22.22	3.70

Chart 4   The public library should be judged on its ability to satisfy public demand

If libraries are to remain pivotal and flourish in the 21st century then they need to some extent to satisfy public demand as well as maintaining a distinctive identity (PG).

We need to satisfy public demand – but in some ways we satisfy by stealth and have to find and satisfy a demand that didn't really know it was there (HoS 31+).

How can such a thing be measured? Where is the public demand coming from? How do they know what they want? From the media for example? Libraries need to acknowledge demand but also go beyond what people think they want, to offer more than what is known (PG).

It [The public library] can do so much more – leading the way to new services and facilities before a demand is ever recognized. It would be a shame to stifle innovation and creativity (HoS 31+).

Chart 5 (The public library has an obligation to educate)

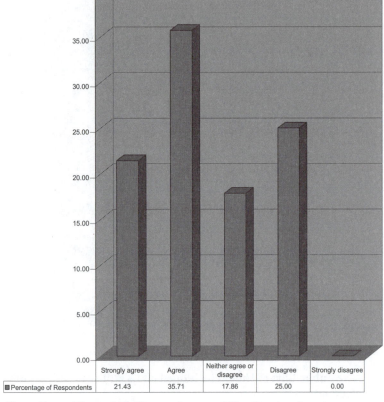

	Strongly agree	Agree	Neither agree or disagree	Disagree	Strongly disagree
■ Percentage of Respondents	21.43	35.71	17.86	25.00	0.00

Chart 5   The public library has an obligation to educate

Summary

Although there was strong support for the general principle implied in this statement many respondents found the terminology inappropriate. Although a quarter of those responding did not agree with the view expressed, most of those did suggest that education/learning should be at least a part of the public library's contribution.

Indicative quotes

Yes, in that it has an obligation to provide educational materials (SP 10+).

Education will always be an essential feature of public library services, though not necessarily on the old "street corner university" model (SP 31+).

It remains one of our core purposes - but there are many ways of educating (Dep 31+).

Although this should not be seen as its only role, PLs should fulfil an educational role by making available the resources/facilities necessary for education (PG).

Educate = provide an opportunity for informal learning (PG).

People should be able to choose what they want/need without there being an educational reason (HoS 21+).

I would challenge the terminology – I think a library has an obligation to support people to learn rather than to educate. Libraries are supportive organizations; they (and the staff) are not the upholders of what is right or wrong in terms of education. The same building can support a migrant worker learning English and a post doctoral researcher (HoS 21+).

Educate is a very old fashioned word here – we are about providing people and communities with choices and opportunities to learn, gain knowledge and develop (HoS 31+).

Learning is implicit in what we do. Education is not our remit (Dep 10+).

We don't have an obligation to educate, in the formal sense, but libraries offer opportunities for self-development and gaining of knowledge, which goes beyond formal education (SP 21+).

Don't like the word obligated. Public library has a role to play in making a positive contribution to the lives of citizens for which it serves, whether this is to promote lifelong learning, improve literacy levels by encouraging reading for pleasure etc. (PG).

Whatever happened to education, information and recreation? Libraries are seen as non threatening so keep them that way and don't alienate people who don't want to be educated, and only want the latest manga title (SP 41+).

Chart 6 (Public libraries should aim to make the best material available)

Summary

There was strong statistical support for this statement, but the comments suggest that many respondents were unable or unwilling to define "the best'. Those who attempted a definition stressed the importance of accuracy in information services and peer review.

Indicative quotes

Libraries should always make the best available, but it does not have to be to the exclusion of all else (HoS 31+).

"Best" in the sense of that material which helps achieve the goals of educating, challenging, stimulating, informing, entertaining – and representing the variety of UK and world cultures. This is a "horses for courses" argument (SP 31+).

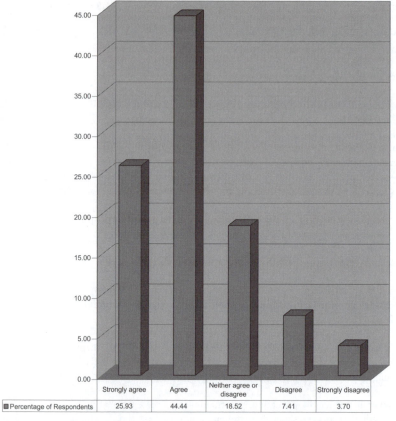

	Strongly agree	Agree	Neither agree or disagree	Disagree	Strongly disagree
■ Percentage of Respondents	25.93	44.44	18.52	7.41	3.70

Chart 6   Public libraries should aim to make the best material available

Should aim to have a balanced and representative range of material available. Within that context, should aim to ensure the "best" is represented, and where "best" is attributed through peer evaluation (e.g. award winning, or academically authoritative, this should be clear to customer (HoS 31+).

The best material in every field – as part of the choices people have available. BUT – funds and space are a problem. Again, the PLSSs on stock may also force us to take a view on what we purchase and choose to retain (HoS 31+).

Who is to say what the best is – let the people decide, even if it's *The Sun* or BNP manifestos. Then we can start having the debate about what is "best" (HoS 21+).

My only concern is who decides what is "best"??? (SP 21+)

I have no idea what this question means (Dep 10+).

Libraries still not very confident in saying that our collections are different to bookshops and why (SP 21+).

What does "the best material" mean? We have an obligation to ensure that we are providing value for money and that the material we have is relevant, up to date and accurate. The most informed material on a subject may be at a very academic level which is inaccessible to the general reader. We must also stock material that people do not see as threatening – e.g., the same material as is available through the supermarkets (HoS 21+).

Chart 7 (It is a waste of public money buying material that is not frequently used)

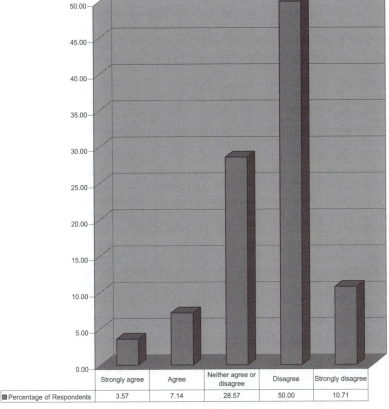

	Strongly agree	Agree	Neither agree or disagree	Disagree	Strongly disagree
■ Percentage of Respondents	3.57	7.14	28.57	50.00	10.71

Chart 7   It is a waste of public money buying material that is not frequently used

Summary

There was little agreement with this statement although some responses suggest that a lack of available resources may lead library authorities to adopt this view. Respondents stressed the importance of promoting high quality material, and the public good, inherent in providing specialist material that might not be freely available elsewhere.

Indicative quotes

> Only the most popular and frequently used materials that meet the needs of local communities should be purchased – the rest can be borrowed via ILL (HoS 21+).

> There are many items that will never be massively popular and yet should and MUST be available for the minority who wish to use them (HoS 31+).

> There is a role for the minority interest – libraries must take a balanced view. Yes the primary stock should be popular, but we also need to offer other stock (SP 21+).

> People need to be able to "explore" and not just what is a bestseller or judged to be an award winner. Librarians are good judges of important materials, using a wide range of criteria. Most stock selection policies I have seen have been impressive and inspiring. However, I do think that some of these issues are not considered at library school anymore, or adequately debated (SP 21+).

> Need a balanced collection, and demand is fickle. Cannot always anticipate demand or cycles of demand. If items go out of print, then holding them in library collections does provide access to the recorded knowledge. However, it is a waste if everyone holds rarely used material, especially in public areas (HoS 31+).

> Difficult to tell how frequently things are used – I've just had a complaint that we have removed books that were consulted rather than borrowed even though they were lending items. Problem re keeping stuff that gathers dust and then appears unattractive, and stuff that is provided because it is good issue fodder. We know that thinning out shelves increases issues, PLSSs drive us down this path (HoS 31+).

> Reference material and specialist material, which may not be frequently used, would not be available for the general public if not stocked in libraries. This material provides alternative sources of information and viewpoints, which would be lost if we stuck to popular material only. We need a range of literary styles to develop readers reading habits (SP 21+).

> I think that a book, if it is of high quality, should be selected even if it is unlikely to generate interest. The book may simply need to be marketed better (PG).

Chart 8 (Public libraries should provide equality of access to the best)

Summary

Respondents' comments indicated strong support for equality of access, but once again many were uncomfortable with the concept of 'the best', and who should make judgements.

Indicative quotes

> I think I strongly agree although the question is open to interpretation. If it means the best of books, information, activity and services then yes (HoS 31+).

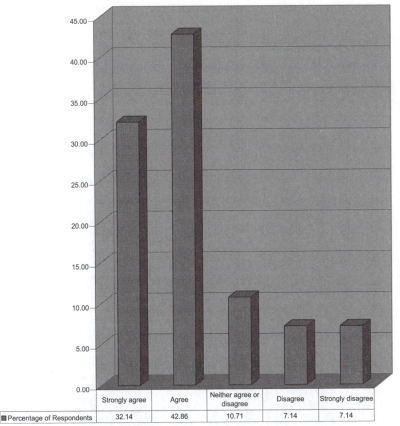

	Strongly agree	Agree	Neither agree or disagree	Disagree	Strongly disagree
◼ Percentage of Respondents	32.14	42.86	10.71	7.14	7.14

Chart 8   Public libraries should provide equality of access to the best

We have a duty to provide a service to all. Everybody's "best" will be different, we are not wise enough to objectively state one "best" (nor should we), and our collections must reflect that (Dep 31+).

It depends on what the community's definition of "the best" is (HoS 21+).

Who determines the best? (HoS 31+).

[Libraries should provide] Equality of access to best resources fit for purpose (HoS 31+).

Libraries are a place where all should have an equal chance, regardless of circumstances, disadvantage or previous negative experiences (SP 31+).

If they are to provide "the best" then this should be done with equality of access (PG).

I am uncomfortable with the word best (SP 10+).

Chart 9 (The culture of self-improvement is a thing of the past)

Summary

The vast majority of respondents stated that self-improvement, although often called something else, is alive and well. However, a minority felt that it was not as significant as in the past.

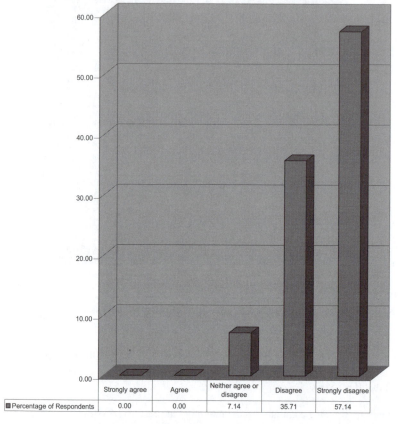

	Strongly agree	Agree	Neither agree or disagree	Disagree	Strongly disagree
■ Percentage of Respondents	0.00	0.00	7.14	35.71	57.14

Chart 9   The culture of self-improvement is a thing of the past

Indicative quotes

Far from it. Continuing high interest in adult education and obtaining new skills (SP 31+).

In many ways and, especially as a result of the cutbacks in adult education, it is more difficult now to study/learn on a part-time basis. The Learning and Skills Council focus on certain age groups also hinders access. Public libraries can help fill in gaps in the market (HoS 21+).

It's just taken different forms, whereby different media are used which are outside current public library remits (and/or funding) (SP 21+).

It's just changed focus – look at all the books on self-help in personal skills. People still want support material for study, and there are people who want to read the definitive work in different subjects (HoS 31+).

All the evidence is that people are being very purposive with their scant leisure time – there is a new wave of "self-improvement" – although people wouldn't necessarily recognize this term (HoS 31+).

Self-improvement is even more important in the age of the Internet and public libraries are the perfect place in which people can realize their dreams (PG).

Evidence from [name of authority] learning partnership surveys shows that people see the library as a non threatening place where they can learn by themselves. Libraries and other providers are key players in raising the aspirations agenda (HoS 21+).

Even if the phrase "self-improvement" isn't used the principle still exists. Perhaps more so in an age of rapid change, especially in ICT. There is definitely a need for people to update their skills (to stay employable) outside of formal education and training (PG).

It is certainly not as significant as in the past, and its nature has changed, but I believe it still exists (SP 31+).

Chart 10 (When libraries promote culture they contribute to the public good)

Summary

Respondents' comments showed that there is almost total agreement with this statement although some reservations about the kind of culture that should be promoted.

Indicative quotes

Culture is the added value to living, it is what makes life worthwhile, but again that is culture in the widest understanding of the word (HoS 31+).

They can break down the exclusivity which surrounds much cultural activity, promote engagement and participation, and ensure that cultural activity reflects all aspects of society (SP 31+).

Widening people's horizons making them aware of opportunities, promoting community engagement, all contribute to the quality of life and to local authorities' general duty of promoting well being. It's what libraries do (HoS 31+).

Depends what is meant by libraries promoting culture – we do promote arts, reading, learning and community events, so fulfil a role of providing information about events, and sometimes even providing the venue. More importantly, libraries have a role to support

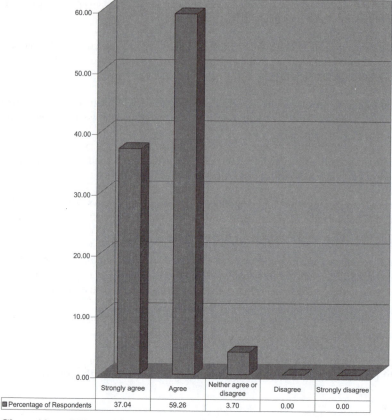

	Strongly agree	Agree	Neither agree or disagree	Disagree	Strongly disagree
▣ Percentage of Respondents	37.04	59.26	3.70	0.00	0.00

Chart 10   When libraries promote culture they contribute to the public good

community development, social inclusion etc. and this is achieved in subtle ways (HoS 21+).

Any participation or awareness of life around you makes a contribution, however you define culture (HoS 31+).

Agree with reserves. The statement implies "high cultures", but *Big Brother* is also culture and I question whether promoting the spin off publications from *Big Brother* would "really" be for the public good for example (PG).

Providing we promote all cultures and not force-feed an isolating monoculture. We are a unique institution for increasing understanding of, and between, the diverse cultures in the UK. This is an aspect of the work we do which is often missed if we rely on hard, financial, value for money performance indicators at the expense of harder to quantify, quality of life research (Dep 31+).

Chart 11 (Public libraries should counteract the negative effects of commercialism in the provision of cultural services)

Summary

Just under half of those responding agreed with this statement but most of the comments came from those who disagreed, and felt that public librarians had to live in a commercial world.

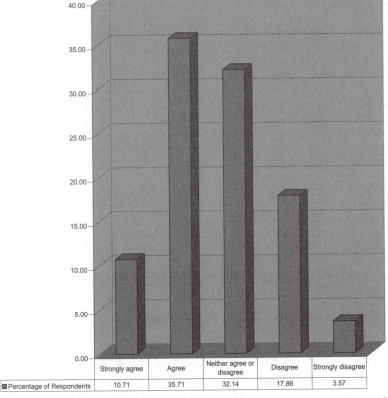

	Strongly agree	Agree	Neither agree or disagree	Disagree	Strongly disagree
Percentage of Respondents	10.71	35.71	32.14	17.86	3.57

Chart 11   Public libraries should counteract the negative effects of commercialism in the provision of cultural services

Indicative quotes

Cultural services should be free at the point of need and untainted by commercial pressures. The guiding principle should be from each according to his / her ability, to each according to his/her needs (HoS 21+).

I think we have an important role in making access to culture equally available to all – especially those who are economically disadvantaged (SP 21+).

Public libraries are "not for profit" organizations (PG).

I think libraries counteract commercialism just by existing and being used. The underlying trust implied by being able to borrow books for free is pretty radical… (PG).

We live in a commercial world. Someone included shopping as a cultural activity – why not? We can't exclude current trends, but we can contribute to people's ability to understand the trends and make their own minds up about their value (HoS 31+).

Maybe – but we can't ignore commercial techniques – otherwise we won't reach people used to a sophisticated commercial world (HoS 31+).

Public libraries have their own role; they do not exist as a foil to commercialism. They can be a complement to it though (evidence that library users buy more books for example) (HoS 31+).

We live in a commercial world and our society is capitalist. We have to live by these "rules" and compete in the same world (Dep 10+).

We live in a culture where the commercial sector has an important influence on individual expectations. In order for the public library to remain relevant and accessible to people, aspects of the commercial sector must be visible in the library. That does not undermine the free nature of the service (HoS 21+).

But there is nothing wrong with some commercial activity in libraries, if it helps support the provision of other key services (SP 31+).

In an increasingly competitive world driven by market forces, in which there are competing services, libraries need to embrace initiatives in partnership with a range of services, i.e. publishers, local business. This will help raise the library's profile. (PG)

Chart 12 (Public library services must be 'customer-led')

Summary

The figures suggest strong support for 'customer-led' services but the comments from respondents suggest that many feel that there should be some restriction on the power of the customer to dictate the direction of the service. Only one respondent commented on the use of the word 'customer'.

Indicative quotes

The library should reflect and be responsive to the needs of its customers, but it should also challenge and innovate. It should offer the new experience and provide opportunities to try something new and different. To stimulate the imagination. However, it should seek to identify what its customers want and seek to provide this to the best of its ability (HoS 31+).

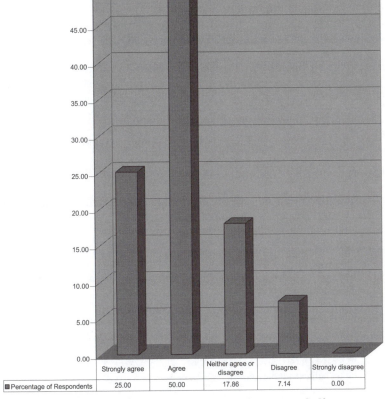

Percentage of Respondents	Strongly agree	Agree	Neither agree or disagree	Disagree	Strongly disagree
	25.00	50.00	17.86	7.14	0.00

Chart 12   Public library services must be 'customer-led'

Agree so long as the concept of customer is very broad – we should not be led by the vocal minority of customers, we should be finding out what current and potential customers need (HoS 31+).

Mostly agree. But we need to do a lot more to know who the customer is and what they really want. Don't just listen to the articulate few. Ask the non user too – but show them what they could have access to in a meaningful way to them (Dep 10+).

Public libraries exist to serve the public. In this sense they must respond to the needs and wants of the public. The challenge is in meeting majority and minority needs (HoS 21+).

It depends on exactly what you mean by "customer led", but any service which knowingly ignored the needs/demands of customers could not be defended (SP 31+).

Customer led, but not customer-dictated. We should focus on our customer but leave room for some professional judgment to ensure that we cater for all and not just the vocal minority (or even vocal majority) and neglect some of the less vocal, but equally important groups (SP 21+).

... sometimes libraries must go out on a limb and anticipate new demands rather than just continuing to provide to the most articulate/vocal (SP 21+).

We must look to meet the needs of the widest number of customers, while also having an eye to our broader, social responsibilities, which may not be perceived by all (Dep 31+).

But public libraries do not have customers (transactional relationship) they have stakeholders (democratic accountability relationship). Libraries must be "needs-led" (HoS 21+).

Chart 13 (Public libraries should help people develop a critical capacity)

Summary

There was strong support for this statement with several respondents emphasizing the need for a critical capacity in contemporary society.

Indicative quotes

Yes, public libraries have a role in encouraging people to question and develop their own opinions and standards (HoS 31+).

Public libraries should help people to think and become empowered and engaged citizens who can challenge the status quo and ask informed questions of the powers that be (HoS 21+).

Isn't this back to "educating the masses"? (SP 41+)

Libraries are neutral safe places where people can develop themselves at their own pace. Libraries should facilitate that process through provision of material, resources such as PCs, and staff help as appropriate – or even just provide the space for people to spend quality time (SP 21+).

We need to provide alternatives to the Internet and materials outside the mainstream – which challenge some "accepted" thinking. So we lead by example – even if we cannot directly teach people how to think (SP 21+).

Why else do we give free access to information from a range of viewpoints? A critical capacity is vital for a full, positive and active engagement with society and the democratic process (Dep 31+).

Opening up the world of knowledge and providing choice will only succeed if people can learn to evaluate between different options, otherwise confusion reigns. We offer the choices and help with developing skills – then it is up to the community to decide which way to go (HoS 31+).

There is a place for populism but libraries should offer the opportunity for people to develop discrimination and informed choice (SP 31+).

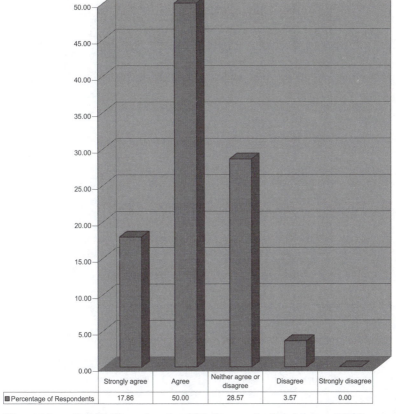

	Strongly agree	Agree	Neither agree or disagree	Disagree	Strongly disagree
▣ Percentage of Respondents	17.86	50.00	28.57	3.57	0.00

Chart 13   Public libraries should help people develop a critical capacity

Chart 14 (The public library is where citizens should be able to find challenging material that may never make the bestseller lists)

Summary

There was almost total support for this statement. Many respondents emphasized that best sellers should also be available and others stressed the importance of selecting material that would stand the test of time.

Indicative quotes

If not there – where will it be found? (HoS 31+)

This may not be new material. The joy of public libraries is the depth and breadth of their collections and the opportunity they provide for people to discover unknown and unfamiliar material (HoS 21+).

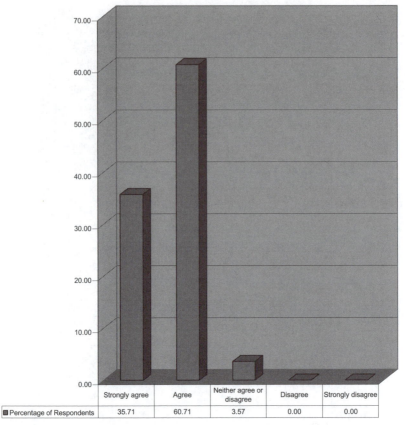

	Strongly agree	Agree	Neither agree or disagree	Disagree	Strongly disagree
■ Percentage of Respondents	35.71	60.71	3.57	0.00	0.00

**Chart 14	The public library is where citizens should be able to find challenging material that may never make the bestseller lists**

Libraries offer a place where people can expand their horizons and take risks in their reading material – in disadvantaged communities, free access to such material may make the difference between trying it out and sticking with something "safer" (SP 21+).

Not everything can be a bestseller, but it's important for recorded words and knowledge to be held somewhere and made accessible. We are not just about the here and now, but about future generations of readers too (HoS 31+).

Libraries should address minority, as well as majority, interests and encourage variety, diversity and experimentation (HoS 31+).

Although public libraries are, of course not the only place, I think it is important for people to be able to access a wide variety of material, including more obscure titles, at their public library! This is perhaps particularly important for people on a lower income who can't afford to buy this sort of material, which can be more expensive (especially compared to bestsellers for £3.99 in Tesco!!) (PG).

This material will broaden people's horizons and promote social cohesion and understanding in all possible levels (local, national, international) (PG).

Agree, but we don't need to go overboard on this (we do tend to traditionally). Better to provide a good range and lots of popular material too, because that is how people will get hooked on self-development / love of literature etc. (Dep 10+).

But only if this material is used and meets local needs – not just because it is "worthy" or "important" or "best" of its kind (HoS 21+).

But that should not mean that our shelves are full of non-issuing mediocre materials bought for balance, etc. – which is sometimes the case now (Dep 31+).

Chart 15 (The professional librarian who knows what quality is should be mainly responsible for what is selected for the library)

Summary

Few respondents agreed with this statement. Many felt that a wide range of people should be involved in stock selection. This could include para professional staff, subject experts and members of the community. There was some comment about a lack of training and education with regard to selection.

Indicative quotes

Would have agreed strongly with this, if I felt there were mechanisms/training available to ensure librarians were taught book selection. I have always objected to approval collections from library suppliers and have found that selection done using different selection methods on a centralized basis is much better. Do you remember all those branch libraries that either had massive collection on railways, gardening, cookery, etc.!! Awful (SP 21+).

The professional librarian has a vital role in the selection of a good, rounded stock, but the person on the counter who deals with the public and their needs on a day to day basis also has a vital role to play. Also, who better to recommend stock for purchase than the service user themselves – particularly those people we sometimes has difficulty identifying with, like teenagers? (HoS 31+)

The professional librarian should manage the process and identify areas of interest for the community to ensure "community needs" are met, but this needs to be regularly tested. No one group holds the answer to what is best (HoS 31+).

Selection should not be carried out by professional staff because they do not reflect local communities – selection should be carried out by the community, with advice and guidance from library workers (HoS 21+).

I would agree that professional or suitably experienced staff should be responsible for drawing up specifications and guidelines, but not that they should necessarily be directly involved in the actual selection (SP 31+).

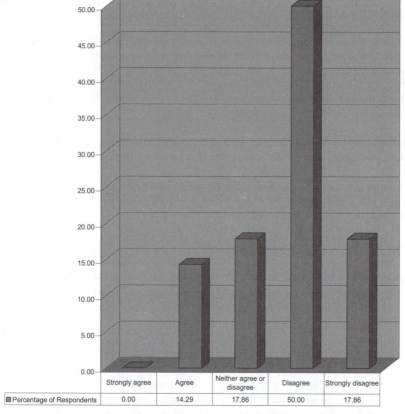

	Strongly agree	Agree	Neither agree or disagree	Disagree	Strongly disagree
▨ Percentage of Respondents	0.00	14.29	17.86	50.00	17.86

Chart 15   The professional librarian who knows what quality is should be mainly responsible for what is selected for the library

The librarian should seek the advice of experts in particular subject areas, teachers and the general public. He or she should nevertheless make an effort to select quality resources avoiding any bias (PG).

In the current financial climate some pragmatism is called for, even to the extent of adopting supplier selection. Contracts and specifications should be carefully complied and suppliers should employ skilled librarians in the task of selecting stock to meet specifications (SP 31+).

Chart 16 (The professional librarian should 'let the customer select')

Summary

The majority of respondents neither agreed or disagreed with this statement while the rest were almost equally divided. There were concerns that customer selection might bias the stock in favour of the more articulate or vociferous.

Indicative quotes

In many ways "yes" Why should middle aged staff select material for 13 year olds? We should encourage more customers to become involved, whilst maintaining a balanced stock (HoS 21+).

Local involvement strengthens links, gives a sense of ownership, extends our understanding of local needs and improves perceptions of relevance (Dep 31+).

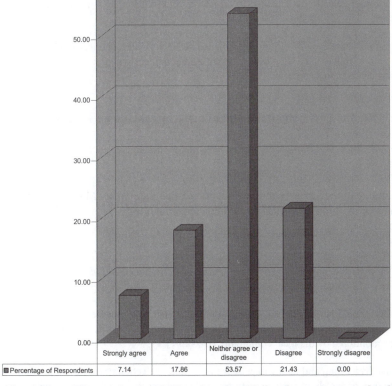

	Strongly agree	Agree	Neither agree or disagree	Disagree	Strongly disagree
Percentage of Respondents	7.14	17.86	53.57	21.43	0.00

Chart 16   The professional librarian should 'let the customer select'

I really believe customer needs should be reflected and have a high priority – but it's important to get the range of stock too, including the more challenging stock and that which caters for the minorities. It should be a balance between customer-expressed choice and professional judgment based on knowledge of the community (SP 21+).

Libraries should be far more open about their stock selection methods and be prepared to discuss them with customers – or even negotiate them. … I have had experiences with adult customer selection and it is usually people with narrow interests – why would they be interested otherwise. Different matter with children and teenagers – lots of good examples of getting help from these groups (SP 21+).

The customer already does this in a roundabout way – look at what issues and what doesn't! (Dep 10+)

Customers should influence selection and in some cases (e.g. young people) participate in selection to encourage their identification with and loyalty to the service; but an important role for the librarian is to ensure that all needs are addressed, not merely the mainstream or the most vociferous (SP 31+).

.... Customer selection could lead to a bias of stock rather than a wide-ranging stock (SP 21+).

This just perpetuates what the stronger minded customer wants, and leads to biased stock – we need to reflect very wide tastes and encourage non customers in – how do we cater for their needs in this scenario? (HoS 21+)

Chart 17 (All but a very small amount of materials should be selected by library suppliers)

Summary

Only a small number of respondents supported this statement. Many stressed the importance of the library service providing a specification.

Indicative quotes

Inevitable in the current financial, organizational, political and commercial climate (SP 31+).

All stock should be selected by library suppliers, based on a specification developed by the local community in partnership with library workers. The quality of selection should also be monitored by the local community (HoS 21+).

We have had a long and happy experience of supplier selection: they are unbiased, have no preconceptions about customers' tastes, and are closer to the publishing industry than we are. But I would also emphasize the need for good specifications for them to work to (SP 31+).

Selection by library suppliers will only be as good as the specification provided by the library authority. Some areas of stock are impossible to specify adequately – nor do suppliers have the expertise. Newly published mainstream material – yes – anything else, probably no (HoS 21+).

The librarian's job is to ensure s/he understands the community's needs and to ensure that this information is constantly updated and tested and translated into a specification. There is a role for supplier selection, but there is no reason why other groups cannot participate (HoS 31+).

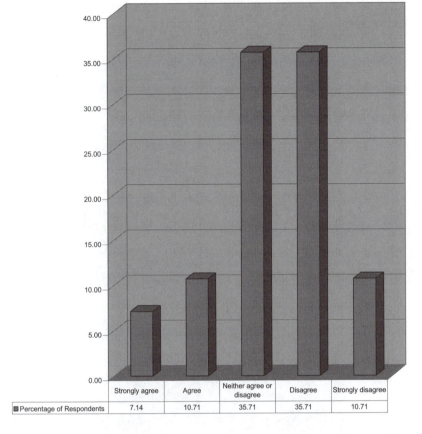

	Strongly agree	Agree	Neither agree or disagree	Disagree	Strongly disagree
▣ Percentage of Respondents	7.14	10.71	35.71	35.71	10.71

Chart 17   All but a very small amount of materials should be selected by library suppliers

Best sellers, popular areas, revision guides etc. are obvious areas for supplier selection, if managed effectively. Library staff knowledge of local community needs and changes in demand can supplement this to provide variety of stock (SP 21+).

For smaller authorities with very tight budgets, selection by staff who have a much greater insight into the needs and requirement of local communities is preferable to supplier selection, however good the profiles are. It is not always possible to circulate stock which has been chosen by suppliers and would not have been chosen by local librarians (SP 41+).

Ideally there'd be a system in place that library staff could select most of the stock ... Less emphasis on commercial supplies ... which ultimately serve only the mainstream people in society (PG).

Chart 18 (The public service ethic provides people with the opportunity to grow and develop)

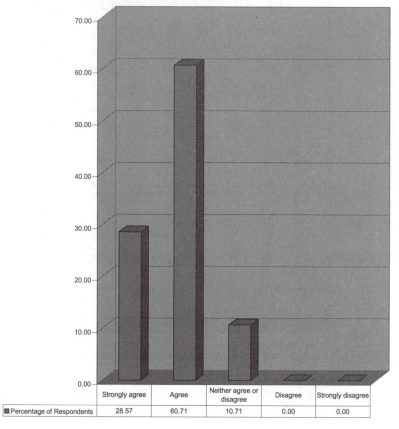

	Strongly agree	Agree	Neither agree or disagree	Disagree	Strongly disagree
■ Percentage of Respondents	28.57	60.71	10.71	0.00	0.00

Chart 18   The public service ethic provides people with the opportunity to grow and develop

Summary

The support for this statement indicated in the figures was reflected in comments from respondents.

Indicative quotes

It certainly should do in its simplest form (SP 10+).

Public goods such as libraries encourage collective growth and development and help to counteract the damaging effects of individualism, materialism and consumerism (HoS 21+).

It also allows people to develop at their own pace, in a non-judgmental environment (HoS 21+).

Engaging with communities, understanding and meeting peoples needs, and seeing them develop does grow and develop staff. We also invest in training and development (HoS 31+).

The elements of free access, neutral spaces, non-judgmental services, and a tradition of positive interactions mean that we do not always have the same connotations as formal education or other agencies (Dep 31+).

It should do, but it is people who support the ethic and these people need to ensure they are challenging themselves on how well they are undertaking this. Tired and jaded public servants will hardly provide the means for others to grow and develop (HoS 31+).

I find libraries and local government a very developmental environment for staff and public (HoS 31+).

Chart 19 (The public library should provide people with the opportunity for reflection and understanding)

Summary

Once again the numbers and the comments from respondents support each other.

Indicative quotes

It does if they choose to do so (PG).

Through access to books, papers and other materials we present different perspectives and we should encourage reflection and understanding through activities and through core service delivery (HoS 31+).

Part of its [the library's] educative role – give people the means to understand the world and form their own judgements (HoS 31+).

This is facilitated through the stock, access to our services, appropriate spaces within the library, and the style in which staff support people .... (HoS 21+)A quiet (ish) place to sit and relax is so important for many people. For older people this provides an opportunity to socialize (SP 21+).

Public libraries are one of the few places which provide free, democratic open space. However, they are not as open to all, "neutral" and welcoming as they could be. They are managed by the white middle class for the white middle class (HoS 21+).

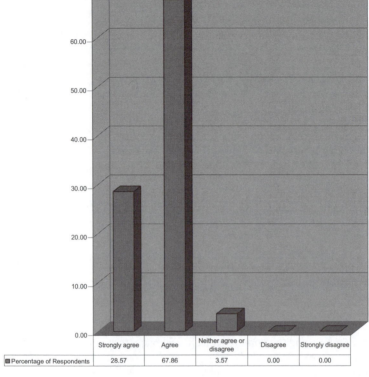

	Strongly agree	Agree	Neither agree or disagree	Disagree	Strongly disagree
■ Percentage of Respondents	28.57	67.86	3.57	0.00	0.00

Chart 19   The public library should provide people with the opportunity for reflection and understanding

Chart 20 (Promoting and prioritising high aesthetic standards would make public libraries culturally exclusive)

Summary

Slightly more respondents agreed with this statement than disagreed. Strong comments were made on both sides of the argument. As in earlier sections several remarks reflected a discomfort with defining standards.

Indicative quotes

These standards should be set by the local community. The current standards are set by the white middle class and are both exclusive and elitist (HoS 21+).

Libraries have this image already and we are trying to overcome this, to encourage more people to join and use the resources (SP 21+).

It would make them exclusive if that was *all* they did …but by doing it alongside other activities is fine …indeed a positive move (PG).

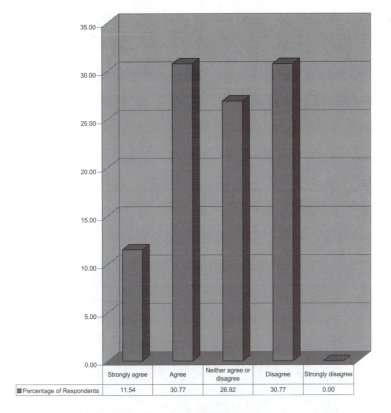

	Strongly agree	Agree	Neither agree or disagree	Disagree	Strongly disagree
■ Percentage of Respondents	11.54	30.77	26.92	30.77	0.00

Chart 20   Promoting and prioritising high aesthetic standards would make public libraries culturally exclusive

We are about range and choice, not high aesthetic standards. Just stocking Booker prize winners is not going to help anyone (HoS 31+).

Nothing wrong with standards – as long as the quality is matched by quality staff, who know their customers and passionately promote the service (SP 21+).

High standards communicate to people that their presence is welcomed and valued, and a high quality environment results in civic pride (HoS 21+).

Not [exclusive] if it is balanced with other cultural, diversity standards. We should seek to offer the best in services and facilities (HoS 31+).

I believe that in this way people will be hopefully introduced to a wider range of cultural choices. This presupposes that a "high" culture is not imposed on people but rather offered as an alternative, whose value is communicated to people (PG).

What are high aesthetic standards? IE do they only apply to opera and classical literature? Or can they apply to graphic novels, popular culture, etc? I think so (HoS 31+).

Chart 21 (Highly qualified personnel will not want to dedicate their working lives to a public library service that does not seek to educate)

Summary

Strong feelings were also reflected in the responses to this question. Half of those responding disagreed with the statement with around 20% finding some truth in the view expressed.

Indicative quotes

Harry Potter walks off the shelf, why bother with a qualification if you are not going to help people develop and grow? (Dep 31+)

Although this statement is hard I believe it could be true up to a point for some librarians (PG).

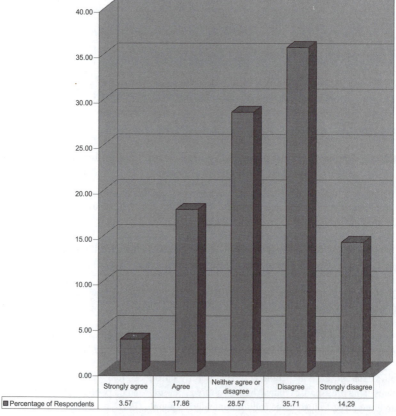

	Strongly agree	Agree	Neither agree or disagree	Disagree	Strongly disagree
■ Percentage of Respondents	3.57	17.86	28.57	35.71	14.29

Chart 21   Highly qualified personnel will not want to dedicate their working lives to a public library service that does not seek to educate

In that case they should work in academic libraries not public libraries. The very name "Public" means that we should be catering for everyone regardless of what they want to read (SP 41+).

Of course they will [want to work in public libraries]. It is even more satisfying to make a change in someone's life however small, when that change is achieved by someone written off by the academic world – or someone who has been led to believe they had no chance to develop (HoS 31+).

I think most professional librarians have similar reasons for working in public libraries. In my experience most are in tune with the new initiatives and greater emphasis on "learning" (SP 21+).

The variety of the work and of the public we meet in our working environments provides the job satisfaction (SP 21+).

As a highly educated person I'm driven by a desire to ensure people aren't socially excluded... education is a bonus. But "seeking to educate" is loaded.... Letting people learn or discover that society does have a place for them is pretty educational in my book (PG).

It depends on the definition of highly qualified – our experience has been that highly qualified library people do not necessarily have the right skills to deal with communities and the challenges of delivering a responsive community based library service. We are looking for highly qualified people in other senses (HoS 21+).

Chart 22 (The public library should actively try to strengthen communities through education)

Summary

There was general agreement with this statement although a minority of respondents appeared to be uneasy with the concept of education.

Indicative quotes

If it [education] means through challenging cultural, ethnic, social and other divisive barriers by providing information and learning to promote wider understanding of other cultures and people – then strongly yes (HoS 31+).

Agree – but I'd perhaps say through participation, which for many is itself a form of education – in the broadest sense of the word (PG).

A key role for libraries is about community engagement and cohesion, and our learning roles are critical to its delivery. We have a unique opportunity in a local authority context to give a lead (HoS 31+).

The public library should actively try to strengthen communities through engagement (HoS 31+).

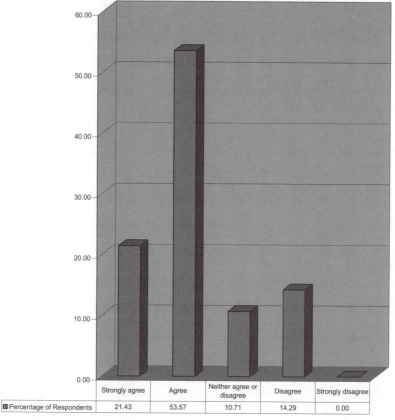

	Strongly agree	Agree	Neither agree or disagree	Disagree	Strongly disagree
◼ Percentage of Respondents	21.43	53.57	10.71	14.29	0.00

Chart 22   The public library should actively try to strengthen communities through education

It is particularly important to reach disadvantaged or excluded communities (PG).

Although there are many reasons why a community may be fraught with weaknesses, taking a library service out into the community can benefit individuals and therefore be a start in the right direction (PG).

Libraries can help to strengthen communities in a number of ways – as a physical community space, by fostering a sense of place, through community projects which can be arts based or learning based. Libraries can help to raise skill levels but they do not have a role to formally educate (HoS 21+).

But education (with all of its negative connotations) should not be the only route. Libraries can strengthen communities through a combination of Lifelong Learning (a more holistic approach to education), Social Inclusion and Community Regeneration (HoS 21+).

Chart 23 (Public library services should seek to renew themselves as cultural institutions)

Summary

There was strong support for this statement but respondents differed in their opinions as to the extent to which it had been achieved.

Indicative quotes

We ARE a cultural institution (although I don't like the word "institution") (HoS 31+).

The library service in **** has renewed itself as a cultural institution. In the past 5 years active users have increased, book issues have remained stable, visitors have increased. This has been the result of a change in service delivery to a more customer responsive, accessible service offering a greater range of choice and quality of material and other services (HoS 21+).

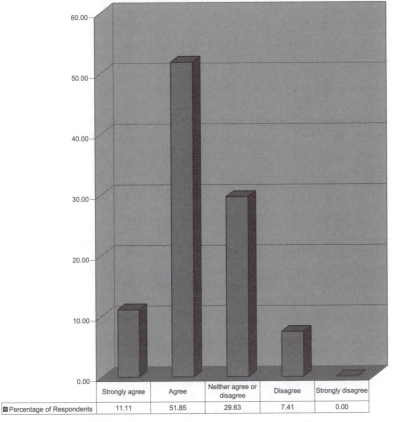

	Strongly agree	Agree	Neither agree or disagree	Disagree	Strongly disagree
▪ Percentage of Respondents	11.11	51.85	29.63	7.41	0.00

Chart 23   Public library services should seek to renew themselves as cultural institutions

They [libraries] already are cultural institutions. They need to ensure their library activities meet the community's needs (HoS 31+).

This is a core role for the service and strikes a chord with politicians, users and communities. For many people the library is their first and most enduring link with culture (SP 31+).

I slightly agree in that the implication is that the "cultural" element of the library remit can be perceived to be lost to the "social inclusion element" but I'd say this is a false dualism … which is interesting to debate but doesn't truly reflect what is happening on the ground (PG).

Libraries have a very important role to play but many of the more traditionally cultural organizations seem to regard libraries as "bit players". We need to have the recognition of our contribution and a place at the table where decisions are made (SP 21+).

This is certainly a key role for the PLs which is often unexplored, many excellent resources/collections under exploited (SP 10+).

They [libraries] need to be completely transformed, repositioned and rebranded as non elitist, non exclusive community based cultural institutions (HoS 21+).

Chart 24 (The public library should be a centre of intellectual life of the area it serves)

Summary

There was substantial support for this statement but a numbers of respondents reflected the UK profession's discomfort with the word 'intellectual'.

Indicative quotes

While not wishing to be elitist, libraries should have a place at the heart of intellectual life! (SP 21+)

The public library should be part of a network of information, learning and relaxation places in communities. If this is intellectual life then the answer is agree. What is intellectual stimulation to one person is different to another (HoS 21+).

But not in a way that excludes community members which do not wish to use certain stock/services/activities (PG).

As long as this can be done without excluding anyone in the community (HoS 31+).

Not just intellectual life, a place where people can satisfy social needs, enjoy themselves, educate themselves depending on their requirements (PG).

But language such as intellectual life should be avoided – they should become centres of community activity and action based on both brain and brawn (HoS 21+).

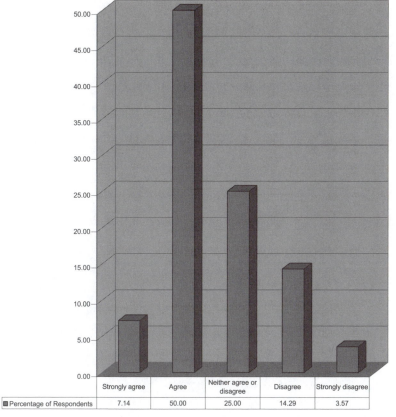

	Strongly agree	Agree	Neither agree or disagree	Disagree	Strongly disagree
■ Percentage of Respondents	7.14	50.00	25.00	14.29	3.57

Chart 24   The public library should be a centre of intellectual life of the area it serves

Chart 25 (The public library is a place where the egalitarian principles of democracy meet the elite claims of high culture)

Summary

The figures and the comments from respondents reflect a very mixed set of views with regard to this statement.

Indicative quotes

This is certainly how the public library came into being – whether today's service could be described as such (or not) is another matter (SP 10+).

Perhaps fairer to say it is a place where they can co-exist (SP 31+).

A library could be a meeting point of different people. I believe that a public library should present a multi variant, pluralistic culture (PG).

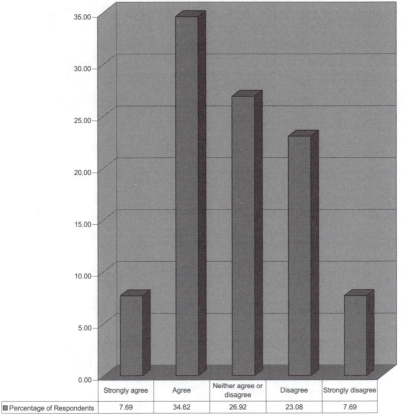

	Strongly agree	Agree	Neither agree or disagree	Disagree	Strongly disagree
■ Percentage of Respondents	7.69	34.62	26.92	23.08	7.69

Chart 25   The public library is a place where the egalitarian principles of democracy meet the elite claims of high culture

Although libraries may provide access to "high culture" …I'm not sure that equality and high culture truly "meet" in a public library (PG).

I disagree because I dispute that high culture is, per se, "elitist" (HoS 21+).

Democracy yes – high culture no (HoS 31+).

But elite claims of high culture strongly outweigh and undermine the library's ability to be both egalitarian and democratic (HoS 21+).

A public library should be a place where the claims of high culture are challenged and where the cultural needs of the whole community are met – a sense of sharing, community and civic values and belonging (HoS 21+).

I no longer know what this means. Openness and personal growth should support democracy but a library cannot socially engineer individuals to choose good over evil. High culture doesn't necessarily mean democracy is promoted – see George Steiner's words on high Nazi officials who spent evenings listening to music played by prisoner quartets while sanctioning gas chambers. (HoS 31+).

Chart 26 (Local authority support for the arts improves residents' quality of life)

Summary

No respondent disagreed with this statement which was supported by 85% of those taking part.

Indicative quotes

This is the quality that adds value to life (SP 31+).

All of the research evidence points to this. Conversely, when cultural services are removed, local communities start to fall apart (HoS 21+).

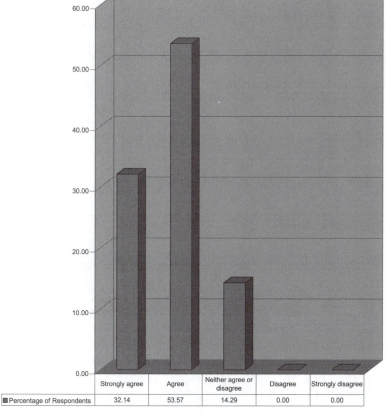

	Strongly agree	Agree	Neither agree or disagree	Disagree	Strongly disagree
■ Percentage of Respondents	32.14	53.57	14.29	0.00	0.00

Chart 26   **Local authority support for the arts improves residents' quality of life**

Art can stimulate, challenge, change perception. It can open doors and broaden horizons (HoS 21+).

The arts bring colour, vitality and vibrancy into people's lives and into the communities in which they live. They can help to raise people's aspirations. Many communities would be denied access to arts without local authority support (SP 21+).

…We will never be a going commercial concern, if the local authority did not provide us, no one else would (Dep 31+).

Without this support, the variety of cultural opportunities would not be available for all members of the community (SP 21+).

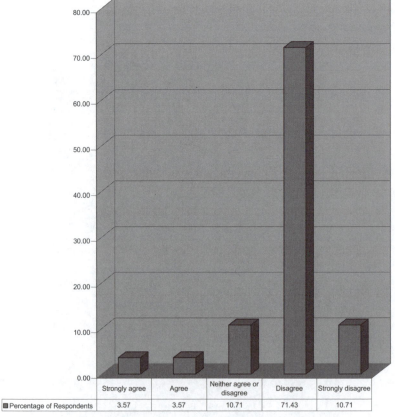

	Strongly agree	Agree	Neither agree or disagree	Disagree	Strongly disagree
■ Percentage of Respondents	3.57	3.57	10.71	71.43	10.71

Chart 27   It is undemocratic to promote high culture at public expense

Chart 27 (It is undemocratic to promote high culture at public expense)

Summary

A large majority of respondents disagreed with this statement. However, many suggested that it should not only be high culture that is promoted.

Indicative quotes

I don't think it is, if it has the potential to be accessed by everyone. It could also be seen to be enabling social inclusion, if by promoting it, it allows previously excluded groups to access it (PG).

Culture belongs to everyone – it should not be considered high or low. Only providing culture that appeals to a narrow group of people is elitist and a waste of public money (HoS 21+).

People who enjoy "high culture" are also part of the community (HoS 31+).

It is the role of public libraries to provide opportunities to or people to access the best (HoS 21+).

How else will those without means be able to experience the best? (SP 31+)

I think this one depends on the scale. It's one thing to offer opportunities to widen access to high culture by promoting and supporting it. However, to sink millions of pounds into minority interest areas is neither democratic nor value for money – rather it becomes a public subsidy of an activity patronized by people who could probably afford to pay for it (SP 21+).

So long as we promote it amongst a range of other appropriate cultures it is still a legitimate interest of some in society, therefore it is their democratic right to be represented in the library (Dep 31+).

But it must be recognized that it is perfectly reasonable for not everything to capture everyone (Dep 31+).

Access to culture at whatever level is important. However, it should not be at the expense of more community based cultural activity (HoS 21+).

Chart 28 (Egalitarian aspirations have hindered attempts to create public libraries as centres of excellence)

Summary

Some respondents were clearly uncomfortable with this and the next statement. The majority disagreed and often expressed this disagreement in strong terms. A significant minority however did express concern at a library service that tried to be all things to all people.

Indicative quotes

I don't think this is bad (PG).

Rubbish – a centre of excellence caters for all needs and aspirations. How can something be excellent if it does not serve ALL its customers? (HoS 31+)

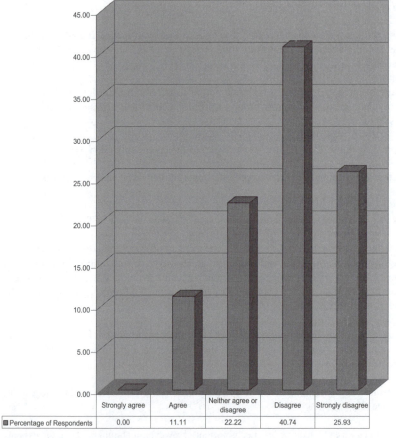

	Strongly agree	Agree	Neither agree or disagree	Disagree	Strongly disagree
■ Percentage of Respondents	0.00	11.11	22.22	40.74	25.93

Chart 28   Egalitarian aspirations have hindered attempts to create public libraries as centres of excellence

That's an incredibly pompous statement. Our libraries aspire to excellence and egalitarianism! (SP 21+)

A public library successfully addressing social inclusion within a particular context is certainly a centre of excellence (PG).

Experience shows that with resources and imagination libraries can demonstrate excellence in many areas – not egalitarian aspirations, but the lack of any aspirations for the service is the problem in some places! (SP 31+)

I think I dispute the interpretation of excellence here. Excellent libraries will be highly egalitarian (HoS 31+).

Equality and equity of access ensure that the public library can aspire to be centers of excellence – it depends on what you mean by excellence. If you are coming from a community point of view, then libraries are excellent community based venues (HoS 21+).

Classless provision is essential to the work of public libraries (PG).

The problem is that egalitarian aspirations have either not existed or have not been actively pursued by elitist and exclusive library managers (HoS 21+).

What is a "Centre of Excellence"? Certainly not an exclusive ivory tower accessible only to a few (HoS 21+).

We have tried to be all things to all people, and lost confidence in our core business of books, and even in the word Library in some places. This was with the intention of "staying relevant". Big mistake. As a result we now have to play catch up (HoS 31+).

Excellence is not necessarily exclusivity, but neither is it trying to offer everything everywhere and diluting scarce resources. There has to be balance (Dep 31+).

Centres of excellence in what? The wide remit of libraries promotes tensions in creating a centre of excellence not the egalitarian aspect (HoS 31+).

We cannot please everyone all of the time. Trying to do this has led to services not delivering the quality expected (SP 21+).

Chart 29 (Some social inclusion policies can be detrimental to public libraries' educational activities)

Summary

A large majority of respondents disagreed with this statement but, as in the previous question, a minority expressed concerns about the impact of some policies.

Indicative quotes

Rubbish – a centre of excellence caters for all needs and aspirations. How can something be excellent if it does not serve ALL its customers? (HoS 31+) (Repeat of earlier answer.)

Social inclusion policies can only strengthen public library activities, educational or otherwise. Inclusion, Learning and Regeneration should be the three pillars of the public library movement (HoS 21+).

Social inclusion is not about a one size fits all service. We offer a range of learning services reflecting a range of needs. Just because we target at certain under-represented groups does not mean that others are necessarily ignored (Dep 31+).

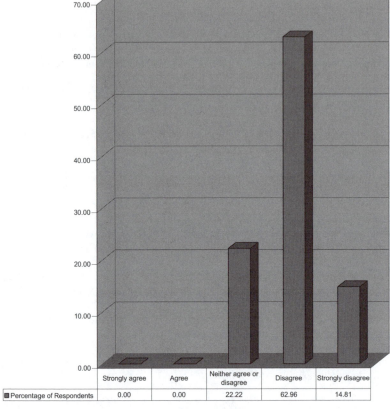

Percentage of Respondents	Strongly agree	Agree	Neither agree or disagree	Disagree	Strongly disagree
	0.00	0.00	22.22	62.96	14.81

Chart 29   Some social inclusion policies can be detrimental to public libraries' educational activities

A library is a place where learning is supported for the whole community. It is possible to meet the needs of a variety of users with a variety of learning needs/levels within the same building. It is a matter of design and priority and an acceptance by the educated elite that all people have a right of access to knowledge at whatever level and whatever subject (HoS 21+).

Social inclusion promotes understanding of diversity, and supports educational activities (SP 21+).

We can't put social-inclusion against education... it's all inter connected!! Blend the things together in more imaginative ways (PG).

There is a tension but not between social inclusion and education since many social inclusion policies are strongly focused on learning. However, social inclusion work is resource intensive and the pressure of targets is to focus on increasing use and visits (HoS 21+).

Don't the "socially included" learn and grow? However, encouragement to smelly tramps to sleep in the library may certainly affect usage! (HoS 31+).

Some social inclusion policies can be time consuming and tie up resources for small numbers of potential users (HoS 31+).

Chart 30 (It is insulting to working class people to suppose they will only use libraries specifically designed to meet their perceived demands)

Summary

Most respondents agreed with this statement and many commented on the need for consultation. As ever there was some disagreement over the concept of class.

Indicative quotes

People want to expand their life experiences and opportunities not be type-cast, or have dumbed down services (SP 21+).

[Libraries should] Challenge, offer opportunities for learning and new experiences. Culture can be appreciated by everyone regardless of their social background (HoS 31+).

We have a responsibility to widen horizons and present the opportunities and services available, not to be solely demand led (HoS 31+).

I don't think we should put labels on people and on libraries. A good public library could be equally good to anyone (PG).

We should not second guess or assume what the needs of working class people are. We should actively engage working class people in the planning, design, delivery and evaluation of library services (HoS 21+).

Second guessing the demands of any group is insulting – you need to consult with that group (PG).

The key here is "perceived". If all groups are fully involved in the planning and design of libraries and services then this is not the case – the service will reflect actual demands, not those which we think people have (Dep 31+).

"Working class" is too broad/vague a definition when trying to identify the demands of non users. While groups of non users may belong to the "working classes" there are probably also many active users from this background. Public libraries should ideally cater for all groups regardless of social/economic class. Obviously there are groups from particular sectors of society, but I think "working class" is too vague a definition (PG).

No class will use facilities that don't meet its needs. The working class? Does it still exist? (HoS 31+)

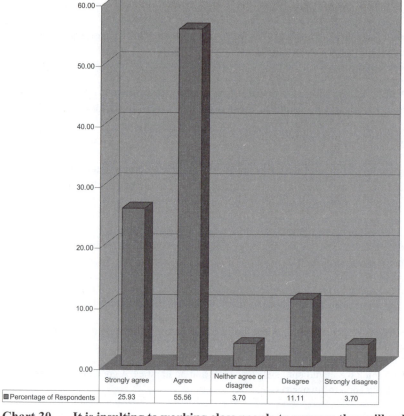

	Strongly agree	Agree	Neither agree or disagree	Disagree	Strongly disagree
◼ Percentage of Respondents	25.93	55.56	3.70	11.11	3.70

Chart 30   **It is insulting to working class people to suppose they will only use libraries specifically designed to meet their perceived demands**

Chart 31 (In the public library populism is perfidious)

Summary

A substantial majority disagreed with this statement which also provoked a surprising amount of comment about the word perfidious, which the present author took to mean 'breach of faith' in the original quotation.

Indicative quotes

> Populism is the answer to the decline in public library usage. Libraries are actively used by less than 20% of the population. 50% of the population is non users. They could be attracted into libraries if they were made more popular (HoS 21+).

> I have no desire to run an unpopular service (SP 31+).

People can enjoy a wide range of interests to suit different moods or needs – populism can easily sit next to high culture. Where is the dividing line? (HoS 31+)

A popular item may be transitory (e.g. Desmond Bagley) or form a major plank of our culture (e.g. Dickens). We need to reflect popular culture and encourage mass use, but also maintain a balanced long-term approach to collection content and service provision (Dep 31+).

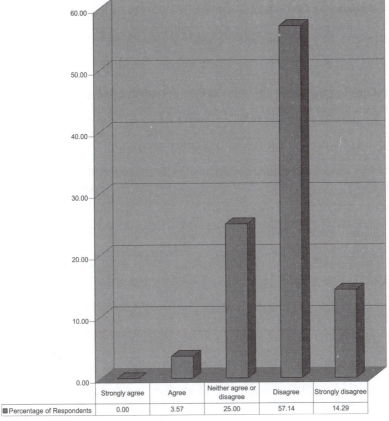

	Strongly agree	Agree	Neither agree or disagree	Disagree	Strongly disagree
■ Percentage of Respondents	0.00	3.57	25.00	57.14	14.29

Chart 31   In the public library populism is perfidious

We should provide a wide range of stock – including the popular genres and titles (for people with reading difficulties, finishing a Mills and Boon is a real achievement) but also offering additional materials which will stimulate and challenge, and then encourage people to try them out (SP 21+).

The library can make itself popular without being trashy (HoS 31+).

[Populism] Undermines choice and variety (SP 21+).

I feel there needs to be an appropriate balance between the two ends of the spectrum in order to broaden the appeal of the service but also to provide the most sustainable service (SP 10+).

I really disagree with the tone of some of these questions – it has never been the role of libraries to dictate a highly cultural/educational model on its customers. For some people a cheap western or romance is the peak of their reading ability and aspirations – we might tempt them further – but if not so be it. Public libraries are for people – whatever their "level" or need. (HoS 31+)

I had to look up "perfidious" outlandish statement! The ethos of the service isn't a religion! (PG).

Chart 32 (Opening up public libraries as requested by policy makers will destroy the quality of the service)

Summary

Three quarters of those responding disagreed with this statement. A significant number suggested that it was a lack of resources that was responsible for a decline in quality.

Indicative quotes

On the contrary I believe it will add to the quality of the library services since its impact will be greater and it will reach a larger part of the population (PG).

Which policy makers? Libraries should be open to everyone – see the first Public Libraries Act (HoS 31+).

Opening up the library will increase the quality of the service to the whole community (HoS 21+).

It can improve the quality of the service by making a wider range of resources and information available (SP 21+).

You can have quality and still encourage more disadvantaged groups to use them. Why should the disadvantaged have poorer access to libraries than the better-off? We should be striving for excellence for all (SP 21+).

All libraries where money has been properly spent on high quality buildings that are then well resourced and staffed, have been very successful. Quality of bookstocks may have suffered, but that is probably down to poor training and recruitment (SP 21+).

Not if extensions to opening hours, new services etc., are properly funded. Trying to get "something for nothing" or relying on staff's good will rather than on properly trained professionals may inevitably damage quality (Dep 31+).

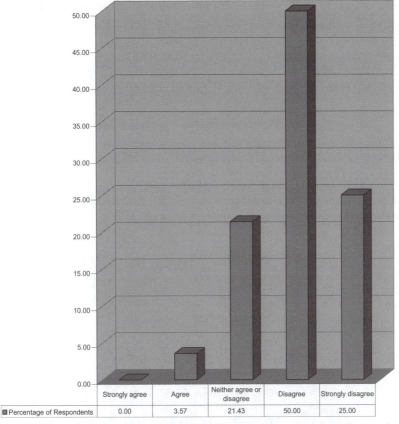

Percentage of Respondents	Strongly agree	Agree	Neither agree or disagree	Disagree	Strongly disagree
	0.00	3.57	21.43	50.00	25.00

Chart 32   Opening up public libraries as requested by policy makers will destroy the quality of the service

Quality isn't destroyed by opening up services, but availability of resources to ensure the best is offered in whatever subject area, will be the key to the provision of a total qualitative service (HoS 31+).

There is no shame in being popular, but the service should not be populist to the exclusion of more serious and purposive goals (SP 31+).

…I think it is important to be cautious in altering any aspects of library service in order not to alienate existing users (PG).

It [Opening up the service…] will certainly constrain the quality of the service (SP 10+).

The service has been destroyed by being kept too closed, elitist and exclusive. Opening it up will make libraries vibrant, dynamic and diverse centres of community activity (HoS 21+).

Chart 33 (The public library should promote an unashamedly popular image)

Summary

Just over 40% of respondents agreed with this statement although many of the comments expressed caveats and stressed the need for 'balance'.

Indicative quotes

There is a need to promote a popular image to encourage non-users through the door (HoS 31+).

There is a strong argument to say that all publicity is good publicity – particularly when libraries in the past have failed to seize the day, it is vitally important in todays hectic and demanding world that libraries promote, promote, promote! (PG)

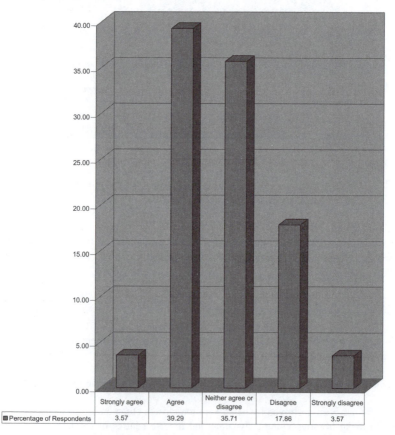

	Strongly agree	Agree	Neither agree or disagree	Disagree	Strongly disagree
■ Percentage of Respondents	3.57	39.29	35.71	17.86	3.57

Chart 33   The public library should promote an unashamedly popular image

The message should be – libraries are for everyone, no matter what your interests, needs and tastes are. The wider the popular appeal the better. Where this approach has been adopted (Cuba, Scandinavia) active use rates are above 80% (HoS 21+).

PLs should be aiming to increase their popularity by improving services (by marketing appropriately to attract new users). In this respect public libraries should be promoting a popular image. However I think it is important that public libraries aim to increase their popularity through providing better services for more people, rather than seeking popularity for the sake of it! I don't think public libraries should "sell out" and seek popularity over quality (PG).

Popular, yes, but there is a danger of not being taken seriously by the decision makers at all levels if libraries are seen purely as popular institutions with no real value. It's important to get the right balance between popularity and credibility (SP 21+).

The public library should promote what it is... a unique service that has something for everyone regardless of whether their tastes are "popular", classical, "Highbrow" or eclectic (HoS 31+).

They should promote a positive modern image – without buying into a completely new ethos or selling out of the current one (PG).

I would disagree with a purely unashamedly popularist approach for all libraries. This may be appropriate for a small local branch, but not for a service as a whole ... (Dep 31+).

The public library should promote an attractive but nevertheless dignified image (PG).

I feel there needs to be an appropriate balance between the two ends of the spectrum in order to broaden the appeal of the service but also to provide the most sustainable service (SP 10+).

Chart 34 (Public libraries' preferred strategy for the twenty-first century)

Summary

Most respondents wanted public libraries to be all of the things suggested by the three options given in the survey. In deciding where the greatest emphasis should be placed there was almost equal division between those favouring 'lifestyle' strategies and those opting for a strategy based on quality services and collections. Access to IT was still regarded as important, but many respondents felt that in the long term such access would be available elsewhere.

Indicative quotes

Libraries should do all these things and there can be little to choose between them. However, if quality and excellence is at the heart of services then the rest will follow as a matter of course (HoS 31+).

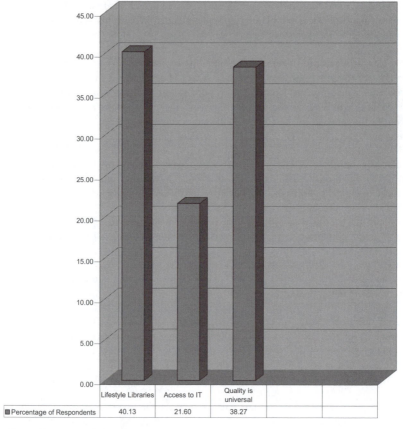

	Lifestyle Libraries	Access to IT	Quality is universal		
■ Percentage of Respondents	40.13	21.60	38.27		

Chart 34   Public libraries' preferred strategy for the twenty-first century

It's hard to have to choose between the options – really, what we need is a combination of the three, where people can relax in a welcoming, comfortable environment, with access to free ICT, and a quality service in all that we do. It's not really an either/or situation! (HoS 21+)

The service will need to be an amalgam of all three statements, but I feel that the most important role will be that of a storehouse / distribution point of knowledge and inspiration, reflected in the collections (whether physical items or on-line resources) and the way in which we provide access to that information, whether in person at the library or through virtual access (Dep 31+).

(1) [The lifestyle library] is the nearest to a Needs Based Library Service:

A Need Based Library Service is predicated on the assumption that everyone has needs and everyone has different needs. Therefore a Needs Based Library Service is a universal concept which can be applied to any library service in any circumstances at any time (HoS 21+).

Lifestyles move on too quickly, so libraries can look out-of-date very quickly. They need to have an air of quality and timelessness. We have a lot to learn from other countries like New Zealand and Singapore (SP 21+).

(Lifestyle) The public seems to want this, where these changes are made, the visits are going up. Is that not good evidence of value? (Dep 10+)

(IT) This may only last for a short period until all people have access to digital services at home. (Quality) Forget this (Dep 10+).

It is important that libraries are places that people want to visit and that they enjoy the experience. Quality and range is also important. IT has a role to play but it should not dominate (SP 31+).

Unless we create the right environment, people will not use us. This doesn't change what we do, just how we attract people to come in and stay – its how they expect to find it, compared with other places they visit. The quality of the collections and staff expertise is our USP, not the access to IT. In the future most will have access in the home to IT, but they will still need the expert staff and collections (HoS 31+).

The ones I've marked 1[Lifestyle] and 2[IT] are inseparable for me at the moment although I believe that 1 will become more significant in the future and, in terms of public funding, is the one that will give us greatest clout – although I think the key issue will be what people use IT for not the simple issue of access to IT which is already available easily for many people.

1.Quality needs to be defined but people deserve to see the best in whichever field or subject they are interested in, populist or elitist. Image will change but quality of service will always be recognized.

2.Image, visual effects and lifestyle are increasingly important, therefore people will feel encouraged to enter and linger in places where the surroundings meet their comfort zone. But if the quality is not there, the surroundings will be an empty shell.

3.Info technology provision is important now in libraries, but eventually it will be as ubiquitous as the TV set. Libraries must not forget their role in presentation of information (HoS 31+).

Lifestyle libraries certainly have a role and are obviously popular with many customers/ users. I don't think this is a bad thing, but it should not be at the expense of a more "serious" role. PLs are the only place that many people have for private study, homework etc. so it is important that this function is still provided – i.e. a scholarly environment that is not intimidating. While the life style library approach can help make libraries less intimidating it should not infringe on those who wish to work quietly etc. (T1).

At the moment from what I have seen in my short time in libraries I feel that for libraries to remain as a popular destination in today's society the strategies should be as marked on the left hand side (1.2.3.) It has to meet the standards and expectations of today's society. Fundamentally, in my own mind, I would like to see the reverse (3.2.1.) which is perhaps a more traditional view, but then I already appreciate the value of the public library service (PG).

Bibliography

Adam Smith Institute (undated) 'Liberating Libraries', http://www.adamsmith.org/culture/index.php/culture/think_piece/liberating_libraries/ (accessed: 29.06.06).

Akey, S. (1990) 'McLibraries', *The New Republic*, 202, 26 February, 12–3.

Alabaster, C. (2002) *Developing an Outstanding Core Collection. A Guide for Librarians* (Chicago: American Library Association.)

Alemna, A.A. (1995) 'Community libraries: An alternative to public libraries in Africa', *Library Review*, **44**(7): 40–44.

Alibhai-Brown, Y. (2007) 'The view from India: Horror at these barbarians', *The Independent*, 22 January, 31.

Allan, T. (2005) 'Opinionated journalists are short-changing electorate', *The Observer*, 4 September, 7.

Americans for Libraries Council (2005) *Designs for Change: Libraries and Productive Aging*, http://www.imls.gov/publications/publications.shtm (accessed: 16.01.07).

American Library Association (undated) *About Roads to Learning*, http://www.ala.org/ala/olos/outreachresource/roadstolearning/aboutroadslearning.htm (accessed: 01.08.07).

American Library Association (2006) *Library Services for the Poor*, http://www.ala.org/ala/ourassociation/governingdocs/policymanual/servicespoor.htm (accessed: 15.09.06).

Anonymous (2006) 'Contribution to: Are our libraries being neglected?' *Times Online*, http://www.timesonline.co.uk/article/0,,564-2099855,00.html (accessed: 09.01.07).

Appleyard, B. (1992) 'Libraries sell out their literary soul to a rash of trash', *Sunday Times*, 1 March, Section 2, 2.

Arrow, K. *et al.* (1993) *Report of the NOAA Panel on Contingent Valuation, Federal Register*, Volume 58, Washington, DC.

Asheim, L. (1953) *Not Censorship But Selection*, ALA OIF website, http://www.ala.org/Template.cfm?Section=basics&Template=/ContentManagement/ContentDisplay.cfm&ContentID=109668 (accessed: 02.04.07).

ASLIB (1995) *Review of the Public Library Service in England and Wales for the DNH: Final Report* (London: ASLIB).

Aspden, P. (2004) 'Stop going on about civilisation', *FT Magazine*, 31 July, 34–36.

Augst, T. (2003) 'American libraries and agencies of culture', in Augst, T. and Wiegand, W. (eds) (2003), *Libraries as Agencies of Culture* (Madison, WI: University of Wisconsin Press), 5–22.

Augst, T. (2003a) 'Introduction' to Augst, T. and Wiegand, W. (eds) (2003) *Libraries as Agencies of Culture* (Madison, WI: University of Wisconsin Press).

Ball, D. and Earl, C. (2002) 'Outsourcing and externalisation: Current practice in UK libraries, museums and archives', *Journal of Librarianship and Information Science*, **34**(4), 197–206.

Ball, M. (undated) *How to Create Literary Fiction*, http://www.absolutewrite.com/novels/create_literary.htm (accessed: 29.09.06).

Ballard, J.G. (2006) *Kingdom Come* (London: Fourth Estate).

Barenboim, D. (2006) *In the Beginning was Sound*, Reith Lectures 2006, http://www.bbc.co.uk/radio4/reith2006/lecture1shtml (accessed: 01.08.07).

Barber, B.R. (1995) *Jihad vs. McWorld: How Globalism and Tribalism are Reshaping the World* (New York: Ballantine Books).

Batt, C. (2003) 'Policy Push, Personal Pull: Trying to Make Sense of the Journey Towards the Information Society', in Hornby, S. and Clarke, Z. (eds), *Challenge and Change in the Information Society* (London: Facet Publishing), 63–82.

Battles, M. (2003) *Library: An Unquiet History* (New York: W.W. Norton & Company, Inc.).

BBC (2006) *History of the Proms*, http://www.bbc.co.uk/proms/aboutfestival/history.shtml (accessed: 15.09.06).

Bennett, A. (2004) *The History Boys* (London: Faber & Faber).

Bentley, M. (2002) *Institutionalised Classism? An investigation into how far public libraries are serving the needs of working class individuals and communities.* A study submitted in partial fulfilment of the requirements for the degree of Master of Arts in Librarianship at The University of Sheffield.

Berelson, B. (1949) *The Library's Public* (New York: Columbia University Press).

Berman, S. (2001) Libraries dumbing down? *New Breed Librarian*, http://www.newbreedlibrarian.org/archives/01.03.jun2001/feature2.html (accessed: 28.04.04).

Berman, S. (2005) *Classism in the Stacks: Libraries and Poverty*, http://www.ala.org/ala/olos/olosprograms/jeanecoleman/05berman.htm (accessed: 16.01.07).

Bernstein, C. (1992) 'The idiot culture', *The New Republic*, 8 June, 22–8.

Binns, R. (2004) Letter to *The Independent*, http://comment.independent.co.uk/letters/article58434.ece (accessed: 04.08.06).

Bishoff, L. (2000) *Interoperability and Standards in Museum/Library Collaborative*, http://www.firstmonday.org/issues/issue5_6/bishoff/ (accessed: 11.10.06).

Black, A. (1999) *Man and Boy: Modifying masculinities in public librarianship, 1850–1950, with a case study of the inter-war librarianship Masonic circle.* Paper delivered to the 'Gendering Library History' Conference, Liverpool John Moores University, 15 May, http://www.lmu.ac.uk/ies/documents/2001-1.pdf (accessed: 06.03.07).

Black, A. (2001) 'The Victorian Information Society: Surveillance, bureaucracy, and public librarianship in 19th-century Britain', *Information Society*, **17**(1): 63–80.

Black, A. (2006) 'Introduction. The public library in concept and reality', in Black, A. and Hoare, P. (eds), *The Cambridge History of Libraries in Britain and Ireland Vol. III 1850–2000* (Cambridge: Cambridge University Press), 21–23.

Black, A. and Crann, M. (2000) *A Mass Observation of the Public Library*, Library and Information Commission Research Report 69.

Black, A. and Crann, M. (2002) 'In the public eye: a mass observation of the public library', *Journal of Librarianship and Information Science* **3**(3), 145–157.

Blacker, T. (2005) 'The nation's libraries are dying from neglect', *The Independent*, 11 March, 37.

Blacker, T. (2006) 'Libraries are not just about books', *The Independent*, 24 March, http://comment.independent.co.uk/columnists_a_l/terence_blacker/article 353283.ece (accessed: 09.03.07).

Blackstone, T. (2004) Lords Hansard text for 17 March, http://www.parliament. the-stationery-office.com/pa/ld200304/ldhansrd/vo040317/text/40317-06.htm (accessed: 16.01.07).

Blair, T. (1996) *New Britain: My Vision of a Young Country* (London: Fourth Estate).

Block, M. (2004) 'In need of a better business model', *Ex Libris* 207, 12 March, http://marylaine.com/exlibris/xlib207.html (accessed: 08.08.06).

Bloom, A. (1987) *The Closing of the American Mind* (New York: Simon & Schuster).

Bob, M.C. (1982) 'The case for quality book selection', *Library Journal*, **107**, 15 September, 1707–1710.

Bolton, G. (2002) *The Tyranny of Ignorance*. Paper to ALIA Conference, Powering our Future. http://conferences.alia.org.au/alia2002/papers/bolton.html (accessed: 01.02.07).

Booth, R. (2007) 'Generation Y speaks: it's all me, me, me', *Sunday Times*, 4 February, http://www.timesonline.co.uk/tol/news/uk/article1329162.ece (accessed: 06.03.07).

Borgman, C.L. and Cross, R.A. (1995) 'The incredible vanishing library', *American Libraries*, **26**(19) October, 904.

Borgmann, A. (1999) *Holding on to Reality: The Nature of Information at the Turn of the Millennium* (Chicago & London: The University of Chicago Press).

Boston Public Library (1852) 'Upon the objects to be attained by the establishment of a public library', Report of the Trustees of the Public Library of the City of Boston 1852, City Document – No. 37, http://www.scls.lib.wi.us/mcm/history/ report_of_trustees.html (accessed: 09.11.06).

Brady, W. (2003) 'Art galleries and museums should not be forced to dumb down', *The Independent*, 18 December, http://www.findarticles.com/p/articles/mi_qn4158/ is_20031218/ai_n12717373 (accessed: 01.01.07).

Brighton and Hove (2006) *Aims and Objectives of the Library Service* http://www. citylibraries.info/information/about_us.asp (accessed: 02.04.07).

Brighton and Hove City Council Library Service (2005) *Stock Policy and Guidelines,* http://www.citylibraries.info/information/documents/stock_policy_may05.pdf (accessed: 01.10. 06).

British Library (2004) *Measuring Our Value*, http://www.bl.uk/pdf/measuring.pdf (accessed: 27.02.07).

Brontë, C. (2006) *Jane Eyre* (London: Penguin Books Ltd).

Brookes, R. *et al.* (2004) 'The media representation of public opinion: British television news coverage of the 2001 general election', *Media, Culture & Society*, **26**(1), 63–80.

Brown, J.S. and Duguid, P. (2000) *The Social Life of Information* (Boston: Harvard Business School Press).

Bryson, J., Usherwood, B. and Streatfield, D. (2002) *Social Impact Audit for the South West Museums Libraries and Archives Council* (Taunton: South West Museums Libraries and Archives Council).

Bryson, J., Usherwood, B. and Proctor, R. (2003) *Libraries Must Also Be Buildings? New Library Impact Study*, The Centre for Public Libraries and Information in Society (CPLIS), Department of Information Studies, University of Sheffield.

Buford, T. (2004) quoted in Alumni School of Information Studies, Syracuse University, http://istweb.syr.edu/alumni/terry_buford.asp (accessed: 16.02.07).

Bundy, A. (1999) *Challenging Technolust: the Educational Responsibility of Librarians*, IATUL Proceedings Technical University of Crete, Chania, Greece, 17th May–21st May, http://www.iatul.org/conference/proceedings/vol09/papers/bundy.html (accessed: 08.03.07).

Bundy, A. (2002) *Changing Lives, Making the Difference: The 21st Century Public Library*. Paper delivered at the annual general meeting of the Friends of Mitcham Library Service (SA), Adelaide, 31 July, http://www.library.unisa.edu.au/about/papers/changinglives.pdf (accessed: 09.03.07).

Burnell, S. (2005) *Library or Video Store? Does anybody read anymore?* http://lists.webjunction.org/wjlists/publib/2005-March/046167.html (accessed: 31.03.07).

Burton, G. (2005) *Media and Society. Critical Perspectives* (Maidenhead: Open University Press).

Buschman, J.E. (2003) *Dismantling the Public Sphere. Situating and Sustaining Librarianship in the Age of the New Public Philosophy* (Westport, CT: Libraries Unlimited).

Byrnes, S. (2005) 'The eff-off society', *The Independent on Sunday*, 23 October, 27.

Cabinet Office (2006) 'Tackling deep-seated social exclusion', News release 13 June, http://www.cabinetoffice.gov.uk/newsroom/news_releases/2006/060613_se.asp (accessed: 21.01.07).

Cabinet Office Social Exclusion Task Force (2006) *Future Plans*, http://www.cabinetoffice.gov.uk/social_exclusion_task_force/future_plans/ (accessed: 21.01.07).

Carey, J. (2005) *What Good are the Arts?* (London: Faber & Faber).

Carter, D. (2001) 'Public intellectuals, book culture and civil society', *Australian Humanities Review*, http://www.lib.latrobe.edu.au/AHR/archive/Issue-December-2001/carter2a.html (accessed: 30.08.06).

Cartwright, H. (2001) *Change in Store? An investigation into the impact of the book superstore environment on use, perceptions and expectations of the public library as a space, place and experience*. A study submitted in partial fulfilment of the requirements for the degree of Master of Arts in Librarianship at The University of Sheffield.

Case, D. (2002) *Looking for Information: A Survey of Research on Information Seeking, Needs and Behaviour* (London: Academic Press).

Chambers, A. (2000) 'Save us from populist tyrants', *The Bookseller*, 14 July, 12, http://www.aidanchambers.co.uk/journalism/journalism1.htm (accessed: 07.01.07).

Childers, T. (1972) 'Managing the Quality of Reference/Information Service', *Library Quarterly*, **42**, 212–217.

Chowdhury, G.G. and Chowdhury, S. (2001) *Information Sources and Searching on the World Wide Web* (London: Library Association Publishing).

Choy, F.C. (2007) 'Libraries and librarians – what next?', *Library Management*, **28**(3), 112–124.

CILIP News (2006) 'The All-Party Parliamentary Group on Libraries and Information Management', 14 June, http://www.cilip.org.uk/aboutcilip/newsandpressreleases/archive2006/news060614a.htm (accessed: 22.02.07).

Clarkson, J. (2006) 'The lost peoples of outer Britain', *Sunday Times*, 2 April. http://www.timesonline.co.uk/tol/comment/columnists/jeremy_clarkson/article701019.ece (accessed: 28.08.07).

Clee, N. (2005) 'The book business', *New Statesman*, 18 July, http://www.newstatesman.com/200507180047 (accessed: 12.07.06).

Coates, T. (2004) *Who's in Charge?* http://www.rwevans.co.uk/libri/downloads.htm (accessed: 23.08.06).

Coe, J. (2004) *The Closed Circle* (New York: Viking).

Cole, N. and Usherwood, B. (1996) 'Library Stock Management: Policies, statements,and philosophies', *Public Library Journal*, **11**(5), 121–125.

Coleman, P. (1987) *Broadcasting and the Media: Report of the Director of Libraries and Information Services on the relationship between libraries and information services and broadcasting.* Sheffield City Council Libraries and Information Sub-Committee, 16 July.

Collini, S. (2006) *Absent Minds. Intellectuals in Britain* (Oxford: Oxford University Press).

Collins, M. (2004) 'White trash, the only people left to insult', *Sunday Times*, 18 July, http://www.kiwirugby.net/krforums/mobile/thread.php?topic_id=7062 (accessed: 10.11.04).

Collins, M. (2004a) *The Likes of Us. A Biography of the White Working Class* (London: Granta).

Comedia (1993) *Borrowed Time: The Future of Public Libraries in the UK* (Bourne Green: Comedia).

Conway, P (2001). 'Foreword' to Train, B. and Elkin, J., *Branching Out. Overview of Evaluation Findings* (Centre for Information Research: University of Central England).

Cooke, A. (2001) *A Guide to Finding Quality Information on the Internet: Selection and Evaluation Strategies*, 2nd Edition (London: Library Association Publishing).

Cookman, N. and Streatfield, D. (2001) 'Volunteers are *en vogue*', *Library Association Record*, **103**(2), February, 108.

Cooper, Y. (2004) 'Left out or left behind', *The Guardian*, 22 March, http://society.guardian.co.uk/socialexclusion/comment/0,11499,1174898,00.html (accessed: 17.01.07).

Coughlan, R.M. (2001) *An Investigation into the Non-Borrowing Use of Public Library Services*, MA Librarianship Dissertation, Sheffield, Sheffield University Department of Information Studies.

Coveney, M. (2005) 'Critical clowns', *Prospect*, November, http://www.prospect-magazine.co.uk/article_details.php?id=7086 (accessed: 01.01.07).

Cowen, T. (2000) *In Praise of Commercial Culture* (Boston, MA: Harvard University Press).

Crabtree, J. (2004) 'The revolution that started in a library', *New Statesman*, 27 September, http://www.newstatesman.com/200409270026 (accessed: 01.08.07).

Cram, J. (1996) *Engaged in Triumphant Retreat? Public Libraries and the Social Impact of the Internet*, http://www.alia.org.au/~jcram/engaged_in_triumphant. html (accessed: 09.04.06).

Critical reading (1994) Brochure for course held at Library Association Headquarters, 17 May.

Crossland, A. (1956) *The Future of Socialism* (London: Jonathan Cape).

Cruise, H. (2006) *Chavs and the Working Class*, http://blogs.warwick.ac.uk/ hollycruise/daily/120406/ (accessed: 03.01.07).

Dainton, F.S. (1977) 'Presidential address. Modern demand for professionalism', *Library Association Record*, **79**(11), 623.

Damiani, M. (1999) *Public Libraries Stock Management Policies (Formal and Informal) and Patterns of Choice in Stock Selection Occurring in Work Situations*. MA, The University of Sheffield.

Danahar, P. (2006) *How TV News is Distorting India's Media*, http://news.bbc. co.uk/1/hi/world/south_asia/5187242.stm (accessed: 01.02.07).

D'Angelo, E. (2006) *Barbarians at the Gates of the Public Library:How Postmodern Consumer Capitalism Threatens Democracy, Civil Education and the Public Good*, http://www.blackcrow.us/ (accessed: 19. 07.06).

Das, A.K. and Lal, B. (2006) Information literacy and public libraries in India, in *Information Literacy and Public Libraries in India*. Delhi Public Library, India, http://eprints.rclis.org/archive/00005697/01/Information_Literacy_Public_ Libraries_India.pdf (accessed: 13.02.07).

Davies, S., Coles, H., Olczak, M., Pike, C. and Wilson, C. (2004) *The Benefits from Competition: Some Illustrative UK Cases*. DTI Economics Paper No. 9, Centre for Competition Policy, University of East Anglia, http://www.berr.gov.uk/files/ file13299.pdf (accessed: 01.08.07).

Davis, G. (2005) 'Public libraries and a decade of democracy: rebirth or rethink?', *Library Review*, **44**(7), 40–44.

Day, M.J. (1978) *The Selection and Use of Serious Fiction in a Public Library System*, MA in Librarianship Dissertation, The University of Sheffield.

Dayton and Montgomery County Public Library (undated) *Library Materials Selection Policy of the Dayton and Montgomery County Public Library*, http:// www.dayton.lib.oh.us/www/selection/matsel.html#Adult (accessed: 01.10.06).

Define Research and Insight (2006) *MLA DCMS Laser Foundation A Research Study of 14–35 year olds for the Future Development of Public Libraries*, http://www. mla.gov.uk/resources/assets//R/Research_study_of_14_35_year_olds_for_the_ future_development_of_public_libraries_9841.pdf (accessed: 04.01.07).

Delingpole, J. (2006) *What are Museums For?* The Charles Douglas-Home Memorial Trust Award 2005, http://www.timesonline.co.uk/article/0,,6-2090955_1,00.html (accessed: 14.04.06).

Department for Culture Media and Sport (1998) *'New Library: The People's Network' The Government's Response* (Cm3887).

Department for Culture, Media and Sport (2001) *Culture and Creativity: The Next Ten Years*, http://www.culture.gov.uk/NR/rdonlyres/E3C16C65-D10B-4CF6-

BB78-BA449D0AEC04/0/Culture_creative_next10.pdf (accessed: 07.03.07).

Department for Culture, Media and Sport (2003) *Framework for the Future: Libraries, Learning and Information in the Next Decade* (London: Department of Culture, Media and Sport).

Department for Education and Employment (1998) *The Learning Age: A Renaissance for a New Britain* http://www.leeds.ac.uk/educol/documents/000000654.htm (accessed: 07.11.06).

Department of National Heritage (1997) *Reading the Future: A Review of Public Libraries in England* (London: Department of National Heritage).

Desjardins, J. (2006) 'Public libraries in France – Policies', Paper to Developing public libraries – National strategies in Europe, London, April, http://www.goethe.de/mmo/priv/1450743-STANDARD.pdf (accessed: 01.08.07).

Devereux, M.W. (1972) 'Libraries in working class areas', *Assistant Librarian*, **65**(11), 170–173.

Dixon, R. (2007) 'The fact is, it's rubbish', *The Times*, 2 March, 5.

Dolan, J. (2006) 'We also love Books', *The Bookseller*, 6 October, 22.

Dolan, J. (2007) *A Blueprint for Excellence Public Libraries 2008–2011. Connecting People to Knowledge and Inspiration*, Museums Libraries Archives Partnership, http://www.mla.gov.uk/resources/assets/B/blueprint_11126.pdf (accessed: 02.04.07).

Donovan, T. (2006) Contribution to 'Are our libraries being neglected?' *Times Online*, 23 March, http://www.timesonline.co.uk/article/0,,564-2099855,00.html (accessed: 05.04.06).

Dorset County Council (2006) Collection Development Policy 2006, http://www.dorsetforyou.com/index.jsp?articleid=160240 (accessed: 05.10.06).

Dorset County Council (2006a) Reader Development Policy, http://www.dorsetforyou.com/index.jsp?articleid=160378 (accessed: 05.10.06).

Dowlin, K.E. and Shapiro, E. (1996) 'The centrality of communities to the future of major public libraries', *Daedalus*, Fall, http://findarticles.com/p/articles/mi_qa3671/is_199610/ai_n8740172/pg_6 (accessed: 06.03.07).

Drummond, J. (2000) *Tainted by Experience: A Life in the Arts* (London: Faber & Faber).

Duncan, A. (2006) 'Maximising public value in the "now" media world', The New Statesman Media Lecture, Supplement to *New Statesman*, 26 June.

Dunn, J. (2005) 'Tigers and tall tales: questions of literary faith in this year's Man Booker winner', *The Oxonian Review of Books*, Hilary 4(2), http://www.oxonianreview.org/issues/2-2/2-2-1.htm (accessed: 29.09.06).

Dyckhoff, T. (2004) 'New readers should start here', *The Times*, 10 August, http://www.newsint-archive.co.uk/pages/free.asp (available via subscription).

Eagleton, T. (2000) *The Idea of Culture* (Oxford: Blackwell).

Egeland, L. (undated) 'The Libraries – Public education and learning. An historic overview of the history of Norwegian libraries as a source of learning', http://www.abm-utvikling.no/om/engelsk/articles/Libraries_education.pdf (accessed: 25.10.06).

Elkin, J. (1996) 'The role of the children's library', in Elkin, J. and Lonsdale, R. (eds), *Focus on the Child: Libraries Literacy and Learning* (London: Library Association), 65–97.

Erickson, S.J. (2000) *Library Design Issues in the Writings of Architects and Librarians*, a Master's paper submitted to the faculty of the School of Information and Library Science, University of North Carolina at Chapel Hill in partial fulfilment of the requirements for the degree of Master of Science in Library Science, http://ils.unc.edu/MSpapers/2581.pdf (accessed: 08.11.06).

Etzioni, A. (1995) *The Spirit of Community. Rights Responsibilities and the Communitarian Agenda* (London: Fontana Press).

Evans, H. (2005) *A Point of View: Good Night, and Good Luck*, http://news.bbc.co.uk/1/hi/magazine/4343006.stm (accessed: 05.08.06).

Evans, M. (2001) 'The economy of the imagination', The *New Statesman* Arts Lecture, 27 June, http://www.resource.gov.uk/information/policy/newstat01.asp (accessed: 03.12.01).

Eyre, G. (1996) 'Promoting libraries and literature for young people', in Elkin, J. and Lonsdale, R. (eds), *Focus on the Child: Libraries Literacy and Learning* (London: Library Association), 174–192.

Ezard. J. (2006) 'Writer rues library changes', *The Guardian*, 11 September, http://books.guardian.co.uk/news/articles/0,,1869583,00.html (accessed: 02.04.07).

Farnham, D. and Horton, S. (1996) *Managing the New Public Services* (Basingstoke: Macmillan).

Fernández-Armesto, F. (2006) 'Opinion', *Times Higher Education Supplement*, 4 August, 13.

Finks, L.W. (1989) 'Values without shame', *American Libraries*, **20**(4), 352–56.

Fitch, L. and Warner, J. (1997) *Dividends: The Value of Public Libraries in Canada*, Toronto Book and Periodical Council, http://www.cla.ca/divisions/capl/Dividends.pdf (accessed: 13.02.07).

Florida, R. (2002) *The Rise of the Creative Class: And how it's Transforming Work, Leisure, Community and Everyday Life* (London: Basic Books).

Fourth International Conference on the Book (2006) Brochure, http://b06.cgpublisher.com/scope.html (accessed: 05.10.06).

Fox, C. (2006) Speech to Orange Prize Libraries' Seminar, http://www.orangeprize.co.uk/opf/news.php4?newsid=13 (accessed: 12.02.07).

Fox, H. (2005) *An Investigation into Political and Professional Attitudes Regarding Commercialised Models of Service Provision in Public Libraries*. A study submitted in partial fulfilment of the requirements for the degree of Master of Arts in Librarianship at The University of Sheffield.

Franzen, J. (1996) 'Why bother' (The *Harper's* Essay), in Franzen, J., *How to be Alone Essays* (London: Fourth Estate).

Frayling, C. (2005) *'The Only Trustworthy Book...' Arts and Public Value*, RSA Lecture 2005.

Frean, A. (2006) 'Plagiarism "is fault of indulgent lecturers"', *The Times*, 18 October, http://www.timesonline.co.uk/tol/life-and-style/education/student/news/articles604093.ece (accessed: 02.08.07).

Front, R. (2006) 'Libraries should be cherished, but the comfortably off are letting the side down', *The Guardian*, 19 July, http://www.guardian.co.uk/commentisfree/story/0,,1823651,00.html (accessed: 19.07.06).

Froud, R. (1994) '1st chance to read... fresh talent', *Public Library Journal*, **9**(1), January/February, 18–20.

Furedi, F. (2004) *Where Have All the Intellectuals Gone?* (London: Continuum).

Fyfe, G. and Ross, M. (1996) 'Decoding the visitor's gaze: Rethinking museum visiting', in S. Macdonald and G. Fyfe (eds), *Theorizing Museums: Representing Identity and Diversity in a Changing World* (London: Blackwell Publishers), 127–152.

Gadelrab, R. (2006) 'Readers tell libraries to fill shelf gaps', *Camden New Journal*, 15 December, http://www.thecnj.co.uk/camden/120706/news120706_23.html (accessed: 15.12.06).

Garceau, O. (1949) *The Public Library in the Political Process: A Report of the Public Library Inquiry* (New York: Columbia University Press).

Garrod, P. (2003) 'Which way now? The future of UK public libraries', *Ariadne*, 35, April, http://www.ariadne.ac.uk/issue35/public-libraries/ (accessed: 29.09.06).

Gascoigne, L. (2000) 'Mumbo-dumbo: cleverness and stupidity in conceptual art', in Mosley, I. (ed.), *Dumbing Down: Culture, Politics and the Mass Media* (Thorverton: Academic), 191–196.

Gibson, J. (1999) 'Fast food TV threatens quality', *The Guardian*, 25 October, 3.

Gibson, O. (2005) 'Tusa attacks "Blue Peter" BBC arts programmes', *The Guardian*, 18 April, http://arts.guardian.co.uk/news/story/0,11711,1462388,00. html (accessed: 11.03.07).

Gladwell, M. (2002) *The Tipping Point: How Little Things Can Make a Big Difference* (London: Abacus).

Glaister, D. (1997) 'Laureate goes off message with throwaway lines', *The Guardian*, 16 October, 1.

Glenn, I. (2004) *The Creativity of Reading Fiction: An Exploration of the Creative Processes and Responses of Fiction Readers*. A study submitted in partial fulfilment of the requirements for the Degree of Master of Arts in librarianship at The University of Sheffield.

Goodman, G. (2002) 'Beware – the ides that march', *British Journalism Review*, **13**(1), 3–6.

Gorb, R. (2004) 'Final curtain falls at the university of the ghetto', *Camden New Journal*, http://www.camdennewjournal.co.uk/120904/f120904_03.htm (accessed: 24.08.06).

Gordon, R.S. (2006) *The Nextgen Librarian's Survival Guide* (Medford, NJ: Information Today, Inc.).

Gorman, M. (2000) *Our Enduring Values: Librarianship in the 21st Century* (Chicago, IL: American Library Association).

Gorman, M. (2002) *The Value and Values of Libraries*. A talk given at the 'Celebration of Libraries', Sheldonian Theatre, Oxford, 20 September, http://mg.csufresno. edu/papers/Value_and_Values_of_Libraries.pdf (accessed: 01.08.07).

Gorman, M. (2006) 'ALA President's Message: "More on Library Education"', *American Libraries*, 5 May.

Goulding, A. (2006) *Public Libraries in the 21st Century. Defining Services and Debating the Future* (Aldershot: Ashgate).

Grade, M. (1999) Comment made during an *Off the Shelf* literature event in Sheffield on Wednesday 20 October, 1999.

Grayling, A.C. (2000) 'The last word on reading', *The Guardian*, 22 July, 12.

Grayling, A.C. (2002) 'A question of discrimination', *The Guardian*, 13 July, http://books.guardian.co.uk/departments/artsandentertainment/story/0,6000,754182,00.html (accessed: 29.09.06).

Grayling, A.C. (2006) 'What's the point of philosophy? (Discuss)', *The Independent*, 17 February, 8–9.

Grayling, A.C. (2006a) 'The equality equation', *Catalyst*, November/December, 4–6.

Gross, R.A. and Borgman, C.L. (1995) 'The incredible vanishing library', *American Libraries*, **26**(10), October, 900–904.

Habermas, J. (1991) *New Conservatism: Cultural Criticism and the Historians' Debate* (Cambridge, MA: Polity Press).

Hafner, A.W. (1993) 'An overview: Complexity, diversity, and the management of modern libraries', in Hafner, A.W., *Democracy and the Public Library: Essays on Fundamental Issues* (Contribution in Librarianship and Information Science Number 78) (Westport, CT: Greenwood Publishing Group).

Hallam, G. and Partridge, P. (2005) *Great Expectations? Developing a Profile of the 21st Century Library and Information Student: A Queensland University of Technology case study*. Paper to World Library and Information Congress, 71st IFLA General Conference and Council, http://www.ifla.org/IV/ifla71/papers/047e-Hallam_Partridge.pdf (accessed: 06.02.07).

Hari, J. (2004) 'Who are you to laugh at chavs?', *The Independent*, 5 November, 41.

Harris, J. (2006) 'Bottom of the class', *The Guardian*, 11 April, http://www.guardian.co.uk/britain/article/0,,1751272,00.html (accessed: 03.01.07).

Harris, M. (1973) 'The purpose of the American public library', *Library Journal*, 15 September, 2509–14.

Haugen, R. (2006) 'The Library of the Molde Labour Association in 1910: Enlightenment and Social Control in a Norwegian Workers', *Library History*, **22**(2), July, 117–122.

Hemsley, K. (2003) *The Booker: Prized in Public Libraries? An Investigation into the Attitudes of Public Librarians Towards the Man Booker Prize for Fiction*. A study submitted in partial fulfilment of the requirements for the degree of Master of Arts in Librarianship at The University of Sheffield.

Henderson, R. (2006) *Why PSB Matters*, http://www.transdiffusion.org/emc/thirdprogramme/whypsb.php (accessed: 08.11.06).

Herman, D. (2003) 'Thought crime', *Guardian Unlimited*, http://arts.guardian.co.uk/features/story/0,11710,1075282,00.html (accessed: 22.10.06).

Hernon, P. and McClure, C. (1987) *Unobtrusive Testing and Library Reference Services* (Norwood, NJ: Ablex).

Heywood, S. (2006) 'Re: Future of multi media in libraries', E-mail sent 11 July 2006 11:49 to: lis-pub-libs@jiscmail.ac.uk.

Hirsch, E.D. Jr. (2002) *The New Dictionary of Cultural Literacy*, Third Edition http://www.bartleby.com/59/3.html (accessed: 01.08.07).

Hockin, C. (2004) Letter to *The Times*, 10 January, http://www.timesonline.co.uk/tol/comment/debate/letters/article1102176.ece (accessed: 28.08.07).

Hoggart, R. (1988) *A Local Habitation (Life and Times, Vol. 1 1918–40)* (London: Chatto & Windus).

Hoggart, R. (1995) *The Way We Live Now. Dilemmas in Contemporary Culture* (London: Chatto & Windus).

Hoggart, R. (1997) 'Head to head: Shhh ... page rage', *The Guardian*, 22 February, 7.

Hoggart, R. (1998) 'Critical literacy and critical reading', in Cox, B. (ed.), *Literacy is Not Enough* (Manchester: Manchester University Press), 56–71.

Holden, J. (2004) *Capturing Cultural Value. How Culture Has Become a Tool of Government Policy* (London: Demos).

Holden, J. (2004a) *Creative Reading*, http://www.demos.co.uk/media/pressreleases/ creativereading (accessed: 15.09.06).

Horner, L. and Bevan, S. (2006) *Public Value*. Presentation given to the Arts and Humanities Research Council Impact Seminar, 15 March 2006. http://www. ahrc.ac.uk/images/4_97703.ppt#256,1, Public Value Arts and Humanities Research Council – 15 March 2006. Louise Horner and Stephen Bevan (accessed 06.08.07).

Hughes, B. (2007) 'I used to be beaten up for reading', *The Independent*, Education, 8 March, 14.

Hughes, R. (1995) 'Take this revolution...', *Time* Special Issue Spring, 70–71.

Humphrey, H.H. (1997) The remark is quoted on many internet quotations sites and has been attributed to various speeches given by Humphrey in early November 1977. See also History of Democratic Party at http://www.arkdems. org/HistoryofDemocraticParty.aspx (accessed: 24.02.07).

Hutton Inquiry (2004) Report of the Inquiry into the Circumstances Surrounding the Death of Dr David Kelly C.M.G. by Lord Hutton, http://www.the-hutton-inquiry. org.uk/content/report/index.htm (accessed: 25.09.06).

Hutton, K. (1990) *A Right to Know or a Right to be Let Alone? A Survey of Privacy and the British Press with Particular Reference to the Coverage of the Hillsborough Disaster, 15 April 1989*. A study submitted in partial fulfilment of the requirements for the degree of Master of Arts in Librarianship at The University of Sheffield.

Hyams, E. (2005) 'Updating the eternal', *Library & Information Update*, 4(6), 18–19.

IFLANET (undated) *Quotations About Libraries and Librarians: Subject List*, http:// www.ifla.org/I/humour/subj.htm (accessed: 09.03.07).

Indergaard, L.H. (2005) *Eenie, Meenie, Miney, Mo. Overview of Norwegian Public Libraries and their Services to Children and Young Adults – And Some Challenges for the Future*. Paper to World Library and Information Congress: 71st IFLA General Conference and Council, http://www.ifla.org/IV/ifla71/papers/130e-Indergaard.pdf (accessed: 04.02.07).

Insight Research (1998) *Lending Libraries* (London: Insight Research).

Isohella, A.R. (2002) 'Trash TV arrives in Finland', *Helsingin Sanomat*, 9 April, http:// www2.hs.fi/english/archive/news.asp?id=20020409IE12 (accessed: 01.02.07).

Issak, A. (2000) *Public Libraries in Africa. A Report and Annotated Bibliography*, Oxford International Network for the Availability of Scientific Publications (INASP), http://www.inasp.info/ldp/libraries/PublicLibrariesInAfrica.pdf (accessed: 02.02.07).

Ivan-Zadeh, L. (2006) 'Banking on Ballard', *Metro*, 18 September, 29.

Jacobson, H. (2004) 'Seeing is disbelieving', *The Independent Arts & Books Review*, 19 November, 2–6.

Jacobson, H. (2005) 'What are libraries for? Tramps, filth and erudition – not soul-destroying detritus', *The Independent*, 22 October, 42.

Jacobson, H. (2007) '*Big Brother* encourages us to embrace a condition far more worrying than racism', *The Independent*, 20 January, 41.

Jacobson, H. (2007a) 'Imagine what Charles Dickens would have done with a character like Jade Goody, *The Independent*, 27 January, 43.

Jatkevicius, J. (2003) 'When "good" books go "bad": opportunities for progressive collection management in public libraries', *Public Library Quarterly*, **22**(4), 31–40.

Jenkins, S. (1998) 'Books do furnish a mind', *The Times*, 22 April, 8.

Jennings, B. and Sear, L. (1986) 'How readers select fiction – a survey in Kent', *Public Library Journal*, **1**(4), Sept/Oct, 43–47.

Jones, B.C. (2004) 'Whose library is it, anyway?' *The Providence Phoenix* http://www.as220.org/stink/weblog/mulch/library.writeback (accessed: 13.02.07).

Jones, J. (1990) 'Introduction' to Simon, B. (ed.), *The Search for Enlightenment: The Working Class and Adult Education in The Twentieth Century* (London: Lawrence & Wishart).

Jordan, P. (1972) 'Social class, race relations and the public library', *Assistant Librarian*, **65**(3), 38–41.

Joseph, J. (2006) 'Last Night's TV', *The Times*, 30 August, 27.

Jowell, T. (2004) Speech to BFI/UKFC/C4 Media Literacy Seminar. Press Notice London Department for Culture, Media and Sport, http://www.culture.gov. uk/global/press_notices/archive_2004/dcms_Jan_2004.htm?month=Januar y&properties=archive_2004%2C%2Fglobal%2Fpress_notices%2Farchive_ 2004%2F%2C (accessed: 22.03.04).

Jowell, T. (2004a) *Government and the Value of Culture*. Department for Culture Media and Sport, http://www.culture.gov.uk/NR/rdonlyres/DE2ECA49-7F3D-46BF-9D11-A3AD80BF54D6/0/valueofculture.pdf (accessed: 07.08.06).

Karim, K.H. (2001) 'Cyber-utopia and the myth of paradise: using Jacques Ellul's work on propaganda to analyze information society rhetoric', *Information, Communication and Society*, **4**(1), 113–134.

Katz, M.L. (1982) 'Critical literacy: A conception of education as a moral right and a social ideal', in Everhart, R. (ed.), *The Public School Monopoly: A Critical Analysis of Education and the State in American Society* (Cambridge, MA: Balinger Publishing Co.).

Katz, W.A. (1980) *Collection Development: The Selection of Materials for Libraries* (New York: Holt).

Keeley, G. (2006) 'Turning rubbish into a television goldmine', *The Times*, 23 May, 59.

Keene, M. (2005) 'Sell off libraries', Letter to *Daily Telegraph*, http://www.telegraph. co.uk/opinion/main.jhtml;jsessionid=5TQTZAQ1GFTRJQFIQMFCFF4AVCBQ YIV0?xml=/opinion/2005/06/07/dt0701.xml#head5 (accessed: 16.04.06).

'Keepers of the Flame or Tuners of the Faucet?' (2002), http://www.geocities.com/ onelibrarian.geo/keepers.html (accessed: 27.08.06).

Kelly, M.S. (2003) 'Revisiting C.H. Milam's "What libraries learned from the war and rediscovering the library faith"', *Libraries & Culture*, **38**(4), 378–388.

Kendall, M. (1998) 'The new public library and lifelong learning', *Learning Resources Journal*, **14**(3), 52–57.

Kenton County Public Library (2005) Collection Development Policy, http://www.kenton.lib.ky.us/aboutus/policies/colldev.htm (accessed: 01.08.07).

Kerevan, G. (2004) 'Despite Google we still need good libraries', *The Scotsman*, 16 December, http://news.scotsman.com/opinion.cfm?id=1434442004 (accessed: 01.08.07).

Kinnell, M. (ed.) (1991) *Managing Fiction in Libraries* (London: Library Association).

Kingrey, K.P. (2002) 'Concepts of information seeking and their presence in the practical library literature', *Library Philosophy and Practice*, **4**(2), 1–14.

Kleiman, A.M. (1995) 'The ageing agenda', *Library Journal*, 15 April, **120**(7), 32–35.

Kleveland, A. (2005) *The Library and the Cultural Political Challenges in a Digital Age*. Paper to World Library and Information Congress: 71st IFLA General Conference and Council, http://www.ifla.org/IV/ifla71/papers/193e-Kleveland.pdf (accessed: 04.02.07).

Knight, I. (2006) 'Don't laugh, this is ugly', *Sunday Times News Review*, 2 April, 4.

Knowsley Library Service Department of Leisure and Community Services (2004) Stock Selection, http://www.knowsley.gov.uk/.../resources/181043/stock_selection.pdf (accessed: 01.10.06).

Kolodziejska, J. (1971) *The Role of Libraries in Shaping the Interests of Readers*. Paper given at 1971 IFLA Library Theory and Research Liverpool (Paper from author).

Kranich, N. (2002) *Libraries: The Information Commons of Civil Society*, http://dlc.dlib.indiana.edu/archive/00000975/00/adingman_Libraries,_Civil_Society_and_the_public_sphere.pdf (accessed: 07.11.06).

Labdon, P. (1991) 'Acquiring adult fiction', in Kinnell, M. (ed.), *Managing Fiction in Libraries* (London: Library Association).

Labour Party (1997) *Create the Future. A Strategy for Cultural Policy, Arts and the Creative Economy* (London: Labour Party).

Lammy, D. (2005) Public Library Authorities Conference Speech – 18 October, http://www.davidlammy.co.uk/da/24531 (accessed: 09.04.06).

Lammy, D. (2006) *An Aspirational Culture*, Speech to the Child Poverty Action Group 18 May, http://www.davidlammy.co.uk/da/36300 (accessed: 01.08.07).

Lammy, D. (2007) in 'Public libraries: a round table discussion', Smith Institute Supplement to *New Statesman*, 12 March, http://www.newstatesman.com/pdf/publiclibraries.pdf (accessed: 19.03.07).

Lanier, J. (2000) 'Agents of alienation. Commercial attempts to exploit information technology threaten the very essence of what it is to be human', in Mosley, I. (ed.), *Dumbing Down: Culture, Politics and the Mass Media* (Thorverton: Academic), 277–286.

LASER (2004) *Public Libraries: A Vision of the Public Library Service in 2015*, http://www.futuresgroup.org.uk/documents/the%20public%20library%20service%20in%202015.doc. (accessed: 04.08.06).

Lawrence Public Library (2001) *Material Selection and Collection Development Policy*, http://www.lawrence.lib.ks.us/policies/materials.html#criteria (accessed: 01.10.06).

Leading Modern Public Libraries (2005) Course reader: Heads of Service and Senior Managers. FPM unpublished

Lebrecht live (2005) 'Should elitism be regarded as a sin?', http://www.bbc.co.uk/radio3/lebrechtlive/pip/j6gz4/ (accessed: 19.03.07).

Leigh, R.D. (1950) *The Public Library in the United States. The General Report of the Public Library Inquiry* (New York: Columbia University Press).

Levy, D. (2000) 'Digital libraries and the problem of purpose', *D-Lib Magazine*, January, **6**(1), http://www.dlib.org/dlib/january00/01levy.html (accessed: 17.04.06).

Library + Information Update (2007) 'Opinion. Are public libraries dumbing down?' **6**(4), 16–19.

Library Association (2001) 'Government. Culture and creativity the next ten years', Comments from The Library Association, http://www.la-hq.org.uk/directory/prof_issues/cac.html (accessed: 02.04.07).

Library Board of Western Australia (1966) *Book Provision and Book Selection: Policy and Practice* (Perth: Library Board of Western Australia).

Libraries for Life for Londoners (undated) *About LLL*, http://www.librarylondon.org/about.htm (accessed: 05.08.06).

Library of Congress (1996) *A Periodic Report from The National Digital Library Program*, http://www.loc.gov/ndl/jan-feb.html (accessed: 27.10.06).

Linley, R. and Usherwood, B. (1998) *New Measures for the New Library. A Social Audit of Public Libraries*. BLRIC Report 89.

Lister, S. (2002) 'Libraries told to turn over a new leaf for survival', *The Times*, 17 May, 10.

Long, S.A. (2001) 'Foreword' to McCabe, R.B., *Civic Librarianship. Renewing the Social Mission of the Public Library* (Lanham, Maryland and London: The Scarecrow Press, Inc.).

Lonsdale, R. (2000) 'The role of the children's library in supporting literacy', in Elkin, J. and Kinnell, M. (eds), *A Place for Children: Public Library as a Major Force in Children's Reading* (London: Library Association), 19–32.

MacArthur, J.R. (2003) quoted in Missouri State Library *News Line*, November/December, 14, http://www.sos.mo.gov/library/newsline/November-December 2003.pdf (accessed: 08.03.07).

Mackelvie, M.J. (1982) *The Treatment of the Brixton Riots in a Selection of British Newspapers, 11/4/81-18/4/81*. A study submitted in partial fulfilment of the requirements for the degree of Master of Arts in Librarianship at The University of Sheffield.

MacKenzie, J. (2002) 'The quiet storm', *The Big Issue*, 501, 12–18 August, 10–11.

Madiman, S.A. and Parekh, H.S. (1978) 'Profile of a village library: Agashi Sarvajanik Vachanalaya', *Timeless Fellowship*, Vol. **12**, 60–65.

Mäkinen, I. (2001) 'The golden age of Finnish public libraries', in Mäkinen, I. (ed.), *Finnish Public libraries in the 20ᵗʰ Century* (Tampere: Tampere University Press), 116–150, http://www.uta.fi/kirjasto/oppimiskeskus/verkkoaineisto/inf/makinen.pdf (accessed: 09.04.07).

Managing Information (2005) 'New Library Located in Tesco Superstore', Managing Information [Online], 26 July, http://www.managinginformation.com/news/content_show_full.php?id=4091 (accessed: 02.09.06).

Managing Information News (2006) 'Libraries are Key to Renewal Says Minister', 14 June, http://www.managinginformation.com/news/content_show_full.php?id=4975 (accessed: 22.02.07).

Mandela, N. (2002) in an interview on the *Oprah Winfrey Show*, 9 May, 2002, http://www.globalvolunteers.org/LINK/link_29.htm#news (accessed: 10.11.04).

Martin, L. (2006) 'Cracker creator blasts "chav" TV', *The Observer*, 27 August, 5.

Martin, L.A. (1983) 'The public library: middle-age crisis or old age?', The 1982 Bowker Memorial Lecture, *Library Journal*, 1 January, 17–22.

Martin, R.S. (2001) *Returning to the Center: Libraries, Knowledge and Education*, Colorado Library Association, 29 October, 2001, http://www.imls.gov/whatsnew/current/sp102901.htm (accessed: 22.08.05).

Matassaro, F. (1998) *Beyond Book Issues: The Social Potential of Library Projects* (London: Comedia).

Matarasso, F. (2000) 'An equal chance to know', *Public Library Journal*, **15**(2), 35–8.

Matarasso, F. (2000a) 'The meaning of leadership in a cultural democracy: Rethinking public library values', *Logos*, **11**(1), 39–44.

McArthur, M. and Nicholson, K. (2005) 'The customer care challenge', *Public Library Journal*, **20**(2), 2–4.

McCabe, R.B. (2001) *Civic Librarianship. Renewing the Social Mission of the Public Library* (Lanham, Maryland and London: The Scarecrow Press, Inc.).

McClarence, S. (2006) Insight in programme for Halle Concert at Sheffield City Hall, 6 October, 13–14.

McCook, K. de la Peña (2001) 'Poverty, democracy and public libraries', in Kranich, N. (ed.), *Libraries and Democracy: The Cornerstones of Liberty* (Chicago, IL: American Library Association), 28–46.

McCrum, R. (1992) 'Quality not quantity, will always win out', *The Observer*, 22 August, http://observer.guardian.co.uk/review/story/0,6903,1288046,00.html (accessed: 09.04.07).

McCrum, R. (2000) in McCrum, R. and Brown, C., 'Prospect Debate. Is too much irony damaging public life?', *Prospect*, July, 18–22.

McDonald, L. (2006) Letter to *Observer*, http://observer.guardian.co.uk/review/story/0,,1799888,00.html (accessed: 04.08.06).

Mchombu, K. and Cadbury, N. (2006) *Libraries, Literacy and Poverty Reduction: A Key to African Development* (London: Book Aid International), http://www.bookaid.org/resources/downloads/Libraries_Literacy_Poverty_Reduction.pdf (accessed: 02.02.07).

McKearney, M. (2004) quoted in http://www.demos.co.uk/media/pressreleases/creativereading (accessed: 15.09.06).

McKenzie, J. (2000) 'When the book? When the Net?', *From Now On: The Educational Technology Journal*, **9**(7), March, http://fno.org/mar2000/whenbook.html (accessed: 20.02.07).

Memorial Hall Public Library (2005) *Collection Development Manual 2005 Circulating Collection Selection*, http://www.lawrence.lib.ks.us/policies/materials. html#criteria (accessed: 01.10.06).

Menzies, H. (1997) *The Virtual Library: Kiosk or Community*, http://www.vcn. bc.ca/bcla-ip/globalization/clamenzies.html (accessed: 01.08.07)

Meredith, P. (1961) *Learning, Remembering and Knowing* (London: EUP).

Metcalfe, F. (2006) 'Future of multi media in libraries', E-mail sent: 11 July 2006, 14:38 To: lis-pub-libs@jiscmail.ac.uk.

Methven, M. (2004) 'President's perspective. We have the will – so let's do it', *Information Scotland*, **2**(6) http://www.slainte.org.uk/publications/serials/ infoscot/vol2(6)/vol2(6)article1.html (accessed: 30.08.06).

Middletown Thrall Library (2006) *Rediscovering Literature*, http://www.thrall.org/ redislit.htm (accessed: 05.10.06).

Miliband, D. (2005) *Social Exclusion: The Next Steps Forward* http://www. davidmiliband.info/sarchive/speech05_14.htm (accessed: 15.01.07).

Miller, J. (2001) *Issues Raised by Having Large Corporate Entities (e.g. AOL/Time Warner) as Providers of Information Resources*, http://www.personal.kent.edu/ ~jimiller/briefing.html (accessed: 08.11.06).

Miller, J.J. (2007) 'Checked out. A Washington-area library tosses out the classics', *Wall Street Journal*, 3 January, http://www.opinionjournal.com/la/?id=110009472 (accessed: 01.08.07)

MLA (2004) *Visitors to Museums and Galleries 2004*, research study conducted for the Museums Libraries and Archives Council by MORI, http:// www.mla.gov.uk/resources/assets//M/mori_visitors_v2_doc_6693.doc (accessed: 09.04.07).

MLA (2006) *Better Stock, Better Libraries: Transforming Library Stock Procurement*, http://www.mla.gov.uk/resources/assets//B/better_stock_better_libraries_10123. pdf (accessed: 07.03.07).

MLA (2006a) *Library Buildings Survey Final Report*, http://www.mla.gov.uk/ resources/assets//L/librarybuildings_10218.pdf (accessed: 11.03.07).

MLA (2007) Press release. MLA funding strengthens Creative & Cultural Skills initiatives for cultural heritage sector, 16 February, http://www.mla.gov.uk/ webdav/harmonise?Page/@id=82&Section[@stateId_eq_left_hand_root]/@ id=4289&Document/@id=27235&Session/@id=D_koyEkvsy5qrGHt1RDNKB (accessed: 21.03.07).

Moore, S. (1989) 'Ten long years', *New Statesman and Society*, 5 May.

Morrison, B. (1992) 'Nobs versus mobs', *The Independent on Sunday*, 5 July, 25.

Morrison, B. (1994) 'Some books are better than others and there's no snobbery in that', *Independent on Sunday*, 27 March, 20.

Morrison, T. (undated) on http://informatics.buffalo.edu/faculty/ellison/quotes/ libquotesdn.html (accessed: 01.08.07) and many other sites.

Mosey, R. (2003) *Dumbing Down or Wisening Up*, speech given to the Society of Editors Conference, 23 November, http://www.bbc.co.uk/pressoffice/speeches/ stories/rogermosey_editors_conference.shtml (accessed: 02.08.07).

Mosley, I. (2000) (ed.) *Dumbing Down: Culture, Politics and the Mass Media* (Thorverton: Academic).

Mostert, B.J. (2001) 'African public library systems: a literature survey', *LIBRES: Library and Information Science Research Electronic Journal*, **11**(1), March, 31, http://libres.curtin.edu.au/libres11n1/mostert.htm (accessed 04.02.07).

Moura, M.J. (2004) *Public Libraries and Development Planning in Portugal*. Paper to World Library and Information Congress:70th IFLA General Conference and Council, http://www.ifla.org/IV/ifla70/papers/161e-Moura.pdf (accessed: 01.09.06).

Muddiman, D. (1999) *Images of Exclusion: User and Community Perceptions of the Public Library*. Public Library Policy and Social Exclusion Working Papers no. 9. (Leeds: School of Information Management, Leeds Metropolitan University).

Muddiman, D. (1999a) *Working Paper 2 Public Libraries and Social Exclusion: The Historical Legacy*, http://www.seapn.org.uk/workingpapers/vol3wp2.rtf (accessed: 25.10.06).

Mullan, P. (2000) 'Information society: frequently un-asked questions', *Spiked*, http://www.spiked-online.com/Printable/0000000053AA.htm (accessed: 16.10.06).

Murdoch, R. (1989) 'MacTaggart Lecture', Edinburgh Television Festival, September.

Nailer, C. (2002) *National Libraries in a World of Threat*. Paper for presentation at 'Global Knowledge Renaissance', The World Library Summit, April 2002. Paper from author.

Nankivell, B. (2006) Contribution to: 'Future of multi-media in libraries', lis-pub-libs@jiscmail.ac.uk, sent 11 July.

The Network (2007) *Tackling Social Exclusion in Libraries, Museums, Archives and Galleries* http://www.seapn.org.uk/network_menu.html (accessed: 02.08.07).

New, D. (2006) Contribution to: 'Are our libraries being neglected?', *Times Online*, http://www.timesonline.co.uk/article/0,,564-2099855,00.html (accessed: 20.02.07).

Newman, J. (2007) 'Re-mapping the public: public libraries and the public sphere', *Cultural Studies* (forthcoming), http://www.open.ac.uk/socialsciences/ccig/ccigsubset/cciginfopops/pm_newmanremappingthepublic.doc (accessed: 09.03.07).

Nijboer, J. (2006) 'Cultural entrepreneurship in libraries', *New Library World*, **107**(9/10), 434–443.

Nilsson, S. (undated) 'Libraries in a chaotic world', http://www.futurum.polyvalent.se/time.htm (accessed: 09.10.06).

Norris, C. (1997) 'Warning: books change lives', *Library Association Record*, 99, 366.

North East Museums, Libraries and Archives Council (undated) 'A preferred place of learning museums, libraries & archives supporting "skills for life" in the North East', http://www.mlanortheast.org.uk/documents/APreferredPlaceofLearning.pdf (accessed: 21.02.07).

North East Museums, Libraries and Archives Council (2005) *Ladder to Learning and Employment*, http://www.mlanortheast.org.uk/documents/NEMLAC-Ladder toLearningContent_000.pdf (accessed: 08.11.06).

Office of Citizenship (2006) *Library Services for Immigrants. A Report on Current Practices*, http://64.233.183.104/search?q=cache:tp4evGkqoNIJ:www.uscis.gov/graphics/citizenship/Library_Services_Report.pdf+Public+Libraries+immigrant s+education&hl=en&gl=uk&ct=clnk&cd=10 (accessed: 07.11.06).

Oli (2005) Contribution to Adam Smith Institute Blog – State libraries in freefall, http://www.adamsmith.org/blog/index.php/blog/monthly/2005/06/P72/ (accessed: 09.04.06).

Olsen, A. and Andersen, R.R. (undated) *The Public Library – How to Include People with Disabilities*, http://www.of.fylkesbibl.no/ostfyb/tb/eng/The%20public%20 library.pdf (accessed: 16.01.07).

Opening the Book (undated) *Reader Development and Social Inclusion*, http://www. openingthebook.com/otb/page.asp?idno=241 (accessed: 07.01.07).

Opening the Book (2006) Quotes taken from website, http://www.openingthebook. com/otb/welcome.asp?idno=1&textonly=0&f=1 (accessed: 29.09.06).

Orange County Public Library (undated) *Our Materials Selection Policy*, http:// www.ocpl.org/about-policy.asp (accessed 01.10.06).

Owens, L. and Palmer, L.K. (2003) 'Making the news: anarchist counter-public relations on the world wide web', *Critical Studies in Media Communication*, **20**(4), 335–361.

Pachter, M. and Landry, C. (2001) *Culture at the Crossroads. Culture and Cultural Institutions at the Beginning of the 21st Century* (Bournes Green: Comedia).

Parkin, F. (1972) *Class, Inequality and Political Order* (St Albans: Paladin).

Parry, N. (2003) *Small Public Libraries Can Serve Big*, http://www.michaellorenzen. com/eric/public-libraries.html (accessed: 18.05.06).

Pateman, J. (2000) 'Are our libraries still a class act?', *Public Library Journal*, **15**(3), 81–82.

Pateman, J. (2004) *Public Libraries and the Working Classes ISC 20*, http://libr. org/isc/articles/20-Pateman-1.html (accessed: 09.03.07).

Pawley, C. (2003) 'Reading versus the Red Bull: Cultural constructions of democracy and the public library in Cold War Wisconsin', in Augst, T. and Wiegand, W. (eds), *Libraries as Agencies of Culture* (Madison, WI.: University of Wisconsin Press).

Phillips, A. (2005) *What, if Anything, Distinguishes 'A Good Read' from 'Literature'? An Investigation into the Roles of 'Quality' and Enjoyment in Reading*. A study submitted in partial fulfilment of the requirements for the degree of Master of Arts in Librarianship at The University of Sheffield.

Philo, G. and Miller, D. (2000) *Cultural Compliance and Critical Media Studies*, http://www.gla.ac.uk/departments/sociology/units/media/cultural.htm (accessed: 19.09.06).

PKF (2005) *Public Libraries: Efficiency and Stock Supply Chain Review Executive Summary* (London: PKF), http://www.mla.gov.uk/resources/assets//F/fff_ efficiency_01execsum_8724.pdf (accessed: 07.03.07).

Poncé, F. (2004) *Public Libraries Section Country Report: France 2003–2004*, http://www.ifla.org/VII/s8/annual/cr03-fr.htm (accessed: 13.02.07).

Postman, N. (1986) *Amusing Ourselves to Death: Public Discourse in the Age of Show Business* (London: Heinemann).

Potter, D. (1994) 'The James MacTaggart Memorial Lecture', Edinburgh Film Festival, 1993, in Potter, D. (1994) *Seeing the Blossom: Two Interviews and a Lecture by Dennis Potter* (London: Faber and Faber), 31–56.

Pratchett, T. (1995) *Johnny and the Dead* (London: Corgi).

Prentaki, E. (2002) *The Public Library as a Resource For People With Learning Disabilities: An Examination into the Impact of Staff Attitude Towards Users With Learning Disabilities.* A study submitted in partial fulfilment of the requirements for the degree of Master of Arts in Library and Information Management at The University Of Sheffield.

Prescott, S. (2006?) *Return to Reading: A UK Bookmark*, http://www.libraries.vic. gov.au/downloads/Reader_Development/return_to_reading_a_uk_bookmark_ notes_shirley_prescott.pdf (accessed: 15.08.07).

Prichard, D. (2003) *Many Lives of the Civic Multitasker*, http://www.metwork.co.uk/ Book%20Review%20Libraries%20and%20Learning%20Resource%20Centres. htm (accessed: 31.10.06).

Proctor, R., Usherwood, B. and Sobczyk, G. (1996) *What Do People Do When Their Public Library Service Closes Down?* BLRDD Report 6224.

Proctor, R., Lee, H. and Reilly, R. (1998) *Access to Public Libraries. The Impact of Opening Hours Reductions and Closures 1986–1997*, BLRIC Report 90.

Proctor, R. and Bartle, C. (2002) *Low Achievers Lifelong Learners. An Investigation into the Impact of the Public Library on Educational Disadvantage*, LIC Research Report 117.

Public Agenda (2006) *Long Overdue: A Fresh Look at Public Attitudes about Libraries in the 21st Century*, http://www.publicagenda.org/research/pdfs/long-overdue.pdf (accessed: 18.08.07).

Public Libraries of New Zealand A Strategic Framework 2006 to 2016 (2006) Wellington Local Government New Zealand, LIANZA, National Library of New Zealand.

Pullman, P. (2006) 'A treasure house for Moomins, Biggles and well-thumbed pages', *The Times*, March, 25, http://www.timesonline.co.uk/tol/comment/columnists/ guest_contributors/article695649.ece (accessed: 09.04.07).

PuLLS (2006) General information, http://www.enterfora.com/QuickPlace/pulls/ PageLibraryC12570D70046020F.nsf/h_Toc/d9f998e79bc0ec39c12570ec0037008a/ ?OpenDocument (accessed: 10.11.06).

The Pulman Guidelines (2003) Second edition, http://www.pulmanweb.org/DGMs/ DGM-English-Ver-Feb03.doc (accessed: 17.10.06).

Public Libraries in France – Policies, http://www.goethe.de/mmo/priv/1450747-STANDARD.pdf (accessed: 13.02.07).

Purves, L. (2006) 'Reader, you're a right dimwit', *The Times*, 30 May, 19.

Raber, D. (1997) *Librarianship and Legitimacy. The Ideology of the Public Library Inquiry*, Contributions in Librarianship and Information Science, no. 90 (Westport, CT and London: Greenwood Press).

Radice, A.M. (2006) Remarks for Big Read Launch as delivered at Carnegie Hall, 9 May, http://www.imls.gov/news/speeches/050906.shtm (accessed: 13.08.06).

Ranney, D. (2005) 'Watergate journalist says media losing public's trust', *Lawrence Journal World*, 16 April, http://www2.ljworld.com/news/2005/apr/16/watergate_ journalist_says/ (accessed: 01.02.07).

Reed, S.G. (1994) *Library Volunteers – Worth the Effort! A Program Manager's Guide* (Jefferson, NC: McFarland & Company).

Research Centre for Museums and Galleries (2003) *Measuring the Outcomes and Impact of Learning in Museums, Archives and Libraries.* The Learning Impact Research Project End of Project Paper https://lra.le.ac.uk/bitstream/2381/65/1/LIRP+end+of+project+paper.pdf (accessed: 02.08.07).

Rikowski, R. (2002) The WTO/GATS Agenda for Libraries Talk, prepared for public meeting at Sussex University, 23 May, http://www.ieps.org.uk.cwc.net/rikowski2002a.pdf (accessed: 21.03.07).

Roberts, J. (2006) quoted in MLA Press release. New web resource for library staff working with disabled people, http://www.mla.gov.uk/webdav/harmonise?Page/@id=77&Section[@stateId_eq_left_hand_root]/@id=4289&Document/@id=23638 (accessed: 16.01.07).

Roberts, E. and McIntosh, L. (2004) *Retail Innovation in Public Libraries: What Can NT Libraries Learn from the NZ Experience?* http://alia.org.au/groups/topend/2004.symposium/retail.innovation.html (accessed: 31.08.06).

Roosevelt, T. (1906), 'The man with the muck rake', http://www.quotedb.com/speeches/man-with-the-muck-rake (accessed: 02.08.07).

Rose, J. (2001) *The Intellectual Life of the British Working Classes* (New Haven and London: Yale University Press).

Ross, C. (2006) 'Adult readers', in Ross, C.S., McKechnie, L.E.F. and Rothbauer, P.M., *Reading Matters. What Research Reveals about Reading, Libraries and Community* (Westport, CT: Libraries Unlimited) 133–241.

Roszak, T. (1987) Speaking at the ALA conference, *Library Journal*, **112**(13), 27.

Roszak, T. (1996) 'Dumbing us down … computers in the classroom are not all they're cracked up to be', *New Internationalist*, December, http://findarticles.com/p/articles/mi_m0JQP/is_286/ai_30344264 (accessed: 09.10.06).

Rothbauer, P.M. (2006) 'Young adults and reading', in Ross, C.R., McKechnie, L.E.F. and Rothbauer, P.M., *Reading Matters: What the Research Reveals about Reading, Libraries, and Community* (Westport, CT: Libraries Unlimited), 101–131.

Rotherham Library and Information Service (2004) *Stock Management Policy*, Third edition, http://www.rotherham.gov.uk/NR/rdonlyres/1BBB2873-BB6C-4860-8771-9922719EEBC3/0/Stock_Policy_2004.pdf (accessed: 01.10.06).

Rushton, K. (2006) 'Lammy answers his critics', *The Bookseller*, 4 May, http://www.thebookseller.com/?pid=30&did=19466 (accessed: 20.07.06).

Sagan, C. (1983) *Cosmos* (London: Abacus).

Santayana, G. (1998) *Life of Reason* (Amherst, NY: Prometheus Books).

Schneider, C. (1987) *Children's Television: The Art, The Business and How It Works.* (Chicago, IL: NTC Business Books).

Schwanck, I. (2003) *Finnish Literature Today*, Virtual Finland, http://virtual.finland.fi/netcomm/news/showarticle.asp?intNWSAID=27006 (accessed: 02.02.07).

Scrogham, R.E. (2006) 'The American public library and its fragile future', *New Library World*, **107**(1/2), http://www.highschoollibrarian.com/SJSU/266/readings/scrogham.doc (accessed 22.01.07).

Sebastian, P. (2004) 'Reading rooms', *The Hindu*, 7 November, http://www.hindu.com/lr/2004/11/07/stories/2004110700370600.htm (accessed: 13.02.07).

Self, W. (1997) 'Ticket to the entire known cosmos', *Daily Telegraph*, 1 November, Arts & Books Section, A6.

Sheffield Media Unit (1987) *The Television Programme* (available at the time from Sheffield City Libraries).

Shenk, D. (1997) *Data Smog. Surviving the Information Glut* (San Francisco, CA: Harper).

Sheppard, B. (undated) *The 21st Century Learner*, Washington Institute of Museum and Library Services, http://igmlnet.uohyd.ernet.in:8000/InfoUSA/arts/visual/pub21cl.pdf. (accessed: 27.08.06).

Shera, J.H. (1949) *Foundations of the Public Library: The Origins of the Public Library Movement in New England 1629–1855*, reprint edition (Hamden, CT: Shoestring Press, 1974).

Shera, J.H. (1969) 'The quiet stir of thought or, what the computer cannot do', *Library Journal*, **94**(15), 1 September, 2875–2880.

Shera, J.H. (1983) 'Librarianship and information science', in Machlup, F. and Mansfield, U. *The Study of Information: Interdisciplinary Messages* (New York: John Wiley and Sons).

Shetland Library (2006) *Shetland Library News*, http://www.shetland-library.gov.uk/ (accessed: 11.10.06).

Singapore National Library Board (2005) *Library 2010: Libraries for Life, Knowledge for Success* (Singapore: National Library Board Singapore).

Skodova, A. (2002) *Diversity in Libraries' Project Fighting Against Racism*, http://www.radio.cz/en/article/35873 (accessed: 16.01.07).

Skot-Hansen, D. (2002) 'The public library in the service of civic society', *Scandinavian Public Library Journal*, **35**(3), http://www.splq.info/issues/vol35_3/05.htm (accessed 11.03.07).

Skot-Hansen, D. (2002a) 'The public library between integration and cultural diversity', *Scandinavian Public Library Journal*, **35**(1), http://www.splq.info/issues/vol35_1/06.htm (accessed: 11.03.07).

Slane, C. (2006) 'Library is the radio star', *Public Library Journal*, Summer, 2–3.

Slough Libraries and Information Service (2005) *Resource Management Practice & Procedure*, http://www.sloughlibrary.org.uk/framesfolder/resource_management.doc (accessed: 01.10.06).

Smidt, J.S. (2005) *The Cultural Dimension in Library Education*. Paper given to World Library and Information Congress: 71st IFLA General Conference and Council Oslo, http://www.ifla.org/IV/ifla71/papers/049e-Smidt.pdf (accessed: 18.02.07).

Smith, A. (1978) *The Politics of Information* (London: Macmillan).

Smith, C. (1997) 'Our oyster', *Public Library Journal*, **12**(6), 117–120.

Spencer, B. (2005) 'Public libraries provide an essential service', Letter, Daily Telegraph, http://www.telegraph.co.uk/opinion/main.jhtml?xml=/opinion/2005/06/08/dt0801.xml (accessed 08.07.06, this link is no longer available).

Spiller, D. (1991) *Book Selection: Principles and Practice* (London: Library Association).

Spiller, D (2000). *Providing Materials for Library* Users (London: Library Association).

Spink, J. (1989) *Children as Readers: A Study* (London: Bingley).

Stainer, C. (1997) *Towards a Philosophy of Stock Management: Entertainment, 'High Seriousness' and the Public Library.* A study submitted in partial fulfilment of the requirements for the degree of Master of Arts in Librarianship, The University of Sheffield.

Standage, T. (1998) *The Victorian Internet: The Remarkable Story of the Telegraph and the Nineteenth Century's On-line Pioneers* (New York: Walker).

Stauffer, M.H. (1999) *Outline on Literary Elements*, http://www.cas.usf.edu/lis/lis6585/class/litelem.html (accessed: 04.08.06).

Stewart, J. (1995) *Innovation in Democratic Practice* (Birmingham: INLOGOV), 15.

Straight Dope (2006) *How Did Public Libraries Get Started?*, http://www.straightdope.com/mailbag/mpublibrary.html (accessed: 22.02.07).

Sweeney, J. (1994) 'Kelvin may have put the Sun in the Sky. But just how bright his is future?', *The Observer Life*, 28–35.

Swire, H. (2006) *Conservative Pledge Action to End Library Decline*, http://www.hugoswire.org.uk/record.jsp?ID=29&type=cchPress (accessed: 29.06.06).

Taber, W. (2000) 'Library policy has a higher purpose', *The Trustee*, April http://www.telenet.net/~billt (this link now appears to be unavailable).

Tawney, R.H. (1964) *The Radical Tradition: Twelve essays on politics, education and literature* (Harmondsworth: Penguin).

Taylor, D.J. (2004) 'The end of imagination', *The Guardian*, 10 August, http://education.guardian.co.uk/higher/comment/story/0,,1279839,00.html (accessed: 07.03.07).

Taylor, D.J. (2006) 'Whoosh! There goes the media don', *Independent on Sunday*, ABC Books, 20 August, http://enjoyment.independent.co.uk/books/reviews/article1220549.ece (accessed: 05.09.06).

Tempe Public Library (2003) *Tempe Public Library Collection Development Policy*, http://www.tempe.gov/library/admin/colldev.htm (accessed: 01.10.06).

The Guardian (1946) 'Plans for the BBC's Third Programme', September 20, *Guardian Century*, http://century.guardian.co.uk/1940-1949/Story/0,6051,105116,00.html (accessed: 01.04.07).

The Network Newsletter, http://www.seapn.org.uk/newsletter.html (accessed: 06.01.07).

The Observer (2006) 'Leader. It's good to pass exams but it's good to learn', too, 13 August, 22.

Thirunarayanan, M.O. (2003) 'From thinkers to clickers: The World Wide Web and the transformation of the essence of being human', *Ubiquity*, 4(12), May, 13–19.

Thompson, D. (1964) *Discrimination and popular culture* (Harmondsworth: Penguin).

Thompson, J. (2006) 'Money turns many pages', *Times Higher Educational Supplement*, 2 November, 27.

Tisdale, S. (1997) 'Silence, please. The public library as entertainment center', *Harper's*, March, http://www.indiana.edu/~ovid99/tisdale.html (accessed: 20.02.07).

Todd, R. (1996) *Consuming Fictions* (London: Bloomsbury).

Tonkin, B. (2006) 'A week in books', *The Independent*, 20 January, 20.

Tonkin, B. (2006a) 'A week in books', *The Independent*, 1 September, 20.

Toyne, J. and Usherwood, B. (2001) *Checking the Books. The Value and Impact of Public Library Book Reading*, report of a project funded by the AHRB, The University of Sheffield (CD format).

Train, B. (2003) *Quick Reads: Reader Development and Basic Skills*, An evaluation report, The University of Sheffield, with Essex Libraries and the Learning and Skills Council, http://cplis.shef.ac.uk/QuickReads%20Report.pdf (accessed: 09.11.06).

Train, B., Usherwood, B. and Brooks, G. (2002) *The Vital Link. An Evaluation Report*, with the School of Education, The University of Sheffield, for DCMS Wolfson, http://cplis.shef.ac.uk/vitallinkfinal.pdf (accessed: 09.11.06).

Truss, L. (2005) *Talk to the Hand: The Utter Bloody Rudeness of Everyday Life* (London: Profile Books).

University of North Carolina (2006) INLS341 Spring 2006 Seminar in Public Libraries Public Library Inquiry, http://ils.unc.edu/courses/2006_spring/inls341_001/session_notes/20050201.political.02.htm (accessed: 13.08.07).

Usherwood, B. (ed.) (1993), *Success Stories: Libraries are Full of Them* (Sheffield: Yorkshire and Humberside Branch of the Library Association).

Usherwood, B. (1996) *Rediscovering Public Library Management* (London: Library Association Publishing).

Usherwood, B., Proctor, R., Bower, G., Coe, C., Cooper, J. and Stevens, T. (2001) *Recruit, Retain and Lead: The Public Library Workforce Study*, Centre for the Public Library and Information in Society, Department of Information Studies, University of Sheffield Resource.

Usherwood, B., Wilson, K. and Bryson, J. (2005) *Relevant Repositories of Public Knowledge? Perceptions of Archives, Libraries and Museums in Modern Britain.* The University of Sheffield, for the Arts and Humanities Research Board.

Vakkari, P. (1989) 'The role of the public library in the Finnish book culture', *Scandinavian Public Library Quarterly*, **2**, 24–31.

Van Riel, R. (1993) 'The case for fiction', *Public Library Journal*, **8**(3), 81–84.

Vestheim, G. (1994) 'Public libraries cultural institutions on the crossroads between purposive and humanistic rationality', in *The Future of Librarianship. Proceedings of the 2nd International Budapest Symposium, January 1994.* Hogeschool van Amsterdam, 81–95.

Vital Link (undated) *Administrative Barriers*, http://www.literacytrust.org.uk/vitallink/Administrativebarriers.html (accessed: 16.01.07).

Walker, C. and Manjarrez, C.A. (2003) *Partnerships for Free Choice Learning. Public Libraries, Museums, and Public Broadcasters Working Together*, The Urban Institute Urban Libraries Council, http://www.urban.org/UploadedPDF/410661_partnerships_for_free_choice_learning.pdf (accessed: 02.08.07).

Wallis, B. (2006) 'Contribution to: Future of multi media in libraries', lis-pub-libs@jiscmail.ac.uk, sent 12 July.

Ward, M. (1977) *Readers and Library Users: A Study of Reading Habits and Public Library Use* (London: The Library Association).

Warwick, C. (2003) 'Electronic publishing what difference does it make?' in Hornby, S. and Clarke, Z. (eds), *Challenge and Change in the Information Society* (London: Facet Publishing), 200–216.

Washington Post (2007) 'Your comments on ... Hello, Grisham – So Long, Hemingway?', http://www.washingtonpost.com/ac2/wp-dyn/comments/display? contentID=AR2007010100729&start=41 (accessed: 06.03.07).

Waterfield, G. (2003) *The Hound in the Left-hand Corner* (London: Headline).

Webb, C. (2003) 'Pillars of creativity', *The Age*, 16 September, http://www.theage.com. au/articles/2003/09/15/1063478110047.html?from=moreStories(accessed: 16.09.06).

Webster, F. (1999) 'Contribution to: Do public libraries have a future? Public Libraries in the Information Age', http://www.librarylondon.org/localgroups/ camden/pdfdocs/Webster.pdf (accessed: 14.02. 07).

Webster, F. (2002) *Theories of the Information Society*, Second edition (London: Routledge).

Weise, E. (2000), Information everywhere, but not the time to think', *USA Today*, 19 October, Sect D, 1.

West, W.J. (1991) *The Strange Rise of Semi-literate England* (London: Duckworth).

White, L. (1971) 'Back to the basics', *New Library World*, **73**(858), December, 153–5.

Williams, A. (2000) 'The dumbing down of the young consumer', in Mosley, I. (ed.), *Dumbing Down: Culture, Politics and the Mass Media* (Thorverton: Academic), 253–255.

Williams, A.A. (2006) *A Capital Library for a Capital City. A Blueprint for Change. Final Executive Summary*, Mayor's Task Force on the future of the District of Columbia Public Library System, http://dclibrary.org/capcon/Executive_ Summary_Nov2006.pdf (accessed: 08.01.07).

Williams, P. (1988), *The American Public Library and the Problem of Purpose* (New York: Greenwood Press).

Winter, M. (1998) 'Garlic, vodka, and the politics of gender. Anti-intellectualism in American librarianship', *Progressive Librarian*, 14 Spring, http://libr.org/pl/14_ Winter.html (accessed: 17.01.07).

Winter, M. (2001) 'Review of: Brown, J.S. and Duguid P. (2000) *The Social Life of Information* (Boston: Harvard Business School Press) *College and Research Libraries* **62**(1)', http://www.ala.org/ala/acrl/acrlpubs/crljournal/backissues2001b /january01/brownbookreview.htm (accessed: 26.01.07).

Winterson, J. (undated) *John Carey*, http://www.jeanettewinterson.com/pages/ content/index.asp?PageID=328 (accessed: 02.08.07).

Winterson, J. (2006) 'Good books are dangerous devices – able to trigger things in your mind', *The Times*, 19 August, Books, 3.

Woolas, P. (2006) Speech on 8 February to the All-Party Parliamentary Group on Libraries at Portcullis House, London, http://www.communities.gov.uk/index. asp?id=1163728 (accessed: 03.08.06).

Woolf, V. (1929) *A Room of One's Own* (London: Hogarth Press).

Worpole, K. (2004) *21st Century Libraries. Building Futures*, a joint initiative between CABE and RIBA, http://www.buildingfutures.org.uk/pdfs/pdffile_31.pdf (accessed: 02.08.07).

Index